THE PROUD 6TH
AN ILLUSTRATED HISTORY OF THE 6TH AUSTRALIAN DIVISION 1939–45

Following Mark Johnston's acclaimed illustrated histories of the 7th and 9th Divisions comes his long-awaited history of the 6th Australian Division: the first such history ever published.

The 6th was a household name during World War II. It was the first division raised in the Second AIF, the first division to go overseas and the first to fight. Its success in that fight, in Libya in 1941, indicated that the standard established in the Great War would be continued. In Greece, Syria and New Guinea, the Division made further significant contributions. Indeed, the 'Good Old Sixth', as General Blamey called it, was still fighting on the war's last day. Blamey and nearly every other officer who became wartime army, corps and divisional commanders were once members of the 6th Division.

Through photographs and an authoritative text, this book tells their story, and that of the proud, independent and tough troops they commanded.

Mark Johnston is one of this country's leading experts on the Australian Army in World War II. Described by the Australian War Memorial's *Wartime* magazine as 'the leading historian on the experience of Australian soldiers during the war', he is the author of six books on the subject, including two with Cambridge University Press, and of five booklets for the Department of Veterans' Affairs series 'Australians in the Pacific War'. Dr Johnston has undertaken research in Egypt, Greece, England and Germany. He is Head of History at Scotch College, Melbourne.

THE PROUD 6TH

AN ILLUSTRATED HISTORY OF THE 6TH
AUSTRALIAN DIVISION 1939–45

MARK JOHNSTON

CAMBRIDGE
UNIVERSITY PRESS

477 Williamstown Road, Port Melbourne, VIC 3207, Australia

Published in the United States of America by Cambridge University Press, New York

Cambridge University Press is part of the University of Cambridge.

It furthers the University's mission by disseminating knowledge in the pursuit of education, learning and research at the highest international levels of excellence.

www.cambridge.org
Information on this title: www.cambridge.org/9780521514118

© Mark Johnston 2008

This publication is in copyright. Subject to statutory exception and to the provisions of relevant collective licensing agreements, no reproduction of any part may take place without the written permission of Cambridge University Press.

First published 2008

Designed by Rob Cowpe Design

A catalogue record for this publication is available from the British Library

National Library of Australia Cataloguing in Publication data
Johnston, Mark, 1960–
The proud 6th: an illustrated history of the 6th Australian Division, 1939–1945 /
Mark Johnston.
9780521514118 (hbk.)
Australian Army History series
Includes index.
Bibliography.
Australia. Army. Division, 6th – History.
World War, 1939–1945 – Regimental histories – Australia.
940.541294

ISBN 978-0-521-51411-8 Hardback

Cambridge University Press has no responsibility for the persistence or accuracy of URLs for external or third-party internet websites referred to in this publication, and does not guarantee that any content on such websites is, or will remain, accurate or appropriate.

From 30 May 1940, all transport of the 6th Division was required to carry this symbol of a white kangaroo over a horizontal boomerang, both in white on a square black background. The kangaroo was consequently identified with the 6th Division, just as the kookaburra, emu and platypus were identified with the 7th, 8th and 9th Divisions, respectively. In mid-1944 the 6th Division established a recreational 'Kangaroo Club' in Wondecla, Queensland.

Contents

List of Maps	viii
Acknowledgements	ix
Conventions and Abbreviations	xi
Introduction	1
1 Origins and Early Days	7
2 Bardia	26
3 Tobruk to Benghazi	46
4 Greece	64
5 Crete	84
6 Syria	105
7 Return to Australia	121
8 Kokoda to the Sea	132
9 Wau–Salamaua	155
10 The Longest Wait: Australia 1943–4	182
11 Aitape–Wewak	192
12 Conclusion	233
Appendix 1: 6th Division Casualties	241
Appendix 2: 6th Division Honours and Awards	246
Notes	248
Bibliography	256
Index	262

Maps

1a	Libya 1941	26
1b	Bardia detail	27
2	Greece 1941	64
3a	Crete 1941	84
3b	Retimo detail	85
4	Syria and Lebanon 1941	105
5	Kokoda to Sanananda 1942–3	132
6	Wau 1943	155
7	Salamaua 1943	167
8	Aitape–Wewak 1944–5	192

ACKNOWLEDGEMENTS

I found it a great challenge to complete this book, and I take pleasure in thanking those people who helped me along the way. If Professor David Horner and Roger Lee had not backed this project it would almost certainly never have been completed, and I am deeply grateful to them. I also thank Roger and the Army History Unit for giving me an opportunity, through the Army History Research Grants Scheme, to travel to Canberra and examine important records at the Australian War Memorial.

I am grateful also to the staff of the AWM, whose work makes books such as this possible. In particular, my thanks go to Joanne Smedley, Mike Cecil, Peter Burness, Steve Bullard, Garth Pratten, Brad Manera and Peter Stanley.

It has been a pleasure to work with Pauline de Laveaux and Jodie Howell, of Cambridge University Press. I thank them for their efficiency and enthusiasm. I am also grateful to Helena Bond for her excellent copyediting. Andrew Richardson of the AHU and cartographer Kay Dancey contributed substantially too.

As in my previous divisional histories, I have sought the help of veterans. Sadly their numbers and their unit associations are declining rapidly, and I feel fortunate to have had the assistance of those still capable of helping. Foremost among them was Ivor White, of the 2/5th Battalion and 6th Division Associations. I obtained some of the best photographs in the book from him or as a result of his efforts to spread word of my project, which he endorsed enthusiastically. Les Bishop of the 2/3rd Field Regiment and Keith Johnston of the 6th Division Cavalry also made substantial contributions of photographs and information that added considerably to the accuracy and comprehensiveness of the book. Alwyn Shilton (2/5th Battalion) generously helped me on this book, as he has on several others. Other veterans who have made substantial contributions are Frank Atkins (2/11th Battalion), Sir David Hay (2/6th Battalion), John Hynes (2/1st Field Regiment), the late KT Johnson (2/11th Battalion), Douglas Margetts (6th Division Signals), Harry New (2/2nd Field Company), John Peart (2/5th Battalion), Brigadier Keith Rossi (2/2nd Field Regiment) and Alf Stone (2/2nd Battalion).

I also received considerable help from widows and descendants of veterans, including Terry Cole, Tony Creek, Jan Donohue, Sue Kirwood, Rex Langthorne, Lillian Manskie, Joan Mawson, Elizabeth Thurston and Lenore Vincent. A special thanks here to John Mole, who allowed me to read his excellent biography of his father Bryan and to borrow his wonderful wartime photographs. My thanks also to Geoffrey Dean, Winston Fairbrother, Major Paul Handel and Bruce Wilson for their help on various aspects of the book. I am also very grateful to the other veterans and relatives who offered material that I was unable to include because of lack of space.

My greatest thanks go to my family, and especially my dear wife Deborah, for their support and patience with me spending many hours pursuing this elusive and valuable subject.

CONVENTIONS AND ABBREVIATIONS

The main discussion of each photograph is in the body of the text, immediately after its number (e.g. 5.4) is printed in bold.

Abbreviations used in the text and footnotes:

AA&QMG	Assistant Adjutant and Quartermaster-General
AASC	Australian Army Service Corps
AAV	Australian Archives (Victoria)
ADMS	Assistant Director Medical Services
AGH	Australian General Hospital
AIF	Australian Imperial Force
Amb	Ambulance
AT	Anti-Tank
AWM	Australian War Memorial
Bde	Brigade
Bdr	Bombardier
BEM	British Empire Medal
BGS	Brigadier General Staff
Bn	Battalion
Capt	Captain
CASC	Commander, Army Service Corps
Cav	Cavalry
Cdo	Commando
CO	Commanding Officer
Coy	Company
Cpl	Corporal
CRA	Commander, Royal Artillery (of the division)

CRE	Commander, Royal Engineers (of the division)
CSM	Company Sergeant Major
DCM	Distinguished Conduct Medal
Div	Division
DSO	Distinguished Service Order
Fd	Field
FOO	Forward Observation Officer
GM	George Medal
Gnr	Gunner
GOC	General Officer Commanding
GSO1	General Staff Officer 1
HQ	Headquarters
Inf	Infantry
L/Cpl	Lance Corporal
LCT	Landing Craft, Tank
Lt	Lieutenant
Lt-Col	Lieutenant-Colonel
Maj	Major
MBE	Member of the British Empire
MC	Military Cross
MID	Mentioned in Despatches
MJC	Mark Johnston Collection (private)
MM	Military Medal
NCO	Non-commissioned officer
OBE	Order of the British Empire
OP	Observation Post
Pte	Private
RAP	Regimental Aid Post
RAR	Royal Australian Regiment
Regt	Regiment
RHQ	Regimental Headquarters
RMO	Regimental Medical Officer
RSM	Regimental Sergeant Major

S/Sgt	Staff Sergeant
Sgt	Sergeant
Sig	Signalman
Sigs	Signals
SLV	State Library of Victoria
Spr	Sapper
TSMG	Thompson submachine gun
VC	Victoria Cross
WOII	Warrant Officer, Class II

Introduction

'Good old 6th Divvy.'[1] Thus wrote a 9th Division private in his diary in Palestine on hearing news of the first Australian land battle of the war, at Bardia in Libya. That battle, in January 1941, was a great victory for the 6th Division and set the tone for the Second AIF's entire war. In short, the 6th's role was pivotal in Australian military history, for its men fulfilled the awesome responsibility of proving that a new generation of Australians could emulate the high achievements of the First AIF. Not surprisingly, then, the 6th Division was a formation that was a household name in Australia throughout World War II.

Yet today the 6th Division is arguably the least known of the four infantry divisions of the Second AIF: 6th, 7th, 8th and 9th. In wartime its members claimed primacy, for theirs was not only the first to fight, but also the first division formed – in 1939, no less. It was a badge of great pride to be a 'Thirty-Niner', and it was a badge often waved in front of men of the later divisions: a 9th Division veteran recalled for me his discomfort when the warmth he showed the first 6th Division men he saw in Libya was met with disdain and accusations of being too slow to join up. Reinforcements to the 6th Division itself often met much the same attitude, at least in the Middle East. Men who joined in 1940 and saw every campaign of the division still smart in the 21st century at the recollection of their treatment at the hands of the originals. Though irksome to outsiders, this pride and sense of superiority helped to ensure that the 6th Division's men continued to fight superbly and risk their lives even when the war was all but won.

Many thousands of the originals did not see out the war with the division, for more than 5000 were captured in Greece and Crete. Their subsequent story, as prisoners of war, is an important one, but falls beyond the scope of this divisional history. After Greece the 6th had to be largely rebuilt, but was able to contribute substantially to victory in the Pacific, especially in New Guinea. The commander of the AIF, General Blamey, could still call it the 'the good old Sixth' in November 1943.

Blamey had been the original commander of the 6th and was one of many illustrious officers in the division. Sufficient leaders passed through its ranks to officer a force five times larger than the almost 20 000 originally raised for it. The 6th needed strong leaders, for of all the divisions, its men contained most of the larrikin type that made Australians infamous wherever they went on overseas leave. Yet if a sizeable minority misbehaved off the battlefield, with few exceptions they fought well in some of the most demanding terrain of the war: from desert plains to snow- and jungle-clad mountains. They fought four of the 'King's enemies' – Italians, Germans, Vichy French and Japanese – and won the grudging respect of all.

The format of this book will be familiar to readers of my earlier histories of the 7th and 9th Divisions, in that photographs provide the stimulus for much of the discussion. I have included as many unofficial photographs as I could, and all readers will find here some photographs previously unknown to them.

Inevitably most of the photographs are official. I have sought wherever possible, and especially with well-known shots, to provide new information about them and the story of the 6th Division. Wonderful though these photographs are, the official captions are often scanty or even inaccurate.

As in my earlier divisional histories, tables showing the division's senior officers, casualty totals and decorations supplement the narrative and photographs.

For readers who would like an explanation of what the 6th Division comprised, the next section of this introduction describes its composition briefly. In the subsequent chapters, the discussion of the photographs is in the body of the text.

What was the 6th Division?

The 6th Australian Infantry Division, like all army divisions, was part of a hierarchy of formations and units. The following table shows the place of the division in that hierarchy, as well as the approximate numbers of men and the rank of commander usually associated with that unit:

Table 1 The Division and the military hierarchy

Component	No. of men	Commanded by
Army	60 000–100 000	General
Corps	30 000–50 000	Lieutenant-General
Division	**16 000–18 800**	**Major-General**
Brigade	3000–4000	Brigadier
Battalion	700–860	Lieutenant-Colonel
Company	120–185	Captain
Platoon	32–40	Lieutenant
Section	8–11	Corporal

For most of its six years of wartime existence, the 6th Division comprised between 12 480 and 18 800 men. Every volunteer accepted into the Australian Imperial Force (AIF) was allotted to one of the military branches, such as infantry, artillery, engineers or signals. If assigned to certain units within those branches, he would be a member of the 6th Division. Approximately 40 000 men were at some stage members of the division during its existence.

Divisions were the main tactical organisation of World War II armies. Although infantry divisions like the 6th also included various 'arms' and 'services', the division's infantry units were its heart. The 6th contained three infantry brigades, numbered 16th, 17th and 19th. Within each brigade were three battalions.

The battalions were numbered too, and given the rather confusing prefix 'Second'. For example, one battalion was the Second Third, written '2/3rd'. There was another Australian infantry battalion, not of the AIF, called the 3rd, and the term 'Second' was used to distinguish the two. The 2/3rd Battalion was composed initially of men from New South Wales, who were identified by an 'NX' prefix to their army numbers. The 2/3rd's first commanding officer, for example, had the number NX6. Many of its reinforcements were from other states (and thus had X numbers like 'VX' or 'QX'). The numbers, brigade groupings and states of origin of the nine infantry battalions of the 6th Division are shown in the table below:

Table 2 6th Division brigades, battalions and states of origin

Brigade	Battalion	State of origin
16th Infantry Brigade	2/1st Infantry Battalion	Sydney/New South Wales
	2/2nd Infantry Battalion	Sydney/Northern Rivers, NSW
	2/3rd Infantry Battalion	West and south-west NSW
17th Infantry Brigade	2/5th Infantry Battalion	Melbourne/Victoria
	2/6th Infantry Battalion	Melbourne/Victoria
	2/7th Infantry Battalion	Melbourne/Northern Victoria
19th Infantry Brigade	2/4th Infantry Battalion	Sydney/NSW
	2/8th Infantry Battalion	Melbourne/Victoria
	2/11th Infantry Battalion	Perth/WA

Each battalion contained four rifle companies designated A, B, C and D, and a Headquarters Company, which included signals, transport, pioneer and mortar platoons. On campaign, each brigade was supported by a 'field regiment' of artillery, a 'field company' of engineers, a 'field ambulance' and several smaller units. With these units it could operate semi-independently as a 'brigade group'.

Units not in or supporting brigades were 'divisional troops', including the 6th Division Cavalry Regiment (an armoured unit, originally called 6th Division Reconnaissance Regiment) and the 2/1st Anti-Tank Regiment. In official order of military precedence the main components of the division apart from the infantry brigades were:

Headquarters 6th Division
6th Division Cavalry Regiment
2/1st Field Regiment
2/2nd Field Regiment
2/3rd Field Regiment
1st (later renamed 2/1st) Anti-Tank Regiment
2/1st Field Company
2/2nd Field Company
2/8th Field Company
2/2nd (later renamed 2/22nd) Field Park Company
6th Division Signals
6th Division Australian Army Service Corps
2/1st Field Ambulance
2/2nd Field Ambulance
2/7th Field Ambulance
2/1st Army Field Workshops
Light Aid Detachments
6th Division Provost Company
6th Division Postal Unit
6th Division Salvage Unit
6th Division Field Cash Office

The battalions and regiments were of great importance to their members. Ask a veteran of the 6th what unit he belonged to during the war and he will probably name his battalion or its equivalent. Men's personal friendships tended to be from smaller units: companies, platoons and sections in the infantry; batteries, troops and sections in the artillery.

The men who led the division and its sub-units were extremely important to its atmosphere and its success on the battlefield. The commanders of the division's main combat units at formation and in its various campaigns are listed in the following table.

Table 3 Senior 6th Division commanders

	Origin	Libya	Greece, Crete and Syria	Papua (Kokoda to the sea)	Wau–Salamaua	Aitape–Wewak
6th Division	TA Blamey	I Mackay	I Mackay	NA	NA	**JES Stevens, HCH Robertson,** *R King*
16th Brigade	**AS Allen**	**AS Allen**	**AS Allen**	**JE Lloyd**	NA	**R King**
2/1st Battalion	KW Eather	KW Eather	IR Campbell	PA Cullen	NA	PA Cullen
2/2nd Battalion	GF Wootten	FO Chilton	FO Chilton	CRV Edgar	NA	AG Cameron
2/3rd Battalion	VT England	VT England	DJ Lamb, JR Stevenson	JR Stevenson, I Hutchison, JR Stevenson	NA	I Hutchison
17th Brigade	**SG Savige**	**SG Savige**	**SG Savige**	NA	**MJ Moten**	**MJ Moten**
2/5th Battalion	TP Cook	H Wrigley, GE Sell, IR Campbell, R King	R King	NA	PDS Starr, NL Goble, TM Conroy	AW Buttrose, JS Maclean, GC Darling, AW Buttrose
2/6th Battalion	AHL Godfrey	AHL Godfrey, *SHWC Porter*	H Wrigley		FG Wood	FG Wood
2/7th Battalion	TG Walker	TG Walker	TG Walker	NA	HG Guinn	PK Parbury
19th Brigade	**JW Mitchell, HCH Robertson**	**HCH Robertson**	**GA Vasey**	NA	NA	**JEG Martin,** *JA Bishop,* **JEG Martin**
2/4th Battalion	PA Parsons	IN Dougherty	IN Dougherty	NA	NA	NWP Farrell, GS Cox
2/8th Battalion	JW Mitchell	JW Mitchell	JW Mitchell	NA	NA	WS Howden, *CL Simpson,* WS Howden

(cont.)

Table 3 (cont.)

	Origin	Libya	Greece, Crete and Syria	Papua (Kokoda to the sea)	Wau–Salamaua	Aitape–Wewak
2/11th Battalion	TS Louch	TS Louch	TS Louch, RL Sandover	NA	NA	HM Binks, *DAC Jackson*, CH Green
2/1st AT Regt	FM St John	NA	FM St John	NA	NA	AL Rickard
2/1st Field Regt	LC Kelly	LES Barker	HGF Harlock	KE O'Connell	NA	KE O'Connell, AG Hanson
2/2nd Field Regt	AH Ramsay	WE Cremor	WE Cremor	NA	NA	RF Jaboor
2/3rd Field Regt	AJ Hobbs	HW Strutt	HW Strutt, VC Burston	NA	NA	GEH Bleby, CE Chapman
6th Div Cav Regt	MA Fergusson	MA Fergusson, JE Abbott, SA Morrison	NA	NA	NA	EC Hennessy
GSO I	SF Rowell	FH Berryman, GA Vasey	RB Sutherland	NA	NA	JA Bishop
AA&QMG	GA Vasey	GA Vasey, CE Prior	CE Prior	NA	NA	WC Murphy
CRA	EF Herring	EF Herring	EF Herring	NA	NA	J Reddish
CRE	CS Steele	LC Lucas	LC Lucas	NA	NA	CE Baird, *BH Buddle*, JC Hay
CO Div Sigs	JES Stevens	JJ Eather	LJ Wellman	NA	NA	LN Tribolet
CASC	NB Loveridge	NB Loveridge	NB Loveridge	NA	NA	J Talbot
ADMS	SR Burston	HC Disher	HC Disher	NA	NA	HM Fisher

Notes: Italics means temporary or acting command. NA means not applicable

CHAPTER 1

ORIGINS AND EARLY DAYS

The story of the 6th Division's origins is the story of the founding of the Second Australian Imperial Force, for the division was the first raised for World War II.

Twelve days after Australia followed Britain into war against Germany on 3 September 1939 the government decided to raise a division for overseas service. Lack of equipment, hesitation about the value of land forces in modern warfare, Labor party opposition, fear of Japanese intentions and uncertainty about the length of the coming European war all delayed the decision. However, on 15 September 1939, Prime Minister Robert Menzies announced in a radio broadcast that a new Australian infantry division would be created to serve at home or abroad. The division would be the nucleus of a 20 000-man special force, to be called the Second Australian Imperial Force, or AIF. Australia already had a militia of 80 000 men who had volunteered for home defence and a regular force of about 2800. Half of the 20 000 vacancies in the new special force were allotted to the militia, but only about 5000 volunteers came forward from that source. Most of the remaining volunteers had no military experience.

Because five militia infantry divisions already existed in Australia, the new division was named the 6th Division. It was, however, the first division of its kind raised for World War II. Inevitably, World War I and especially the First AIF loomed large in the minds of politicians and soldiers of all ranks as the new force was organised. For example, the first entry in the war diary of one of the division's three infantry brigades says:

> Today the years between the demobilisation of the famous 1st. A.I.F. and the formation of the 2nd were bridged when Bde Cmdrs and Bde Majors attended a Divisional conference at Army H.Q., Victoria Barracks, St. Kilda Rd.[1]

The brigade was the 16th, which, like the 1st Brigade of the 1st Division in the First AIF, was to be raised in New South Wales. The 17th Brigade would, like the 2nd Brigade, be raised in Victoria, and the third brigade to be raised for the new division, the 18th, would be raised in the smaller states, as was its earlier counterpart. Shoulder patches for the units were identical to those of their equivalent in the First AIF, except that a narrow grey border was introduced. That grey line distinguished the unit from its numerical counterpart in the militia, as did the prefix 'Second' or '2/'. Thus, the AIF's 'Second Third' or '2/3rd' Battalion was not to be confused with the Third Battalion of the militia.

1.1　　　　　　　　　　AWM 001427

The Great War experience was also a major consideration in the appointment of the new division's senior officers. Thomas Blamey, at left in **Photograph 1.1**, was promoted to the rank of lieutenant-general on 13 October and appointed to command the division. A regular soldier in 1914, he had landed as a major with the 1st Division at Gallipoli and by war's end was a brigadier-general and chief of staff in the headquarters of General Monash, who greatly appreciated Blamey's organisational skill. Although his interwar years had been turbulent, culminating in being sacked as Commissioner of the Victoria Police in 1936, at the outbreak of war he was chairman of the Commonwealth's Manpower Committee, Director of Recruiting and well placed to lead the wartime army.

Blamey may have been the 6th Division's first commander, but he would never lead the 6th Division into action. In February 1940 the War Cabinet decided to raise the 7th Division, which with the 6th would form the nucleus of a new corps. Blamey was appointed corps commander and took four senior 6th Division officers with him. Major-General Iven Mackay, previously commanding the 2nd Division of the militia, was appointed to replace Blamey. Mackay, at right in the photograph, taken as he prepared to leave Melbourne with a convoy in April 1940, was a citizen soldier. The official historian considered him 'shy, bleak, sometimes fussy and pedantic', but acknowledged too that he had 'great qualities of mind and

ORIGINS & EARLY DAYS

1.2   AWM 019443

character'.[2] He had been twice wounded at Gallipoli, commanded a battalion at Pozieres and the 1st Brigade in 1918.

Blamey, Mackay and other senior 6th Division commanders were impeccably qualified, but the regular soldiers of the Staff Corps were greatly disappointed that, in accordance with government policy, no one from their ranks was initially appointed to brigade or unit commands in the 6th Division. However, by the time **Photograph 1.2** was taken, in December 1940, a regular had been appointed to a senior position in the division. He was Brigadier HCH Robertson, known to his men as 'Red Robbie' (far right, front row). He commanded the 19th Brigade, which on being created in Palestine in May 1940 had become part of the 6th Division, replacing the 18th Brigade. The components of the brigade were determined partly by Australia's decision to remodel its divisions in accordance with British practice, so that each brigade would comprise three rather than four battalions. Each existing brigade would contribute one battalion to the 19th Brigade. The 2/4th, 2/8th and 2/12th were slated to go, but because the 2/12th's convoy to the Middle East was diverted to England, the 2/11th took its place in Palestine. The latter, formed in Western Australia, would be the division's only battalion not raised in New South Wales or Victoria.

Next to Robertson in the photograph is General Mackay and at far left is Brigadier AS 'Tubby' Allen, the popular, brave but difficult commander of the 16th Brigade. Behind Allen is Colonel Frank Berryman, the division's GSO1, the chief planning officer. At centre rear is Brigadier Stan Savige, commanding the 17th Brigade, and at top right Colonel George Vasey, Assistant Adjutant and Quartermaster General. These men, like the 6th Division's other early commanders, would figure prominently in the Second AIF as it expanded. Mackay would eventually command an army, Savige and Berryman a corps, and Allen, Vasey and Robertson would be divisional commanders. Berryman would become chief of staff at Advanced Land Headquarters.

By the time this photograph was taken, well over a year after the division was raised, the 6th was at last about to be sent into action.

Before looking at that period, we will examine briefly how the first year of the division affected the common soldiers who were its main component. Men who enlisted with the AIF did so for the period of the war and 12 months thereafter. None could have suspected that the war would last nearly six years.

Government and press expected an initial rush to enlist, but this did not eventuate, largely because of the government's publicly expressed uncertainty about how the new force would be employed and anxiety about the potential impact on the militia. Nevertheless, by 30 November, apart from officers and NCOs and from some medical and ordnance units, the division had reached 'war establishment'. The officers would mostly be promoted from the ranks in February and March 1940.

Photograph 1.3 depicts new recruits at the Melbourne Showgrounds in November 1939. Keith Carroll, a lieutenant allocated to look after 120 men there in October, described them thus:

> All sorts of men from every possible calling and trade, good and bad but on a casual glance an excellent type of chap showing great enthusiasm and will eventually become good soldiers.

Carroll, who would ultimately be a captain in the 2/6th Battalion, enthused even at this early stage: 'I think they will become the finest fighting force to leave these shores'.[3]

Despite the smiles for the camera, many were initially bewildered by their treatment on enlistment. 'Chaos reigned there', said one concerning the Showgrounds.

> 'Everywhere you went there seemed to be people shouting at you. You were in crowds for this and queues for that. Straw palliasses on the floor, and in general it was disorderly. As you came in there were people shouting at you "You'll be sorry", and to tell the truth, we were sorry . . .'[4]

ORIGINS & EARLY DAYS 11

1.3 AWM 000177

In late October there was even a suicide among the troops at the Showground: a man taunted by others over his physical deficiencies. Generally, however, regrets were only temporary.

What had motivated them to don the slouch hat? Partly what that hat symbolised: success on the battlefield and adventure abroad. Duty to empire was an important motive, but there were often personal considerations too, such as being with one's mates. At left in Photograph 1.3 one man has his hand on another's shoulder, perhaps signifying a friendship. Labor politician EJ Ward argued that many soldiers were enlisting merely to earn 5 shillings a day with food and accommodation, an improvement on the 8s 6d a week dole available to single unemployed men. It was, Ward said, 'a form of economic conscription'.[5] No definitive proof exists on this point, though an interesting piece of evidence arises in the 16th Brigade war diary. On 4 November, the diarist, Roland Hoffmann, wrote:

> Rumors that recruits were to receive no pay until next week caused a good deal of uneasiness among the men . . . A large number had enlisted from the unemployed ranks and had entered camp a fortnight before with little, and in some cases, no money.[6]

1.4   Courtesy Lillian Manskie

Bill Morse, the soldier pictured in the centre of the proud group in **Photograph 1.4**, joined because he was on the 'susso', or dole, at the outbreak of war. On enlistment as a private he was 34 years old and a champion walker. Here photographed in 1940 as an NCO in the 2/5th Battalion, he would soon be earning his keep in the division's first battle, at Bardia. Indeed, he would become one of the first Australian soldiers decorated in the war. After being chiefly responsible for the capture of an Italian machine-gun post, five tanks, a headquarters and 500 or more men, Sergeant Morse received the Distinguished Conduct Medal and the nickname 'the one-man army'.

Whether or not the division contained a high proportion of unemployed men, there was certainly a higher proportion than in the later divisions of men who could be described as larrikins or independent spirits. 'Jo' Gullett, an 'original' himself, argued that the 6th 'attracted the most adventurous as well as the most reckless elements in the community', and that these gave the division a unique style and character.[7] Nevertheless, the 'reckless' formed a minority. The majority of initial recruits shared pride in being the first to enlist. The 'Thirty-Niners', those who volunteered in 1939, formed an exclusive fraternity.

In **Photograph 1.5**, recruits are becoming soldiers, again at the Showgrounds. They are carrying Lee-Enfield rifles and wearing the notoriously ill-fitting cotton working dress, or 'giggle suits'. They were lucky to be this well equipped in early November, for the 16th Brigade was in camp for two weeks before it received rifles, and by the end of November some men still had no working dress, and fewer than half had uniforms. The dapper soldier drilling them is a member of the Australian

ORIGINS & EARLY DAYS   13

1.5   AWM 000171

Instructional Corps. The emphasis in early training was on physical 'hardening', establishment of units and sub-units with the idea of creating esprit de corps, and individual training.

Early in November, the 16th and 17th Brigades moved into semi-permanent hutted campsat Ingleburn and Puckapunyal, respectively. Conditions there were initially primitive. In an extraordinary incident on 20 November soldiers angry at excessive prices and poor service burnt down a hut at Ingleburn near the 2/1st Battalion lines. Lieutenant-Colonel Eather, the 2/1st's normally stern CO, apparently made no effort to halt or punish the arsonists.

The 16th Brigade were keen trainers: in mid-November troops were lining up after evening mess to refresh voluntarily what they had done during the day. The brigade diarist surmised that 'this extraordinary keenness throughout the ranks . . . certainly will be reflected when the men make their first appearance on a public parade'.[8] That belief was vindicated on 4 January 1940, when the 16th Brigade marched through Sydney streets thronged with an enthusiastic crowd. The smiles on the faces of the men in **Photograph 1.6** probably reflect their delight and

14   ORIGINS & EARLY DAYS

1.6   AWM 000664

surprise that the population had treated them so warmly. Not that the march was easy. One participant outlined the route in a letter home and added: 'all this was done non-stop and we had our heavy uniforms on and it was about 100° in the shade and by hell it was hot'. The worst part, he said, was when they passed a brewery, where 'a beautiful smell rose to greet us and didn't our tongues hang out'. However, he added that on this march he saw 'the biggest crowd I have ever seen. They gave us a great reception and a lot gave us chewing gum and the flags they were waving and didn't the good sorts give us a hoy'.[9]

The official historian talks of a 'defiant pride' that had developed on the basis of animosity towards the militia and a perception that the public considered them a force of 'the rag-tag and bobtail of the people'.[10] That perception had a basis in fact: several civilians were brought before police courts for insulting soldiers as 'Five bob a day killers'.[11]

No doubt the joy apparent here also reflects the growing esprit de corps of the division and its units. A parade of the 17th Brigade in Melbourne on 24 January was similar, leaving one officer to claim that 'their serious efficiency has impressed many with the feeling that they will out-do the first A.I.F.'.[12] However, a man in

1.7   Courtesy Sue Kirwood

the ranks who made a similar comparison also admitted that he understood why the men were not 'let loose' in the city after the march but returned directly to camp: there were, he said 'a lot of bad eggs in the Brigade'.[13]

In **Photograph 1.7** Gunner Lloyd Searle of 2/2nd Field Regiment practises on a Lewis gun at Puckapunyal. Life in this camp had initially been Spartan and dusty, with many succumbing to an epidemic of 'Pucka throat'. By February the weather was hot and it remained, in the words of an officer, 'a desolate spot'.[14] Gunner Searle is wearing an overcoat as well as his giggle suit, suggesting the photograph was taken in March or April 1940. By then, the unit was reasonably well equipped, though the obsolete weapon he is using reflects the continuing shortage throughout the division of up-to-date weapons. Of far more concern to his unit was the antiquity of its artillery pieces, which were 18-pounders. They were an upgrade of the World War I model, but had inferior range to the new British 25-pounder, of which there were none in Australia. Indeed, unlike the division's other two field regiments, in Libya the 2/2nd continued without 25-pounders, and at Bardia was initially allocated gun positions from which it could not hit the enemy.

16 ORIGINS & EARLY DAYS

1.8　　　　　　　　　　　　　　　　　　　　　　　　　　　　AWM 000678

By the time this photograph was taken, the first convoy had arrived in the Middle East, carrying the 16th Brigade group. While training and receiving equipment there, the Australians could release British troops for Europe. On departing, the 16th Brigade men did not know their destination, but naturally they reflected on whether they would return. For family men like the soldier in **Photograph 1.8**, the parting was especially affecting. Such farewells were to be experienced by thousands of 6th Division men during the war.

In **Photograph 1.9** 16th Brigade members wait to board the *Otranto*, one of four luxury liners converted as troopships. Most of these 2/2nd Battalion men enlisted in Newcastle in 1939, including the tallest man here, Lieutenant Gerry Connor. He would be Mentioned in Despatches for 'gallant and distinguished services' in the South-West Pacific. He would also be one of the first Australians to find evidence of Japanese cannibalism on that front. The photograph was taken on 9 January 1940, the day before the convoy left Sydney Harbour.

In **Photograph 1.10** the second convoy is arriving in the Middle East, at Kantara, Egypt on 18 May. An Arab policeman watches troops of the 2/5th Battalion, whom the second-in-command called his 'loveable cutthroats', disembarking from the

ORIGINS & EARLY DAYS   17

1.9 Courtesy Alf Stone

1.10 AWM 041663

crowded *Ettrick* after a five-week voyage.[15] The first soldier's bag bears the name 'Brooker'. Two men of that name, both from Kerang, joined the battalion in 1939. John Brooker would die in New Guinea in June 1945. No doubt they were relieved at getting off the ship early that morning, but they still had an eight-hour train journey ahead of them that day. By nightfall most of the 17th Brigade was in camp at Beit Jirja, Palestine.

All three brigades of the division would assemble in Palestine: the 16th in February, the 17th and 19th in May. The operational employment of Australian troops was ultimately an Australian political decision but because Palestine was administered by Britain the Australian troops there were under overall British command. Hence, it was appropriate that General Sir Archibald Wavell, the British General Officer Commanding in the Middle East, should address the 16th Brigade when they arrived. When he did so on 20 February, he praised the achievements of Australian soldiers in the Middle East in the previous war, but emphasised that Australians had also left there 'a reputation of another kind, for a lack of restraint and discipline, which I am sure you will not wish to maintain but to remove'.[16] Australian indiscipline was a theme to which Wavell and other British generals would return, with reference to the 6th Division. A large minority of 6th Division troops misbehaved on leave in Palestine. 'Our troops have been behaving . . . as the *Bulletin* and *Smiths* [*Weekly*] and other papers have illustrated them as behaving for the last 25 years', wrote an exasperated Colonel George Vasey, the chief administrative officer of the division in March 1940. Vasey said that the men's 'larrikinism, thefts and making a general nuisance of themselves' in Jerusalem and Tel Aviv made him 'ashamed to wear the uniform' and kept him and Allen busy trying to 'pass it off with the British army people'.[17] Many of the worst offenders were sent home as 'Snarlers' (SNLR, or 'Services no longer required') before their units reached the front.

In his speech Wavell also mentioned the possibility, which he called remote, of Italy joining the war on Germany's side. He hinted that if this happened it would 'vitally affect' the use of the Australian troops, who were stationed near Italy's African possessions. He was right, but the remainder of 1940 lay ahead before this possibility bore fruit on the battlefield. In the meantime, the 6th Division had to train, acclimatise, fraternise and train again. **Photograph 1.11** encapsulates several elements of the 6th Division's new experience. The soldier, Corporal Bill Ryan of the 2/2nd Battalion, was the son of an Australian Light Horseman who had fought in Palestine. The civilian, Hanna Bisharat, was a Transjordan Arab who, according to the original caption, 'was an ally of the AIF in 1918'. Taken near Jersualem in March 1940, it would have met General Wavell's approval as retaining a focus on the best Anzac traditions. Ryan looks superb in his uniform, with the

1.11　　　　　　　　　　　　　　　　　　　　　　　　　　AWM 001474/09

purple over green patch, rectangular like those of all the division's battalions. He would continue to do his part, leading a group of stranded Australians on a daring escape from Crete, and as a lieutenant leading his platoon on the Kokoda Track until he was wounded in the stomach. He seems to have been 18 years old at the time of the photograph – like many others he had 'put up' his age to enlist.

Long route marches were common in Palestine. In July, for example, the 2/2nd Battalion marched 72 miles in a week. In **Photograph 1.12** members of the 2/4th Battalion are marching through Gaza, some 25 kilometres from their camp at Julis. That day, 8 March, saw the rifle platoons practising attack. The battalion war diary noted that the men were very keen on any training 'allowing use of initiative'.[18] The battalion had arrived in Palestine as part of the 16th Brigade but would in May be allotted to the 19th. This was something of a wrench, but it had the consolation of remaining within the 6th Division. Uniquely among the four AIF infantry divisions, all nine of the 6th Division's infantry battalions were allotted to it from the time of its creation.

Australian soldiers generally considered Gaza and other Arab villages filthy. Many showed compassion towards Arab children, but also a deep suspicion of

1.12   AWM 001474/14

their proclivity to steal. Senior officers were especially concerned about the danger of Arabs stealing rifles.

In **Photograph 1.13** 2/7th Battalion troops in summer dress at Beit Jirja on 26 May are engaging in equally time-honoured and rudimentary training, with the bayonet. This image looks clichéd in a war where the bayonet was generally useless, but the 2/7th would use their bayonets in a famous charge a year and a day after this photograph was taken. The unit's mantra, 'As ye train so shall ye fight', would prove true. Weapons other than rifles were in short supply. In May, for example, the 2/5th Battalion had only nine Bren light machine guns. Wooden representations were employed in training.

The Bren gun that 2/7th Battalion men were photographed using at the Jaffa Range in June in **Photograph 1.14** is real, however. From March new weapons had begun arriving for the Australians, who were keen to practise with them. At this time the battalion spent four days practising with live ammunition at the impressively constructed range. Men out on desert patrols during this bivouac found souvenirs of fighting from the last war. Private Ernest Reynolds is on the gun, while Corporal Douglas 'Jock' Taylor looks on. Taylor would be badly wounded and win a Distinguished Conduct Medal at Buna for 'conspicuous gallantry' in an attack by Bren carriers.

ORIGINS & EARLY DAYS 21

1.13 AWM 001947

In the midst of the training men took leave and occasionally mixed training with pleasure in sporting events. On 22 June the 2/1st Battalion organised a Surf Life Saving Carnival, which the war diary proudly called the first ever held in Palestine.

1.14 AWM 002249

Damien Parer's **Photograph 1.15** shows the start of the beach sprint with young Australians giving their all in a typically Australian event. This photograph is both striking and poignant, when one considers the fate of the five men identified. Two spent four years as prisoners of war (Jack Whittle, second from left, and William Cooper, far right), a third was killed on Crete (Frank Wood, far left), another died of illness in

1.15   AWM 002195

1944 (John Reid, falling). Just one, John Burrell – wearing a shirt – survived the war unscathed. Burrell was battalion adjutant by 1945.

By June 1940 the war was coming closer to the Australians in Palestine. On 11 June Italy declared war on the Allies, and shortly thereafter France capitulated. Lebanon and Syria passed into the hands of the pro-German Vichy French government, and Italy's control of Libya made Britain's territories, especially Egypt, seem insecure. As Wavell had predicted in his February speech, this had implications for the Australians in the Middle East. Precautions were taken against sea and air invasion. One extraordinary measure was to combine the 2/1st Field Regiment and the 2/4th Battalion into two anti–aircraft (AA) regiments, called 'X' and 'Y', with the role of protecting Haifa's oil refinery and port. These temporary regiments were still training for their role when the fears behind their creation were vindicated. On the night of 15 July, 40 Italian bombers set alight four oil tanks in Haifa. The Australians suffered no casualties, but one bomb fell some 300 metres away – 'too close to be pleasant', according to the 2/4th Battalion's Lieutenant Cecil Chrystal. For most involved it was their first experience of enemy action. 'Today for us the war began,' wrote Chrystal.[19]

1.16   Courtesy Elizabeth Thurston

The 2/4th reverted to infantry in August, but in August–September the '2/1st Field Regiment (AA)' gained valuable experience using anti-aircraft guns to protect locations in Egypt. In **Photograph 1.16**, members of 'Peter's Force', one of the regiment's detachments, are manning a 3.7-inch gun at Port Fouad on the Suez Canal. At far right is Bombardier Ted Fulton. When the regiment reverted to its field artillery role in late September, it had no guns. It had arrived from Australia with 24 obsolescent guns, which on becoming an AA force it had handed to the then gunless 2/2nd Field Regiment. In November the 2/1st Field Regiment did get their new 25-pounder Mark II guns. The 2/2nd would have to wait.

The third field artillery regiment of the division, the 2/3rd, and its 1st Anti-Tank Regiment, had been diverted to England with the third convoy. Both units had arrived there in June without guns, and their status as artillery had been in doubt. After some training as infantry, the 2/3rd was issued with 25-pounders in July, making it the first Australian unit to receive these exceptional new weapons. The anti-tank regiment was broken up, only to be reconstituted in September. In **Photograph 1.17** members of the two regiments are seen with King George VI during an inspection of Australian troops at Colchester on 30 October. On the king's right is Lieutenant-Colonel Horace Strutt, who would command the 2/3rd Field Regiment for most of the war. On his left is Lieutenant-Colonel Francis

1.17 AWM 004569

St John, CO of the Anti-Tank Regiment. It had all its 48 anti-tank guns by the time the two regiments departed for the Middle East, in mid-November. Both arrived in the Middle East at the end of December just as the other two regiments were about to go into action.

The 6th Divisional Engineers experienced similar difficulties to the artillery in the Middle East: shortage of equipment and the absence through the third convoy of some of their number. The 2/1st and 2/2nd Field Companies travelled with the first two convoys. The third convoy carried the division's 2/3rd Field Company and 2/1st Field Park Company. In their place the division was permanently allotted the 2/8th Field Company and the 2/2nd Field Park Company. 6th Division Signals had a similar experience, with half the original unit sent to Britain and a new one constituted mainly from signallers in the battalions and regiments in Egypt and Palestine. The division's engineers and signallers would be prominent in the action looming at the end of 1940.

In early September 1940, most of the division moved to Helwan in Egypt. On 13 September Italian forces crossed the Egyptian/Libyan frontier. Tension soon arose between Australian and British commanders over the question of the detachment of the 16th Brigade to an operational role. After consulting Wavell, General Blamey told the Australian government that the 16th Brigade would have a month's training and be provided with full equipment before being allocated such a role. The upshot of this tiff was that the division was not moved to Amiriya, on the edge of the Western Desert, till October and November. Its men were still not fully equipped, but were now well trained. In November and December there were full divisional exercises. Nearly all 6th Division officers and sergeants had attended training schools in the Middle East, and units and brigades had trained alongside British regulars. Leaders and men were confident that they could give a good account of themselves in whatever action lay ahead. The human material in the division was excellent. Whether the deficient equipment, the materiel, would suffice was another question. After one three-day exercise a gunner of the 2/2nd Field Regiment, which at Helwan fired the only live ammunition it was spared between departing Australia and going into action, wrote to his wife that the slit trenches they had dug 'looked uncommonly like graves'.[20] Within weeks the 6th Division would be digging graves as well as slit trenches in the desert.

CHAPTER 2

BARDIA

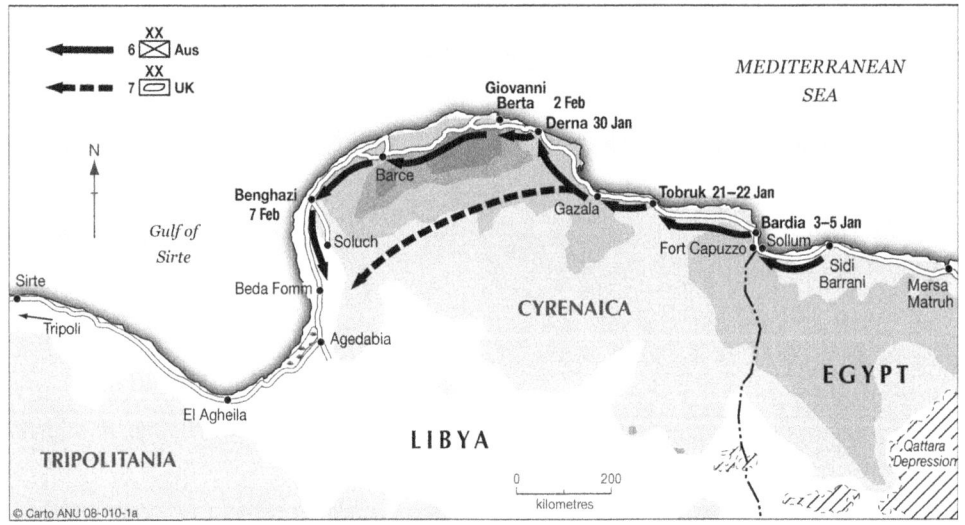

Map 1a Libya 1941

In December 1940, the 6th Division at last entered the front line. On 9 December the Western Desert Force of General O'Connor, comprising chiefly the 7th Armoured and 4th Indian divisions, attacked the Italian invaders of Egypt and, after thrashing them at Sidi Barrani, threw them back across the Libyan border into the province of Cyrenaica. Before this offensive began, Wavell had decided that within a week of its commencement he would replace the 4th Indian Division with the 6th Australian Division. The first exchange of ground fire involving the

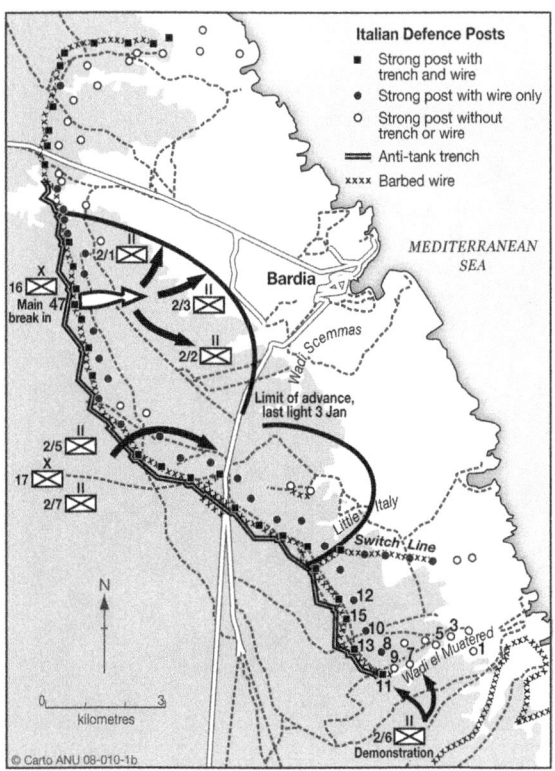

Map 1b Bardia detail

6th Division, and indeed the Second AIF, occurred when a squadron of truck-borne 6th Division Cavalry raided an isolated Italian frontier post at Garn el Grein on 11 December. The following day the 16th Brigade started to move forward, hoping there would still be some enemy to fight. The British command felt that the Italians were finished and, buoyed by their army's first land victory of the war, were determined to continue the advance. In fact, the Italians had fallen back in strength to Bardia, a fortified town 24 kilometres across the frontier. O'Connor's staff believed that the enemy might well abandon Bardia, and the 19th Brigade was ordered to prepare to move by sea from Alexandria to occupy Bardia should the enemy depart without a fight.

However, by 20 December, when the 16th Australian Brigade was in position outside Bardia, it was apparent that the Italians intended to hold the town. British intelligence estimated the Italian strength at 18 000–20 000: in fact, it was more than twice this. O'Connor ordered Mackay, whose 17th Brigade would arrive on 27 December, to use the 17th and the 16th Brigades to finish the supposedly demoralised Italians in Bardia, and to keep his third brigade in reserve for an advance on Tobruk, the next major Italian town on the Libyan coast. In their first battle, the Australians would have to attack a numerically superior enemy entrenched in well-established defences.

Photograph 2.1 depicts newly arrived Australians of the 2/1st Field Company standing around a downed Italian aircraft near Sollum, about 20 kilometres along the coast from Bardia. One diarist said his group were 'tickled to bits' when they saw Australian aircraft shoot down several Italian planes.[1] The clothing looks warm and incongruous for the desert, but as men soon found, nights and early mornings in Libya were bitterly cold. In his diary, Sapper Richard Beilby of this field company noted the detritus of battle and the equipment and supplies left by

2.1 AWM 004924

a fleeing enemy. On the day of the photograph, as they prepared to move closer to Bardia, he wrote of one of five air raids they had endured in the past two days: 'They lay a stick of bombs across the plain and scared the hell out of us all, we could hear the lumps of steel bouncing off the rocks over our heads'. One sapper had already gone out with 'shell shock' occasioned by the bombing or the enemy's shelling. They would face more as they drove forward. Before they did so, their officer told the men they had the honour of being first into action. 'From today we will know whether we have guts or not,' Beilby wrote.[2]

The 2/1st Field Company was given a vital role in the planned attack on Bardia, for the town's 29 kilometre arc of concrete underground posts was protected by an anti-tank ditch and barbed wire defences that had somehow to be breached. Contrary to Australian expectations, in the coming battle enemy aircraft proved to be 'conspicuously absent'.[3] The same could be said of much of the equipment the men needed. Wire-cutters – captured from the enemy – and gloves would only arrive within hours of the attack.

On the road from Sollum to Bardia, Beilby and his mates passed Fort Capuzzo, 'or what was left of it'. He described its remains as including the Italian victory

2.2 AWM 005264

arch depicted in **Photograph 2.2**. Standing on it and directing traffic is Lance-Corporal William Brooks, of the Provost Corps 6th Division. The provosts, or military police (MPs), were not on a pedestal as far as many other members of their division were concerned. Such was the poor reputation of the MPs of the First AIF that in 1939 it had proved difficult to recruit provosts – some who joined felt they were 'shanghaied' or tricked by the nice sound of the name 'provost'.[4] Ken Clift, who would win a DCM in the weeks ahead, so hated provosts that he refused to bury a dead one in New Guinea. He happily recounted a ditty sung in his unit:

2.3 AWM 005307

> Ladies have babies,
> And have them with ease.
> Harlots have babies
> And make them M.P.s[5]

The MPs' reputation improved later, after they demonstrated their value in Greece. On the day of this photograph, General Mackay would have liked to have more trucks to send past Brooks' post at Fort Capuzzo. There was a chronic shortage of vehicles, which would be crucial if the advance were to proceed beyond Bardia. Borrowed and captured vehicles were indispensable.

The 2/1st Field Regiment had enough vehicles to bring its guns into position on 23 December. A sandstorm was raging and the following morning the men found that one of their two batteries was open to enemy observation. They fired throughout the day, with surprisingly few enemy responses, and withdrew to a safer position that night. **Photograph 2.3** depicts one gun and crew of that 1st Battery in their new positions. They are manning one of their new 25-pounders, the last of which the regiment received on 2 December. The guns' arrival had been a source of great joy to the men, who had initially missed meals just to familiarise themselves with the new equipment. General Mackay had twice visited the unit to see them. On the shells, the men chalked messages, the most benign of which was 'Merry Xmas, Musso'. Only 10 rounds of observed fire were allowed per day, to preserve ammunition. A higher expenditure was allowed on harassing fire at night. The camouflage net was a necessary precaution against enemy aircraft, which did raid the guns on 27 December, only to lose three planes. The men have also camouflaged their helmets, as well as adorning them with the artillery corps symbol and the colour patch of their beloved regiment. The gunner at far left, 21-year-old Eric Hillcoat, would be killed in Greece. The man next to Hillcoat, Gunner John O'Sullivan, and William Smith, a crewman of this gun not visible here, would both be killed by enemy shelling outside Derna within a month. Even before the action began, life was tough for the artillerymen at Bardia. One wrote to his wife that the men were sleeping fully dressed, filthy, bearded, cold and tired. Nevertheless, he said on 29 December, when this photograph was taken, 'we are all in good spirits'.[6] By then the guns were taking a toll of enemy artillery and of enemy infantry who unwisely showed themselves. Moreover, artillery observers, aerial reconnaissance, and aggressive and enterprising patrols had built up an accurate picture of enemy dispositions.

The Australians' own dispositions were uncomfortable rather than dangerous, although enemy air attacks had killed about 20 men by Christmas Day. Not only were the nights cold, but the wind blew up clouds of dust. Water was rationed to a salty half gallon per day. There was just one hot meal daily. The ground was also rocky and resisted attempts to dig, though the Australians' positions were beyond the range of most Italian guns.

Some of the headquarters, including General Mackay's, were moved into ancient cisterns. **Photograph 2.4** depicts the Divisional Signals and post office, located in a cavern next to Divisional Headquarters. Mail, an immeasurably important factor in soldiers' morale, was distributed from here to the troops until the eve of battle, although not all got through. One artilleryman wrote to his beloved wife on the last day of 1940 that the destruction by fire of two weeks' airmail from Australia was 'the worst catastrophe that has befallen me since I left Australia'.[7]

O'Connor used the 7th Armoured Division to contain Bardia to the west, as he did not wish to risk their tanks against the Italian guns. However, he did give Mackay practically all his available artillery – more than 160 guns – and the 25 Matilda tanks of the Royal Tank Regiment.

Mackay ensured that the 19th Brigade arrived at the front on 1 January, but its task was to exploit towards Tobruk with the armoured division on the third day of the battle. The infantry fighting for Bardia would fall to the other two brigades, and particularly the 16th. Mackay's staff planned the attack meticulously, like an assault in the previous war. As in those attacks, artillery was considered

2.4   AWM 004950

crucial, and at Mackay's insistence the assault was delayed until 3 January 1941 so that 125 rounds per gun had been brought forward. The 2/1st Field Regiment moved secretly into new positions on the night of 1/2 January so that they could provide effective support to the assault. This movement of guns and the requisite ammunition ensured that the gunners had no sleep.

At 5.30 am, before first light, on 3 January 1941 ninety-six guns heralded the Australian army's first battle in World War II. It was the first bombardment most men of the 6th Division had ever heard. As planned, the guns pounded a narrow section of the enemy's perimeter to the west of the town and Lieutenant-Colonel Eather's 2/1st Battalion and parties from the 2/1st Field Company advanced. The sappers were carrying Bangalore torpedoes made up by 2/2nd Field Park Company, to blast the wire. They also had to break down the anti-tank ditch, so that vehicles could pass through. Sapper Eric Loubet, who was in one of the parties thus tasked, called it a 'suicide squad'. After crawling close to the tank traps and listening to their own 'hellish' barrage, they endured 'drop shorts' from the enemy barrage. Lieutenant Dawson, who was responsible for giving the signal to blow the gaps, was stunned by a shell fragment that pierced his helmet. 'Then', Loubet wrote, 'into the traps and work like hell with the tanks waiting around'.[8] After a delay,

2.5   AWM 134446

Lieutenant-Colonel Eather ordered the engineers to blow the gap in the wire, which was up to six metres thick. He then directed men forward through the gap with his walking stick.

Photograph 2.5 probably shows the initial attack. Two days before, more than 11 000 sleeveless leather jerkins had been brought up, and those who received them willingly wore them over or under their woollen tunics, as well in many cases as a greatcoat. They wore helmets and carried ammunition, grenades, three days' rations and, initially at least, picks and shovels. They waited tensely at the start-line, which the brigade diarist called 'the start line of the Australian soldier in this war'.[9] Though some found the noise appalling, the sound of the guns lifted their morale, as did the issue of rum to most men of the two brigades. The official historian records that men were 'calling, singing, and shouting defiance at the enemy', though the guns drowned their voices.[10]

A British gunner saw some 200 Australians march through his gun positions just before the assault. It was dark, but he noticed their toughness, 'studied indifference'

2.6　　　　　　　　　　　　　　　　　　　　　　　　　　　　　　AWM 069223

and nonconformity: even as they advanced, one private was giving colourful backchat to his company sergeant-major, who promised to knock the miscreant's 'bastard teeth out'.[11] The insouciance was 'studied', for as one infantryman remembered: 'Everyone seemed to have frequent cause to stop for a nervous wee, a problem that passed as we settled down and actually started to do something constructive'.[12]

Photograph 2.6 was taken in what the caption calls 'an Italian tank trap' during the battle. It is one of several famous British photographs of the battle that are tantalisingly difficult to identify. The bombardment of the enemy defences is proceeding in the background. Vehicles are visible too. Signalman Tom Neeman was in a truck sending and receiving messages in a wadi, or dry watercourse, that morning. In a letter home he described hearing the scream of approaching shells, seeing them explode through the opening at the back of the truck and hearing stones rattle on the canvas hood like hail. He thanked heaven the fragments went straight up in the air instead of sideways 'in the good old Australian style'.[13] He called the bombardment 'thrilling', and this may not have been just bravado: Neeman won the Military Medal for bravery under fire at Bardia. The presence of

2.7 AWM 069222

vehicles and daylight in the photograph suggest that it was taken later in the battle, but it well illustrates the nature of the anti-tank ditch. More than four metres wide and more than a metre deep, it could stop the Matilda tanks. Nonetheless, a 2/1st Field Company section made two crossings in the ditch within just five minutes, then checked for mines with bayonets to clear the gap between the wire and the ditch.

Photograph 2.7 shows one of the ditches bridged and sappers watching as a Bren carrier goes through. These men have not been issued with leather jerkins but are armed, and not merely for self-defence. Sapper Richard Beilby wrote that after his group had made crossings, 'they fixed bayonets and raced after the infantry'.[14] At 6.35 am the British tanks and the 2/2nd Battalion moved through a gap made by the engineers on either side of Post 47. Contrary to the laws of war, the sappers recruited captured Italians to assist in this work. The British CO of the 7th Battalion Royal Tank Regiment was deeply impressed by the gallantry and efficiency of the sappers, whose work was so important to the survival of his vehicles and men.

In the famous image, **Photograph 2.8**, Australians are advancing, perhaps in the half-light, as the 2/2nd Battalion did. A story arose and entered 6th Division

2.8 AWM 069221

folklore that men sang 'The Wizard of Oz' as they advanced, but the official historian says that Captain Woodhill of the 2/2nd Battalion made this up, and that in fact the singing was a ribald parody of 'South of the Border'. The 16th Brigade diarist wrote that 'Comin' through the Rye' and 'Please don't burn our . . . house down' were sung.[15] Not everyone had the heart to sing. A cavalryman claimed to have heard some 16th Brigade infantrymen crying, but still advancing. The 2/2nd's CO, Lieutenant-Colonel Chilton, later said of Bardia that there was great tension that morning, with not only individuals but the whole unit – and we might add, the whole division – wondering whether they could 'take it'. He added: 'It is not just an individual experience, but a mass phenomenon which, depending on many circumstances, can produce great achievement or panic'.[16] From the early hours, great achievement seemed more likely, as the initial attack went without a hitch.

While the 2/1st Battalion fought its way along the perimeter north of its breakthrough, the 2/2nd went south. The 2/3rd soon followed and advanced east. Italian resistance was sporadic, some Italians giving up without a fight, while other batteries and posts resisted hard. Nevertheless, by midday 6000 Italians had been captured and the Australians were realising that the size of the garrison had been

2.9 AWM 004914

greatly underestimated. In **Photograph 2.9** one prisoner is receiving help from an Australian, probably Private David Roberts of the 2/3rd Battalion. Roberts himself would be captured later in 1941. One of the Italian prisoners, Lieutenant Carrera, assisted in treating Australian and Italian wounded at the battalion RAP. A makeshift hospital was set up in the anti-tank ditch, where Sapper Beilby saw 'some hideous wounds'. He gave his last cigarette to an Italian with 'one shoulder shot off'. In return he got the pen with which he wrote his diary entry.[17] Several hundred Italian prisoners were released when six Italian tanks came forward and attacked the 2/3rd Battalion. As the tanks menaced the battalion headquarters, they encountered three anti-tank guns mounted on trucks. Led by Corporal Arthur Pickett of the 16th Anti-Tank Company, the gunners destroyed all six tanks. Some time that day, Lieutenant-Colonel Jerram, CO of the British tank battalion, sent a message to Mackay: '16th Brigade infantry is bloody marvellous!'[18]

Shortly before noon, the 17th Brigade began its assault, when the 2/5th Battalion and several companies of the 2/7th attacked on the 16th Brigade's right. The 2/5th were already tired from a long night march; the subsequent fighting did not go according to plan. Close range enemy artillery fire, the late arrival of the tanks and lack of artillery support all slowed the advance. Anxiety rose at brigade and divisional headquarters, but determined officers and men improvised and by early morning of 4 January had reached their objectives deep inside the fortress, with little help from the allotted tanks. Along the way they took thousands of prisoners, nearly 3000 metres of the enemy perimeter, and at least 60 artillery pieces. **Photograph 2.10** shows men of the 2/7th Battalion, probably at the end of 3 January, after they had passed their first great trial as soldiers in a fight around the Capuzzo/Bardia Road. One participant, Philip Hurst, described the assault as like 'a war movie with our chaps advancing through a pall of smoke and dust, shells bursting amongst them and the sun glinting on their fixed bayonets'.[19] The battalion's A Company captured six posts and widened the breach in the enemy line by 2000 metres. B Company took about 2000 prisoners and captured numerous machine guns and artillery pieces.

2.10   AWM P00643.007

Hurst added:

> Some men were going down but amazingly getting up again and moving on, all the time maintaining their line and spacing. I was proud to be part of it. It was an inspiring sight to me but must have been frightening to the watching enemy . . .[20]

The Italians' later testimony vindicated this supposition. Private Norman Kerslake, at far right, is wearing one of the leather jerkins that convinced the Italians facing the seemingly inexorable advance that this shiny clothing was bullet-proof. It was not, of course, and some men were hit. Hurst saw one distraught member of another battalion crying while cradling his mortally wounded brother. B Company lost four officers within minutes. Such losses, and prisoner escort duty, reduced the company's 120 or so men to 45 men by dusk, and A Company to 66.

Although they could not know it after their first success at Bardia, the men still standing in this photograph faced a tough fate. All three would be captured on Crete, and Ian MacDougall (centre) would die in German imprisonment in 1945.

On the extreme right of the assault on Bardia, the 2/6th Battalion had been given the demanding job of making a diversionary attack at the southern end of

2.11 Courtesy Harry New

the fortress on 3 January. This necessitated crossing the deep Wadi Muatered and attacking the heavily armed and fortified Post 11. Some of the most intense fighting at Bardia raged around this post, which was still holding out at the end of a day that cost the gallant 2/6th 27 killed and 32 wounded. The battalion did capture some 550 metres of the wadi's north bank.

By the end of 3 January about two-thirds of Bardia's perimeter was under the control of the 6th Division, which had penetrated approximately two kilometres into the fortress. In **Photograph 2.11** two 2/2nd Field Company sappers congratulate each other late that day. At left is Sapper Jack Nicholson, a hardworking 'Don R' (motorcyclist). Sergeant Alec Crawford (right) would receive a Military Medal for the 'great courage and coolness' he had shown that day. His subsection constructed two crossings of the anti-tank ditch under fire and then, when his section commander was wounded, Crawford ensured that the mine disarming continued successfully. By war's end Crawford was a captain with 2/8th Field Company, with an MBE for outstanding work in New Guinea. Nicholson's hat, the sign and clock are his souvenirs of the day.

In **Photograph 2.12** 6th Division men are examining a bigger souvenir – the gun in an emplacement inside the fortress. The photographer has shown no dead Italians, but Australians saw them everywhere. The gun is a 20 mm Breda Model 35 cannon, an anti-aircraft weapon that could also be used against ground targets. This gun was probably adopted by an Australian unit in the months ahead. The walls of stones, sometimes long breastworks, at other times smaller 'sangars', appear in many photographs taken at Bardia. They were characteristic of the inner defences rather than the perimeter posts, which were concreted and level with the ground. The typical concrete post comprised a large underground bunker

2.12 AWM 041688

connected by concrete trenches to two weapon pits at each end. The pits contained machine guns and anti-tank guns, but no overhead cover, so when under fire their occupants were tempted to retreat into the shelter, away from the fight. Post 11 was of the latter type, though it held many more men and weapons than was typical. An officer who looked over the captured positions on 4 January saw 'Dagoes lying about dead and dozens of Breda and Anti Tank guns around in solid concrete pillboxes – terrific defences'.[21]

On 4 January the 16th Brigade was ordered to take Bardia town, which was partly located on a clifftop, partly on a beach below. The 2/2nd Battalion took the low road, supported by British tanks and machine gunners, while the 2/3rd took the high road with tanks and the cavalry squadron's Bren carriers. The 2/1st would advance on the left. All three faced some stiff fighting and marching. The tanks proved invaluable as the 2/2nd first captured a fort and then, while taking thousands of prisoners, entered the lower town. Meanwhile the 2/3rd entered the upper town behind the tanks and cavalry regiment's carriers, which sped through desultory shellfire to get into the town. The tanks fired occasionally into the windows of the white-walled buildings. **Photograph 2.13**, originally captioned 'Troops

2.13   AWM 006083

rushing through the streets of ruined Bardia in search of stray enemy' was apparently re-enacted by 2/2nd Battalion men soon after the actual event.

More than 30 000 Italians had been captured, but the battle was not quite over. Brigadier Savige was sure that his 17th Brigade would end Italian resistance in the south that night, even though his men had been fighting hard through the previous day and night. Nevertheless Mackay halted the 17th around midday and ordered the 19th Brigade to pass through them to attack south on 5 January. When they did, the 19th Brigade enjoyed artillery support on a scale not previously available to the 17th. Resistance was generally half-hearted and the brigade suffered only three wounded.

The 2/11th Battalion led the advance with tank support. One participant remembered that when ordered to fix bayonets, the men cast 'somewhat nervous grins at one another', as the war for which they had trained so long was at last with them.[22] **Photograph 2.14** depicts unidentified troops of this brigade. The original caption says they captured three generals and their staff in a wadi, which suggests that they were the 2/11 Battalion's B Company: it captured two divisional headquarters. The canvas haversacks the men are wearing on their chests were for gas masks. Though smiling, the 2/11th were footsore, had come under heavy shelling and had

2.14 AWM 041691

seen some horrible aspects of what one dubbed the 'intimate side of war'. He was horrified by the sight of a headless Australian corpse.[23]

Post 11 was still under fire from the 2/6th Battalion, but the Italian commander decided to surrender when tanks approached. Lieutenant-Colonel Godfrey sought him out and shook his hand. It was discovered that the post had sheltered 350 men – 10 times more than usual – with numerous weapons, including eight artillery pieces and 39 machine guns. No wonder the 50 Australians who attacked it with rifles and grenades on 3 January had not captured it. Mopping up and pursuit of Italians fleeing westward ended the battle of Bardia on 5 January.

The Australians' nagging concern as to whether the 6th Division could meet the standards of its illustrious predecessors in the First AIF now vanished. 'Tell all the old diggers I have a collection of stories that will knock any of theirs bandy legged,' one exultant private wrote home.[24]

General O'Connor praised the 'excellence of the Staff of the 6th Australian Div'. The division's success, he said, was 'thoroughly deserved'.[25] By any measure, the 6th Division's first battle had been a great victory. One yardstick was the vast number of Italian troops captured. A small proportion of the 40 000 captured is depicted with just one captor in **Photograph 2.15**. At left, guarding them without

2.15   Courtesy Elizabeth Thurston

a weapon, is the 2/1st Field Regiment's Bombardier Ted Fulton, who we last saw bare-chested on a guncrew in Egypt. He recalled later that this group had come out to the guns and waited a while, relieved to know they had survived, before being ushered on. One offered Fulton a crust of bread from his overcoat pocket. Fulton considered it 'stupid' that just hours earlier his troop had been blasting these same men with high explosive.[26] Private James Atock wrote home after the battle that watching the streams of thousands of Italian prisoners escorted by one or two Australians had in the last few days been amusing, though the days before that were 'not so amusing'.[27]

Bardia's commander General Bergonzoli had boasted to Mussolini before the battle that the fortress was 'impregnable'. Given the numbers of men defending it – reportedly three men per metre of front – it should have been formidable. These men had plenty of materiel with which to fight: the attackers captured more than 400 artillery pieces, more than 100 tanks and, most valuable to the transport-strapped Australians, 708 motor vehicles. Some British officers unfairly alleged that Australian soldiers wilfully destroyed much of the equipment they captured. This was unlikely in an army desperate for the equipment their British suppliers had been unable to provide.

There was some unmilitary behaviour, as for a few days men ran wild, gathering rings, badges, watches, binoculars, pens and pistols as souvenirs. In an atmosphere of hilarity, they discovered and drank alcohol, gallivanted about in captured

2.16 AWM 004921

vehicles and played with grenades and pistols. General Mackay complained on 10 January that 'civilianism' was beginning to break out. As evidence of a growing 'picnic spirit' he cited: 'promiscuous firing of enemy rifles and pistols and exploding of bombs ... dressing in articles of Italian uniform like clowns and not like soldiers, [and] collecting of dogs'.[28] He may not have been amused by the behaviour of the 2/2nd Battalion men in **Photograph 2.16**. Three men are wearing Italian headgear. One man is holding a dog. Yet that soldier is also wounded. The soldier in the fez, Private Tom Harvey, later won the Military Medal for evacuating three wounded comrades under fire at Sanananda. The flag they are holding is from the Bardia Town Hall, and their battalion did as much as any other to secure the capture of that central point. In short, if some behaved wildly after the battle, they had done their job wonderfully during it. Inevitably some had paid a price: 130 Australians were killed and 326 wounded. Corporal Alf Parsons had 'the unpleasant duty' of burying Australian and British dead in a cemetery across the Egyptian border. It took three days and nights.[29] After Bardia, in the words of a 17th Brigade publication, 'not only did we have to be worthy of the old A.I.F.; we now had to be worthy of our own dead. We had our own tradition'.[30]

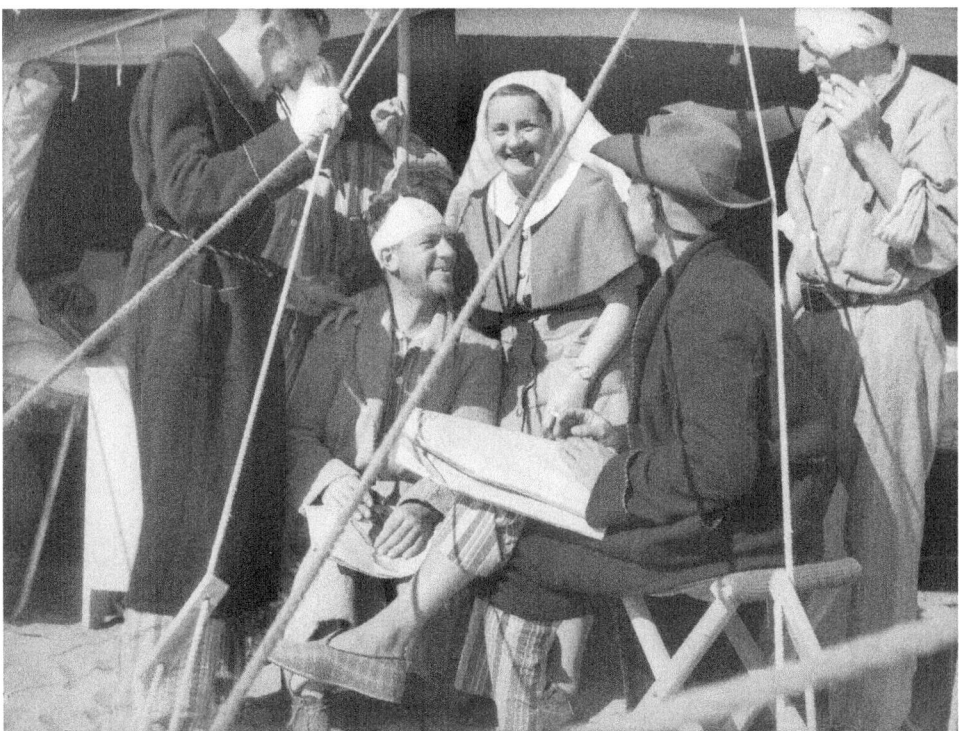

2.17 AWM 005227

In **Photograph 2.17** casualties of the battle are talking about Bardia to an Australian sister at the 2/2nd Australian General Hospital at Kantara, Egypt, on 10 January. Another member of the 2/2nd AGH noted as he helped transport casualties by sea from Bardia to Alexandria how the wounded Australians did not complain of their pain, and indeed descriptions of Australian casualties as either uncomplaining or positively cheerful are common.[31]

The pictured casualties are obviously having a good laugh. At centre with the head bandage is Sapper Albert Bower, of the 2/1st Field Company. The caption says that in Palestine he had been largely responsible for capturing a German spy, and that despite his wound he was keen to return to the front. By the time of the photograph, the front had moved to Tobruk.

CHAPTER 3

TOBRUK TO BENGHAZI

Three days after the fall of Bardia, the 16th and 19th Brigades had moved some 150 kilometres west along the Libyan coast and were outside the perimeter defences of Tobruk. While the Australians enclosed the eastern side of the fortress, the British 7th Armoured Division covered the roads leading south-west and west from Tobruk. Tobruk's 25 000 defenders were surrounded, but were well protected by an anti-tank ditch, wire and underground concrete posts. For more than two weeks, nocturnal Australian patrols secretly gauged the defences. A captain wrote of this period that his battalion were living on bully beef and army biscuits twice a day, with water rationed to one quart every 24 hours.[1]

The attack that opened before dawn on 21 January was modelled on the Bardia operation. Engineers blew gaps in the wire and disarmed mines so that the British tanks – now numbering just 12 – could cross. Sapper Loubet declared Bardia a picnic compared to Tobruk, where his party were caught in enemy shellfire.[2] There was another formidable supporting artillery bombardment, this time from even more guns, including a battery of the newly arrived 2/3rd Field Regiment. Again the 16th Brigade led the advance, this time with the 2/3rd Battalion in the van. By capturing five posts as planned, it cleared a breach for tanks and infantry to enter. While the 2/3rd continued marching west and capturing posts, the 2/1st entered the gap and pushed east, and the 2/2nd fanned out north beyond the perimeter. The Australians advancing towards Tobruk in **Photograph 3.1** are possibly members of the 2/2nd. As the photograph shows, a cloud of dust, whipped up by shells, wheels and tracks, hung over the point where they entered the perimeter. Encountering relatively light resistance, the battalion captured 10 batteries and covered more than 3 kilometres in 2½ hours. The Bren carrier pictured may be that of

TOBRUK TO BENGHAZI   47

3.1   AWM 128411

Captain Bill Laybourne Smith of the 2/3rd Field Regiment, who was a Forward Observation Officer with the 2/2nd Battalion that morning. He wrote to his wife that an important lesson he learnt in this battle – his first – was the great comfort the infantry took in having their own shells falling 'accurately and thickly in front of them'. The other was the courage and cheerfulness of those infantry. He gave a lift to at least 12 of them on this first morning. Each was:

> laughing and using filthy language, four days beard on their faces but never a thought that they had done enough or that someone else should be brought up to carry on ... [They] rode along for a while talking and joking with me and then quietly faded off to carry on with their job.³

The 2/6th Battalion, attached to the 16th Brigade for the assault, entered the perimeter behind the 2/2nd and took a place on its right.

The 2/7th had the task of entering the perimeter east of the original breach and to take over from the 2/1st, on the right flank of the advance. **Photograph 3.2** is a fine study of the 2/7th's men as they gathered at a gap in the wire to fulfil that role. On his helmet one man wears goggles, a useful aid in the frequent dust storms of this period. Most have the bayonets that we saw their battalion training with in

3.2 AWM 128410

Chapter 1. At far left is the battalion's Regimental Medical Officer, Captain Norman Godby, who would have a relatively easy battle. The 2/7th had none killed and only nine wounded, though as one member wrote home, there were dangerous moments: 'I had the pleasure of fourteen shells landing within about fifteen yards of me, but apart from dirtying my nose in an endeavour to get closer to mother earth, got out of it quite whole'.[4] The men look relatively relaxed here, probably anticipating that all will go smoothly. For many that would not be the case in the near future. All but three of the men pictured would be prisoners of war by June. Godby would be captured in Crete and Mentioned in Despatches on three occasions. The man next to him, 'Meggsie' McDonald, was one of the battalion's great characters and soldiers. He had enlisted as a private in November 1939, risen to become sergeant by the time of this photograph and would be a lieutenant by 3 February 1943 when, to the sorrow of his battalion, he would be killed trying to rescue wounded comrades in New Guinea.

Dead Italian soldiers feature in **Photograph 3.3**, taken soon after the assault on Tobruk. The Italians here were often said to have been even less determined than those in Bardia, but the pictured men seem to have died at their posts. Laybourne Smith saw some machine-gun posts where the men had stuck to their task till shot

3.3 Courtesy Winston Fairbrother

dead. He said this was 'the only time in this first day' that he had not 'concentrated mechanically' on his task. He left the scene rapidly.[5] Sapper Loubet was among a group blasted by Italian artillery on the first morning, and saw Australians 'with their guts blown right out and others with heads and legs right off. It looked like a slaughter yard'.[6]

Determined defenders met the left flank of the 19th Brigade when it followed through the gap made by the 16th Brigade and set off from its start line 4.5 kilometres inside the perimeter. Behind a heavy barrage, its three battalions advanced in open order. The 2/8th Battalion came under fire from more than 20 dug-in Italian tanks. The Australians fired back and stormed them, putting 14 out of action and capturing the remainder. Sergeant Jim Burgess jumped on one tank to throw a grenade into it. A machine gun mortally wounded him, but he had the presence of mind to put the pin back in the grenade, thus saving nearby 'cobbers'. An eyewitness then 'had the pleasure of seeing the M.G. that got him wiped out by about 3 Aussies on the end of steel'.[7] Sergeant Ron da Fonte neatly summed up the battalion's action: 'Dago fought well, but nothing could stop the boys'. He called it 'a Great show', but a costly one.[8]

In the centre of the 19th Brigade advance, the 2/4th suffered some casualties in capturing the enemy sector headquarters, including General Manella, commander of the Tobruk garrison. The 2/11th Battalion, on the right of the advance, suffered no casualties in reaching its objective, the escarpment on which a group of them are standing in **Photograph 3.4**. Most are members of 14 Platoon, commanded ably by the irrepressible Lieutenant KT 'Katie' Johnson, at centre middle row with his hand on his hip. The man at front centre holding the Bren is Corporal 'Blue' Pauley. Described in the battalion history as 'ever-aggressive', he would be wounded attacking enemy trenches on Crete, and subsequently captured. Behind him to the right and next to Johnson is the latter's enterprising runner, Private Dave Rogers. He would soon be wounded at Derna, and his brother Bernie at Tobruk. Dave Rogers, Pauley and Johnson would all be wounded and captured in Crete. Indeed Crete would bring disaster upon most of this cheerful group. Of the 29 men who can be identified, the vast majority would be captured, six wounded and three killed in Crete. Corporal David Brand, the soldier with his right hand near his collarbone at centre-back, would be wounded in Greece, though he would make a good recovery and eventually be Premier of Western Australia, the state from which all these men hailed.

From the photographed position these Western Australians could look over the town, and some Italians who saw them up there on 21 January drove up in lorries to surrender. Abandoned enemy guns and emplacements are in the background.

As can be seen in the photograph, black plumes were rising on the horizon by the end of the day. That sight and the lack of sound from the enemy guns suggested that the Italians were finished. By nightfall, all but isolated pockets in the eastern half of the fortress had been captured.

Further west the 2/3rd Battalion had been fighting all afternoon against tough opposition on the perimeter, and at dusk they were just west of the El Adem Road. Some Australians, especially in the 17th Brigade, had marched more than 30 kilometres that day. So it was a tired but content division that rested where it could that night at Tobruk.

A full-scale attack was planned for 22 January, but proved unnecessary. On the perimeter the 16th Brigade's task soon became a matter of collecting prisoners as the attackers marched from post to post. Two Bren carriers of the divisional cavalry led an advance into the town itself. An Italian officer approached Lieutenant Hennessy of the cavalry, offering to surrender the town. Hennessy met Admiral Vietina, ready to hand over his sword. Hennessy waved aside the offer with the comment: 'You keep it mate. I've got enough souvenirs'.[9] Hennessy sent for Brigadier Robertson, who came forward with Brigadier Morshead, who was there as an observer and who would later be the Australian most identified with Tobruk. In the naval headquarters, Admiral Vietina surrendered the town and naval station to the two brigadiers and about 10 cavalrymen. More carriers and a company of the 2/4th Battalion soon arrived and in a famous

TOBRUK TO BENGHAZI 51

3.4

3.5 AWM 005414

gesture, seen in **Photograph 3.5**, one or more Australians removed the Italian flag and ran a slouch hat up the flagpole outside Admiral Vietina's headquarters. The incident and photograph are well-known, but there are at least four different stories identifying the 2/4th Battalion soldier who owned and raised the 'flag'. The official caption identifies the man as Corporal Eldrick Grant, who served with the 2/4th in Libya, Greece and Crete before transferring to the 2/17th Battalion, with which he was killed near Jivevaneng, New Guinea, in 1943. Chester Wilmot called the gesture in this photograph 'the real token of the fall of Tobruk'.[10]

The 6th Division, with support from British tanks and troops, had captured Tobruk within 29 hours of piercing the perimeter. The Italian resistance was slight, but the speed, aggression and skill of the attackers were significant too. So was the planning of the commanders, especially General Mackay, whose concern to preserve the lives of his men found expression in his refusal to attack until he was satisfied with the reconnaissance of the enemy defences and 500 artillery rounds had come forward for each gun.

The gunners had done a wonderful job, as British General O'Connor surmised when he heard how low the casualties were. 'Row terrific gun hot' was one gunner's simple description of the firing between 5.30 and 8 am.[11] In **Photograph 3.6** infantrymen are admiring the Australian artillery's handiwork: an Italian anti-aircraft gun knocked out by a direct hit. Of the 13 infantrymen who can be identified – all from the 2/11th Battalion – seven would soon be killed on Crete, but thanks largely to their artillery support, the unit suffered only one fatality at Tobruk. Conversely the enemy had many, as Eric Loubet recorded that day: 'You should have seen the dead dagoes. They were everywhere. Blown to pieces'.[12] The 2/8th suffered 104 casualties, nearly one-third of the division's losses at Tobruk. A member of the battalion who went over the ground that the

3.6 AWM 005612

2/8th had taken exclaimed after re-examining the Italian defences: 'We did the impossible'.[13]

The division's anti-tank regiment, the 1st, was still in Egypt, but anti-tank support was provided at Tobruk by three anti-tank companies, one from each brigade. **Photograph 3.7** shows some of these gunners entering Tobruk on 23 January. They are riding 'portees', mounted 2-pounder anti-tank guns of the type described in Chapter 1 as being so effective at Bardia.

The division's artillery still had some hard fighting ahead in this campaign. Its vehicles also had plenty of driving ahead. In **Photograph 3.8** two members of the 6th Division Supply Column are working on the engine of a 1 ton Australian-made Chevrolet General Service van called Joyce. The windscreen has been removed to prevent reflection that might attract enemy aircraft. The Service Corps of which this unit was part faced a formidable task in supplying the division in this campaign. British and New Zealand supply units helped significantly, but the divisional supply column's transport was stretched to the limit. Indeed, the addition of captured Italian trucks from Mersa Matruh and beyond, many of them 5 to 10 ton, was

3.7 AWM 005394

vital to the provision of ammunition reserves at Bardia and Tobruk. About 200 vehicles were captured at Tobruk, with about 25 000 Italians and much other war booty that would prove invaluable.

An example of that war booty is apparent in **Photograph 3.9**. Here a relaxed-looking signaller, Matt Hamilton of 'K' Section Signals, stands with ammunition for a 75 mm or 100 mm gun captured at Tobruk, or possibly Bardia. The empty cartridge cases on the ground reveal that this gun has been in action. An infantryman expressed a common opinion when he wrote home that the Italian artillery was 'good, except the ammunition . . . in which there were a great many duds'.[14] Captured weapons would be turned against Axis troops in the defence of Tobruk and Crete in the months ahead. Note that Hamilton has his forage cap flaps down for protection against the wind, which could be bitter in January in the Western Desert.

Photograph 3.10, also taken at Tobruk or Bardia, shows another signaller, Mick Berryman, holding a piece of Italian signals equipment, taken from the Italian suitcase at left. The truck is a 15 cwt Ford, with a steel frame

3.8　　　　　　　　AWM P02399.015

over the rear supporting a heavy canvas covering and an inner canvas to act as a blind for blackout curtaining. Inside, a crew of two worked a 101 wireless set, one per battalion and one at brigade headquarters. The antenna, visible in the background, was fitted to the frame. The '16', white numbers on green, represents 'K' Section Signals. The camouflage appears to be a version of the British Caunter 'splinter' pattern of green, sand and light blue. 6th Division Signals laid nearly 200 kilometres of telephone cable at Bardia and a further 250 kilometres at Tobruk. They won three decorations for bravery at Bardia, while Corporal Ken Clift won a DCM and Signalman McKeague an MM at Tobruk for capturing 60 enemy soldiers.

As the Australians entered Tobruk town, the British 7th Armoured Division was driving west again. On the same day, an advance guard of the 6th Division, comprising primarily a squadron of the divisional cavalry and a battery of the 2/1st Field Regiment, was ordered to move on Derna, another 220-odd kilometres west along the coast. Mackay hoped that they might be able to take the town by 26 January, which, depending on one's state of origin, was Australia Day or Anniversary Day. In case this was not possible he ordered the 19th Brigade, with artillery, engineer and machine-gun support to advance to Derna.

By 25 January the cavalrymen under Major Macarthur-Onslow had reached Derna and come under fire that signified this as a job for the infantry. The 2/11th Battalion began arriving that day, and in the afternoon Lieutenant-Colonel Louch sent forward two companies for his battalion's first really testing action. Brigadier Robertson had assured him that although the cavalry had come under artillery and machine-gun fire on reconnoitring the aerodrome, a swift, vigorous assault should push the Italians out. In fact, the Italians had been holding their fire. They occupied

3.9 Courtesy Douglas Margetts

high ground overlooking the bare plain across which the leading company, under Captain Ralph Honner, had to advance after dismounting from its trucks and making a long approach march. **Photograph 3.11** was taken during the advance. The 6th Division men in it are only specks, but this is a rare action shot, a still from film Damien Parer was making of the assault. The single shellburst visible at left was soon followed by many more, and even Parer took cover. One shell landed a metre from Private Ern MacLeod, who was very grateful that it, like about one-third of those that he had witnessed landing at Tobruk, was 'really poor'.[15] Honner, a dynamic, courageous and highly intelligent officer, risked his life to bring a mortar into action. He and three of the men in Photograph 3.4 of 14 Platoon at Tobruk – Lieutenant Johnson, and Privates Rogers and Graffin – played leading roles in getting into forward positions to determine where the enemy were, to bring fire on enemy artillery and to call the company forward. After dusk and a brisk fight, Honner's company occupied the hangars on the aerodrome. Another 2/11th company moved onto the escarpment overlooking Derna on the coast. Of this day, an Australian gunner wrote with admiration of the infantry his regiment supported: 'They are the ones!'[16]

The 2/4th Battalion arrived at nearby Martuba that day and Robertson ordered it to gain control of the huge Wadi Derna, which ran south from the town. By dawn on Australia Day, 14 men of the battalion got across the wadi and, after a bloody skirmish, established a foothold. They held off determined counter-attacks and were eventually joined by two companies.

Robertson hoped for a swift victory at Derna on 26 January, but found the enemy still determined to resist. In **Photograph 3.12** Robertson is conferring with

3.10 Courtesy Douglas Margetts

another man vital to this operation, Lieutenant-Colonel Barker of the 2/1st Field Regiment (at left). 'Doag' or 'Holy Joe' Barker, who had won an MC in 1918, was tall, alert and daunting; his men's initial dislike gave way successively to admiration and adoration. He was 'the gamest soldier you could ever meet', explained one gunner, as he described Barker's reaction to the destruction of one of his guns at Derna. He saw Barker stroll to the gun position, move one gun to an approximate line on the enemy position, then stand on an ammunition trailer and correct the fire until it silenced the enemy piece.[17] Derna is pictured below them on the coast: 'a beautiful sight from top of scarp'.[18] The Australian artillery's accurate fire quelled enemy counter-attacks and supported Australian advances, but was limited to 10 rounds per gun per day. The Italian artillery was more numerous and Lieutenant-Colonel Louch declared its fire very heavy even by 1918 standards.

27 January was a terrible day for the 6th Division Cavalry, on the far left of the Australian line. In an Italian ambush four of its finest NCOs were killed, including Sergeant George Mills, who had been Mentioned in Despatches for work that included a prominent role in the drive into Tobruk. Three others were captured. **Photograph 3.13,** taken near Derna a few days later, shows one of the regiment's carriers with its distinctive camouflage. It appears to have a wireless aerial, though lack of functioning wireless had contributed to the disaster of 27 January. The photograph is dated 30 January, the day on which Macarthur-Onslow found the lost carriers. Mills lay dead beside his vehicle, with a note of farewell in his diary.

58 TOBRUK TO BENGHAZI

3.11 AWM 127946

3.12 AWM 005675

3.13 AWM 044257

Taken on the same day, **Photograph 3.14** portrays members of 2/11th Battalion advancing down the road into the town of Derna. Enemy shells were exploding in the distance, but Private Norm Duff (later captured in Crete) has taken time to turn round and exchange banter with watching members of the unit. The leading troops, under Captain Honner, found that the Italian rearguard had at last evacuated Derna and an Australian could write in his diary, 'Infantry in the streets, ours!'[19] The rest of the 19th Brigade and the hard-marching 17th tried fruitlessly to cut off their retreat. A signaller with the 17th Brigade reported accurately that the infantry were almost marched off their feet trying to catch the retreating enemy in this campaign.[20] A gunner driving past infantry on the way into the town recalled an 'infanteer' with a harelip calling out: 'Have you bastards got corns on your arse, like I've got on my fu–ing feet?'[21]

While some Australians rested in Derna, others busily helped themselves to what the Italians left behind. How much looting they did is disputed. Italian troops and Libyans had apparently been ransacking the town before the Australians arrived.

3.14   AWM 005647/11

The Australians were soon proving their military worth again on what one called 'the long but not open road' before them.[22] Even before the Australians took Derna, their engineers had needed to open the cratered road into the town. On the road out of Derna, hundreds of mines had to be cleared and craters bypassed before the Australians could drive up the road on the escarpment that led to the 240 kilometre-long plateau of the Jebel Achdar. With the 16th Brigade still in Tobruk, the 17th and 19th Brigades advanced in a pincer movement on Giovanni Berta, the administrative centre for the region, but on 2 February found the town unoccupied. The division possessed insufficient vehicles to move more than a brigade forward at a time, even when all the hard-pressed AASC transport was employed on the task. The 19th Brigade was chosen to lead the Australian advance across the Jebel Achdar on 4 February. Barce fell the next day, and on 6 February Onslow and some of his cavalry Bren carriers drove into the major city of Benghazi. The following morning Lieutenant-Colonel Louch led a force, based on his 2/11th Battalion, south towards Beda Fomm, but they arrived too late to participate in the great British victory there. In the meantime, Brigadier Robertson led part of the 2/4th Battalion into Benghazi. **Photograph 3.15** depicts Robertson's car, with the divisional kangaroo-over-boomerang symbol prominent, driving past the Guard of Honour – provided by the 2/4th Battalion – just before the official handing-over ceremony. These tall, sunburnt men in drab,

3.15 AWM 005848/29

unadorned greatcoats and helmets impressed the thousands of civilian onlookers, who cheered the Australians. Their joy was multiplied when, after the ceremony, the soldiers proceeded not to loot the town, but to pay for what they wanted – especially butter and rolls – with the Italian money they had picked up in the previous month. By that evening, most of the brigade was heading south towards Agedabia.

That day, Bombardier Harold Adeney was lying on a stretcher in the 2/2nd Field Regiment's RAP. He had fallen ill, probably due to the rain, frosts and biting wind of the previous few days. He was eager to get back to his gun crew, and wrote home that: 'Up to date we haven't succeeded in catching up with the dago and it looks as if it's all over as far as Libya's concerned'.[23] Complete victory in the Libyan campaign did indeed beckon, for if O'Connor's army advanced and captured Tripoli, the Axis would be unable to continue the campaign. However, this was not to be. Winston Churchill and his Chiefs of Staff had long considered the Libyan campaign as primarily a defensive operation to safeguard the British base in Egypt. Their higher priority was preventing Greece from falling to the Axis, and they repeatedly offered forces to help the Greeks. When the Greeks accepted in February, the die was cast for the 6th Division. General Wavell initially planned to leave the 'seasoned' 6th in Cyrenaica for defence and send it after a month or so to join the 7th Australian Division in Greece. However, Blamey convinced him that the 6th should go first, as the 7th was insufficiently trained and equipped.

The 6th Division had performed marvels in its first campaign. It created a new Australian military tradition, which the other three AIF infantry divisions aspired to uphold. It also took the pride of the 6th to new heights.

Giarabub oasis

While the 6th Division was crossing Cyrenaica, one of its components was in action some 230 kilometres south of Bardia, on the edge of the Sahara Desert. There lay Giarabub, an oasis occupied by some 1500 Italians. In December, Wavell had sent the headquarters and two squadrons of the 6th Division Cavalry to Giarabub, where despite being outnumbered by 10 to 1 they forced the enemy from their outposts into defences around the oasis itself. Raids by the advance party of this group in mid-December were among the first actions of the Second AIF. Under the command of the tough Lieutenant-Colonel Fergusson, and using trucks rather than the less durable carriers, they mounted a three-month siege. In mid-March 1941, the 18th Brigade sent an augmented battalion group to Giarabub, days after Italian shells critically wounded Fergusson. Nevertheless, the cavalrymen

3.16   Courtesy John Mole

3.17 Courtesy John Mole

contributed to the subsequent fight at Giarabub, which fell to the Australians on 21 March.

It was after the fall of Giarabub that **Photograph 3.16** was taken. It shows members of the regiment's RAP using one of their trucks to transport a cavalryman for burial. The body, wrapped in a sheet, is that of Corporal Eric Trounce, who had been killed on a reconnaissance patrol that came under heavy fire on 31 December 1940. His body had been buried in the sand by the Italians, and it was not until the siege was over that the sombre group pictured – some wearing their distinctive black cavalrymen's berets – could find and rebury Trounce's body. Trounce and Trooper Fuller, killed on the same patrol, were the regiment's only fatalities in the three-month siege. Six others were wounded. The two cavalrymen also had the sad distinction of being the second and third members of the AIF killed in this war, just two days after Corporal Eric Goble, who had been killed patrolling outside Bardia.

In **Photograph 3.17** cavalrymen of the RAP are basking in their victory, with conquered Giarabub behind them. The two Australians pictured are enjoying playing with some of the captured equipment: Italian AA and anti-tank guns. More than 25 artillery pieces and 10 000 shells fell into the victors' hands. The success and low casualties of the 6th Division Cavalry Regiment at Giarabub exemplified the triumph of their division in Libya.

CHAPTER 4

GREECE

Map 2 Greece 1941

An advance party of the 6th Division sailed with the first elements of 'Lustre Force', as the force for Greece was called, on 5 March 1941. At that time the 16th Brigade was in Tobruk, the 17th and 19th in western Cyrenaica, so it was some weeks before they were ready to sail from Alexandria. The 16th was first to return to Egypt. On the night of 17 March, when hundreds of its men were enjoying well-earned leave in 'Alex', military policemen came through the streets shouting that they must return to camp, as they were moving the next morning. On 18 March they embarked. When Italian aircraft attacked the slower ships in the convoy, the Australians fought back with Brens and captured Bredas. The ships

4.1 AWM 006824

remained afloat, but the passengers' experience was ominous. The 19th and 17th Brigades followed in early April.

Greece made a great impact on the Australians: its greenery and beauty stood in stark contrast to the desert. Moreover the Greeks were very welcoming and soon won the division's sympathy. **Photograph 4.1** depicts a friendly local giving directions to Australians on Athens' Acropolis. The soldier at right is a member of the 6th Division AASC. At far left is Sergeant George Bauer, of the 2/1st Field Ambulance, who had served in the Medical Corps in World War I, and lowered his age at enlistment to serve in World War II.

Australians were welcomed wherever they went. In **Photograph 4.2** an Australian Bren carrier is driving through the village of Daphni, where the Australians had a staging camp. Among the cheering onlookers, a child in the foreground is giving the thumbs-up sign, a common Allied gesture. One young local likened the Australians to heroes from Greek mythology.[1] This carrier may belong to the 16th Brigade group, which was moving north on 27 March. On the Greek roads, the carriers' brakes wore out quickly and steering became enormously difficult on the numerous sharp turns.

Photograph 4.3 shows Greek villagers greeting Australian troops. The caption does not tell us where or exactly when this was taken, but the slouch hats suggest it was before operations began. The Australians may be of 19th Brigade Headquarters. Their Bren gun is mounted on a tripod for anti-aircraft use, a necessary precaution in the weeks ahead.

The arrival of modern guns and equipment must have been comforting to the locals, especially when they saw big 25-pounders like those of the 2/3rd Field Regiment in **Photograph 4.4**. They are driving north through Larissa just one day before the German invasion began on 6 April. Larissa would later feel the full force of the German invasion. Even on 7 April it was showing signs of earthquake damage and recent Italian bombing. News of the German invasion did not daunt

4.2 AWM 006841

4.3 AWM 007758

most Australians, including the member of the regiment who wrote: 'Whacko! The game is on'.[2]

On 6 April the 17th Brigade was still in Egypt. Moreover, Wavell had decided, because of German pressure in Libya, that the 7th Division and other units would not follow the 6th as planned. The only other Commonwealth forces in Greece were the New Zealand Division, a British armoured brigade and the headquarters of I Australian Corps. They and the brave but ill-equipped Greek army could not possibly halt

4.4 Courtesy Les Bishop and 2/3rd Field Regiment

the 27 divisions the Germans made available for conquering Greece and Yugoslavia. The only Australian formation in the forward area was the 16th Brigade, which on the day of the invasion moved to the Veria Pass on the Vermion–Olympus Line. By 9 April, the Germans had seized Salonika from the Greeks.

The British–Greek army on the Vermion–Olympus Line faced attack from the east, but also anticipated a German assault from the rear, through the Monastir Gap and down the Florina Valley. To forestall this possibility, 'Mackay Force' was created on 8 April. As well as New Zealand and British elements, it included components of Mackay's division: the 19th Brigade (minus the 2/11th), the 2/3rd Field Regiment and 2/1st Anti-Tank Regiment. This force came directly under British General Wilson, while Corps Commander Blamey commanded the New Zealand Division, parts of the 6th Australian Division and the 12th Greek Division. These complex and unwieldy command arrangements typified this campaign, as did the numerical inadequacy of 'Mackay Force' for its allotted task.

At the conference where Mackay Force's composition was determined, it was decided to move the 6th Division back to the Olympus–Aliakmon Line, which would be harder to outflank. Accordingly, the 16th Brigade began moving on 10 April.

That day the 6th Division fired its first shots of the campaign. The 2/4th and 2/8th Battalions were in new positions at Vevi, in the Florina Valley. They were already exhausted, having spent the previous night covering wide fronts in the snow without shelter. A 2/4th Battalion private asserted, credibly, that unlike the Germans, 80 per cent of the unit had never before seen snow. On preceding days they had long road and rail journeys, as well as exacting marches in full gear. A narrow mountain pass at Vevi and lakes to its east made it a formidable defensive position, but the rugged terrain hampered communications and transport.

When, 'like a dark grey caterpillar on a great green lawn', a German column approached the position on 10 April the 2/3rd Field Regiment reacted.[3] Captain Laybourne Smith, a Forward Observation Officer at Vevi, wrote home:

> My orders flew over the wire and the first rounds screamed through the air . . . A few furious moments and back went the Hun, but five trucks stayed on the road as silent witness that my Troop can really shoot.[4]

The Germans did not press their attack further that day.

Photograph 4.5, the only official photograph taken at Vevi in this period, shows Lieutenant-Colonel Dougherty of the 2/4th (at right) on 11 April. With him is the commanding officer of the flanking Greek battalion. The weather is in stark contrast to that of the 2/4th's previous campaign. Dougherty's battalion was covering more than 6 kilometres of front, with one company held elsewhere and only the carrier platoon as a reserve. Within his battalion was a pervading sense of bafflement about the situation. Blizzard conditions on 11 April added to the confusion, which the Germans exploited to manoeuvre close to the Australians. The 6th Division infantrymen now fired their first shots in Greece, and were glad to see their small arms and the supporting British and Australian artillery drive off the attacking infantry. The German artillery responded in kind. Private Cade of the 2/4th

4.5 AWM 128423

saw one man who lost an arm; Lieutenant Chrystal saw another who was 'just about off his head'.⁵

The defenders held throughout the 11th, but Wilson had ordered Mackay to hold until the night of 12/13 April, so that the transport-strapped Greek forces could withdraw. On 12 April, the position of the three rearguard infantry battalions – the 2/4th, 2/8th and the inexperienced British 1st Rangers – became perilous as the Leibstandarte Adolf Hitler Brigade attacked. When the 1st Rangers fell back unexpectedly, two guns of the 2/1st Anti-Tank Regiment and those of the British 2nd Royal Horse Artillery engaged the advancing Germans over open sights. They delayed the enemy advance in the centre. The 2/3rd Field Regiment also fought the Germans from just a few hundred metres away as the Australian infantry were forced back. German tanks were in the 2/8th's positions by dusk, and the battalion fell back 'in some confusion'.⁶ Most reached their transport, while the artillery transport sought to save their forward guns. With fire support from their 5th Battery, the 2/3rd Regiment managed to save all but two bogged guns. Brigadier Herring, the CRA, stated that this regiment and the 2/1st Anti-Tank, inspired by the British Royal Horse Artillery, had 'done wonders'.⁷

4.6 AWM 007647

Photograph 4.6 depicts members of the anti-tank regiment with one of their 2-pounder guns in an idyllic setting, apparently the day after the fight at Vevi. In that fight the regiment, which had sited its guns well forward with the infantry, had lost heavily: 16 guns and 79 men captured. It was a sanguine introduction to battle for a unit that would receive few other chances to fight. The 2/4th Battalion had also suffered badly when one company had unwittingly walked into German positions and been captured. That night the 2/8th could assemble only 250 men, many without weapons. Only in the sector defended by the 2/4th did the defenders of Mackay Force hang on until the appointed hour of 8 pm, although the battalions had, as planned, fallen back to fight another day. This was partly due to the commander of the infantry rearguard, Brigadier Vasey, who remained cool amidst the disaster.

Later, he, General Mackay and others were critical of the 2/8th. Nevertheless, as the official historian explains, the critics took little note of the unit's exhausting rush from the desert and its 4-kilometre long front above the snowline. This front it defended effectively for two days until, with invulnerable enemy tanks in its company areas and no flank support, it had fallen back. One 2/8th participant in the action felt the unit fought well: on 11 April he described the forward companies as, 'clashing with Jerry and just slaughtering them'; on 12 April, 'Battle royal started today and did our boys give 'em hell'.[8] He spoke of the retreat beginning only with an order to retire. Another says that after being ordered to retreat, the scattered men did not think of surrender, but of rejoining their unit.[9] Captain Bill Laybourne Smith summed up the feelings of many on this retreat when he said 'all we wanted was another smack at Gerry'.[10]

On the same day as this withdrawal, Blamey announced the formation of an ANZAC Corps, comprising the 6th Australian and the New Zealand divisions, under his command. Evocative as this term was, its existence was unknown to many members of the division until after the campaign or, for many of those captured, after the war.

On 13 April, a courageous British rearguard enabled Mackay Force to reach its designated positions on the left of the Olympus–Aliakmon Line. Meanwhile the 16th Brigade had been falling back from the Veria Pass to the right of that line. **Photograph 4.7** shows 2/2nd Battalion men after crossing the Aliakmon River that day. Like the troops at Vevi, these men had been suffering from fatigue and intense cold before they began their withdrawal on 11 April. The route was more than 50 kilometres long and mountainous, so mules and donkeys like the one pictured were invaluable. Even with the donkeys' help, the pictured men are carrying a great deal of equipment. The battalion were justly proud that in their 'Long March' they jettisoned no weapons or equipment, though some laden donkeys had fallen over a precipice while negotiating thick snow. Sappers of the 2/1st Field Company had ferried them across the swift-flowing Aliakmon. The flat-bottomed punt they used, guided by a wire rope and adjusted to the current, is just visible behind the greatcoated men in the foreground. In none of their later campaigns would 6th Division men need such warm clothing.

On 15 April, with the defenders of the Olympus–Aliakmon line in their allotted positions, new plans rendered the dispositions irrelevant. General Wilson had decided, with Blamey's concurrence, that the disintegrating Greek army could not hold its positions on the western flank. Consequently the 2/5th and 2/11th Battalions were sent to guard the flank at Kalabaka as part of Savige Force, named after

4.7 AWM 007844

Brigadier Savige. His 17th Brigade battalions and the 2/11th had only arrived in Greece on 12 April.

Wilson also decided that, although the Germans were not in contact with the 'British Imperial' forces on the Aliakmon Line, these troops must fall back to a line that they could hold without Greek support. Wilson and Blamey chose a position some 150 kilometres back, astride the passes at Brallos, Delphi and Thermopylae.

On this fateful 15 April the senior British commanders in the Middle East determined that Lustre Force would have to be evacuated altogether from Greece. Meanwhile, Australian and New Zealand forces halted a German advance on the Servia Pass. Laybourne Smith recalled: 'We did some very pretty shooting and my troop alone stopped an attempted attack . . . catching the poor bloody huns crossing the icy cold river and absolutely wipeing [sic] out the whole show'.[11] The Anzac forces retreated the following day.

On 16 April it became apparent that the main German thrust was now hitting the British right flank, where if they captured Pinios Gorge they could cut the road to Larissa and thereby block the escape route of virtually all British forces in Greece. Blamey ordered Brigadier Allen to take to Pinios Gorge a brigade group based on the 2/2nd and 2/3rd Battalions, the Bren carriers of the 2/5th and 2/11th

4.8   Courtesy Rex Langthorne

Battalions and a New Zealand battalion and artillery. In **Photograph 4.8** tired-looking men of the 2/2nd Battalion Carrier Platoon pause for a meal. Two of the unit's eight carriers would travel over 300 kilometres in the campaign, by the end of which the platoon would all be serving as footsoldiers.

For Australians driving on the congested roads, poor weather offered the only protection against rampaging German aircraft. Mist and rain on 17 April allowed four of the seven forward brigades to withdraw through Larissa to the new defensive line. The defenders in the Pinios Gorge prepared to fight.

That night, 2/2nd Battalion patrols skirmished with Germans near Tempe. The full force of the German assault hit the 16th Brigade on 18 April. First, German tanks forced back the New Zealanders. Then, in the afternoon, 35 aircraft attacked the Australians, before tanks and infantry assaulted the 2/2nd Battalion. The Australians' Bren guns and 3-inch mortars took heavy toll of the German infantry crossing the Pinios River. 'Our fellows bowled them over in hundreds and thousands' wrote a lieutenant, 'but he seemed to have millions to send at us'.[12] When tanks came down the road into the Australian positions defeat was certain. The fate of troops retreating elsewhere depended on how long the Anzacs at Pinios Gorge could fend off that defeat. There are no photographs from this day of vital fighting, but **Photograph 4.9**, taken in 1945 from positions held by the 2/2nd Battalion in 1941, gives an impression of the ground looking towards

4.9   AWM 130534

the road and river that were keys to the battle. The fighting here was confused, with some units ordered to withdraw, others to stand. New Zealand 25-pounders knocked out several tanks, but the surviving Panzers gradually forced the 2/2nd back, destroying trucks as they went. Enemy aircraft also strafed the infantry and supporting Bren carriers. Australians vainly fired their small arms at planes and tanks. At one point 15 men surrounded a tank, which, impervious to their bullets, ran over two Australians. The survivors and other Australians fell back towards the trucks. Some became cut off in the hills.

The 2/3rd's trucks took the men back 1000 yards, where they disembarked and formed a new line in the dark. Within minutes a Panzer appeared, its commander standing in the turret. Australian fire soon riddled him with bullets. The battalion CO, Lieutenant-Colonel Lamb, urged his men to keep firing, as the tanks could not fight in the dark. Both sides fired ineffectually at each other, until Brigadier Allen ordered Lamb to withdraw.

Despite a German ambush, by dawn most of the 16th Brigade was making its way south. The 2/2nd Battalion had suffered 105 casualties (including 61 prisoners), the 2/3rd 100 (including 60 prisoners). As Brigadier Allen said of this surreal, confused battle: 'We had to hold this position until after dark and thanks to the morale of our force it was done'.[13]

6th Division troops fought another significant battle that day to facilitate the Allied withdrawal. At Elasson, the 2/3rd Field Regiment's 25-pounders and New Zealand and British artillery were ordered to hold off German tanks and infantry through the 18th. Captain Laybourne Smith recalled:

> ... I do not think we were expected to get out and we ourselves almost gave up hope when we saw the massed tanks come down the pass ... For twelve hours we fired continuously and ... let off 7000 shells that day ... the men played their part like something possessed and our fire did not slacken ... our Regt held up the whole German army.[14]

The 2/3rd's historian called the Elasson battle 'the Regiment's finest performance as a unit in the war'.[15] The gunners' effort allowed a night withdrawal, and by 19 April all but the troops in the hills at Pinios Gorge had made it south of Larissa.

Wherever they travelled during daylight hours they were now subject to air attack. These attacks required iron nerves from drivers, but one, Private Felix Craig, showed extraordinary courage at Pharsala, when a convoy came under attack from about 12 dive bombers. The AASC history says: 'Craig continued to respond with a machine gun, making himself a target until killed, providing a diversion which allowed most vehicles to get away'. The AASC's historian is plainly angry at the 'vacillation' that deprived Craig and the AASC of a Victoria Cross.[16] Scenes like that in **Photograph 4.10** were repeated all over southern Greece for the next week. With their truck under a camouflage net and a tree, resigned-looking members of 6th Division Signals are resting. Signaller Tom Neeman MM wrote that with this unit in Greece, 'we learnt what a hell on earth aeroplanes can make'. He noticed, like many others, that the bombing and strafing destroyed few vehicles. He found it 'surprising how much shrapnel and bullets can pass through a car and still leave it in running order'.[17] Apart from air attack, 6th Division Signals suffered from shortages of equipment, especially motorcycles. All available bikes broke down in the rough conditions and on one occasion a rider used four separate bikes to deliver one message. The unit suffered shortages of rations, found its visual signalling gear virtually useless, and did not use its vehicles close to the front, necessitating arduous carrying of cables and stores which had constantly to be moved as the front receded.

On 22–23 April detailed orders were issued for the withdrawal of Lustre Force from Greece. A covering force would occupy the road to Athens while troops were evacuated from beaches near Athens and in the Peloponnese. Rearguard actions

4.10 AWM P02053.001

would continue to be vital, as would activities like that pictured in **Photograph 4.11**, where 2/8th Field Company sappers are preparing to crater the main road in the Erithrai Pass on 24 April. A ridge south of Erithrai was one of the designated covering positions for the withdrawal. The 17th and 16th Brigades passed successfully through this position and towards the beaches. While the bulk of 2/8th Field Company withdrew, its headquarters were left to fire charges on five hairpin bends on the Erithrai road. Following this, they set off in two vehicles to catch up with their unit. On halting for a passing train at a railway crossing on the outskirts of Athens, they were astonished to see German troops sitting in the box cars, their legs dangling. Fortunately, the Germans did not react and the Australians were soon driving south. As a sapper from the company said after the campaign, 'I certainly know what they mean when they say the Engineers earn their money in a retreat'.[18]

Like the engineers, the artillerymen were vital to successful withdrawal. **Photograph 4.12** shows smoke rising from the barrel of a 2/1st Field Regiment gun as it fires on German troops, probably on 24 April. Only one of the regiment's two batteries, 1 Battery, and RHQ had arrived in Greece for the campaign, which went awry before the second could be sent. They had spent a week

4.11 AWM 044637

negotiating chaotic road and rail conditions and avoiding enemy air attack. So effectively were the guns dug in and camouflaged at Brallos Pass that when first emplaced on 21 April they were not even attacked by the enemy aircraft that flew low overhead. However, the men were suffering. On 20 April one had written: 'God! Are we absolutely all done in. No sleep for a week to speak of ... I've had enough'.[19]

The pictured gun came under command of 2/2nd Field Regiment near Brallos. The 2/2nd's guns fought an extraordinary action on 22 April, when two precariously positioned guns threw back attacking enemy columns. The pictured gun's troop was part of the 19th Brigade's rearguard on the Thermopylae Line. It was to this rearguard that Brigadier Vasey gave a famous order: 'Here we bloody well are and here we bloody well stay'.[20] The gunners made their own wisecracks as they waited for the attack, telling each other what 'good stiffuns' their corpses would make or telling others to get out of their trenches to give the bombs a chance.[21]

The skeleton detachments manning the 2/1st guns endured an exhausting night repositioning their weapons. After firing registration rounds as soon as light

4.12   AWM 069879

allowed, the guns in the area underwent a two hour 'saturation bombardment' from up to 60 aircraft.²² At 10 am the men emerged from their slit trenches and gun pits to find their guns scarred and dusty but still serviceable. Within an hour enemy troops were in range, advancing in the open. The guns and the supporting 19th Brigade infantry's small arms drove them to cover. By nightfall the rearguard was under great strain but still holding on. So was the New Zealand rearguard on the coast of the 'Thermopylae Line'. Had either rearguard position fallen quickly, catastrophe would have followed for the retreating troops.

Instead, Lustre Force's evacuation occurred relatively smoothly over the period 24–29 April. The 19th Brigade departed on Anzac Day from Megara and Marathon, the 16th and 17th Brigades from Kalamata on the night of 26 April. 'Anzac Day and we are doing just the opposite to the old Diggers', one injured soldier wrote on board ship.²³ On 26 April Australian guns were still in action, and one of them can be seen in **Photograph 4.13**. The 2/3rd Field Regiment was acting with Australian anti-tank gunners, engineers and machine gunners and the 4th NZ Brigade as a covering force at Erithrai, or more precisely Kriekouki, where since 22 April it had been tasked with preventing an enemy penetration south to Athens. On 26 April its test came. Enemy aircraft reconnoitred the area fruitlessly, and

4.13   Courtesy Les Bishop and 2/3rd Field Regiment

when late that morning about 100 enemy vehicles, including tanks, approached in a tight column from Thebes they presented a perfect target for the gunners.

The pictured gun is at full recoil, with the road along which the Germans travelled visible in the background. The Germans retreated, leaving eight vehicles behind. Their aircraft soon reappeared and the gunners took to their slit trenches, though one guncrew reportedly had the immense satisfaction of seeing a Dornier run into one of their shells and crash on the plain below. So effective was the regiment's camouflage that it suffered not a single casualty that day. That night this force was ordered to embus and move to Porto Rafti, east of Athens, for evacuation. Disturbing news came earlier that day of a German parachute landing at the Corinth Canal, where two companies of the 2/6th Battalion were among the troops who sought vainly to prevent the numerically superior Germans from cutting the road that linked the main British forces.

Photograph 4.14 was probably taken at about the same time, as the 2/5th Battalion retreated towards evacuation. The unit had a frustrating campaign, caught up in the withdrawal without being given a chance to show their fighting ability. On 19 April, which they dubbed 'Black Saturday', enemy aircraft repeatedly attacked the unit's convoy from 7.30 am, killing 15 and wounding 24. This nerve-tearing ordeal was repeated on a smaller scale in succeeding days, but the unit eventually boarded their evacuating ships with their personal arms, ammunition

4.14 Courtesy Ivor White and 2/5th Battalion

and sangfroid intact. The picture shows men able to smile despite the frustrations of a defeat far too big for them to reverse. Many felt upset that they could not be the saviours the Greeks had hoped they would be. The generous farewells given by many civilians made that feeling all the more poignant.

For the 2/3rd Field Regiment, 27 April brought frustration as they waited in exposed positions at Porto Rafti. The Germans entered Athens that morning. The gunners had to destroy all vehicles except the quads that pulled the guns. Laybourne Smith's troop, which had not lost a gun or suffered a casualty in two campaigns, was less than a kilometre from the beaches when:

> thirty feet above the trees the air became black with planes . . . and they gave us the doing of our lives. Before a man could move every vehicle in my troop was on fire. True we saved one gun but nothing else. The vehicles blazed and the ammunition in them exploded and the bastards came back and back until the ground around seemed alive with explosive bullets. The final count showed one man killed, fifteen wounded . . . and everyone scared stiff.[24]

The surviving gun and its smouldering quad are visible in **Photograph 4.15**. After the attack, a cry went up that someone was trapped in a burning quad and Gunner Alwyn Colman risked exploding ammunition to go back and check. The man was not there, and Colman was injured, but still assisted in mustering the wounded. He received a DCM. So did Sergeant Douglas Russell, who is pictured standing near the gun's breech, his back to the camera. This gun had been the last to leave the Kleidi Pass, Vevi, on 12 April, and enabled nine other guns to escape. Four of the five pictured men who can be identified had 'DX' numbers, meaning they enlisted in Darwin. Now, as the surviving guns could not be evacuated, the gunners used them one last time to drive back approaching Germans, then destroyed them before embarking aboard HMS *Ajax*. Wherever they were evacuated, artillerymen left behind their beloved guns, drivers their cherished trucks. Most men carried only ammunition and weapons.

Danger persisted when the ships left Greece, as **Photograph 4.16** attests. The pictured transport ship *Costa Rica* was taking 2500 Australians to Alexandria

80 GREECE

4.15 Courtesy Les Bishop and 2/3rd Field Regiment

4.16 AWM 069346

when aircraft attacked on 27 April. An Australian on board counted 70 machine guns, probably including those pictured, and wrote of tremendous noise as they opened fire.²⁵ Another Australian on the nearby *Dilwarra* recalled the fascination of watching:

> your own and other tracer bullets endeavouring to get a direct hit. It was hard to believe how close some of the bombs came to hitting us, instead of just exploding in the ocean nearby. I am not bull-shitting when I say some actually came between the ships' funnels and then just cleared the side of the deck.²⁶

At about 2.40 pm an enemy aircraft came out of the sun and dropped a bomb that detonated close to the *Costa Rica*. She was soon sinking. Although most troops were below deck, in darkness, they followed orders and waited their turn quietly to go aboard an approaching destroyer. Within 45 minutes all had been transhipped. Many were taken on to Crete rather than Egypt. As they were disembarked, the soldiers gave three cheers for the Navy, a sentiment apparently shared by every Australian evacuated from Greece.

4.17   AWM 007604

Photograph 4.17 depicts an Australian who, like the majority of the division, returned to Egypt. With his recently issued Thompson submachine gun in Alexandria on 28 April, Private Clive 'Commander' Armstrong of the 2/3rd Battalion seems to epitomise defiance in defeat. The war-time caption says: 'Yeah, they nicked me this time . . . but just wait . . . we'll get even . . . we'll be meeting up with 'em again'. Corny though this sounds, other Australians were saying much the same.

Australian and other Commonwealth troops tended to inflate the number of German casualties in Greece wildly. They officially totalled only 1160 killed and 345 missing – as compared to thousands of

Greek losses and 903 Commonwealth deaths, including about 320 Australians. More realistic was a feeling that had the odds been fairer, and with more British air support, the Australians could have performed better. The 2/4th Battalion RMO reported that it was 'the universal opinion that given air equality they would take on the Hun 3:1 and beat him'.[27] Nevertheless, a perceptive Australian infantry officer was probably close to the truth when he stated in his memoirs that the Germans had in fact 'outclassed' the still inexperienced Australians in Greece.[28]

Nearly 1500 members of the 6th Division went into captivity in Greece. The vast majority would never fight again. While the official historian called the fighting withdrawal of some 500 kilometres 'an outstanding military achievement', General Mackay was critical of his division's performance.[29] He argued that one reason for the defeat in Greece was that troops became too anxious about being outflanked, and consequently worried about self-preservation. He said that far fewer Australian troops were brave than was thought: just four or five in each platoon. He harangued his officers about the need for better road convoy discipline and responses to dive-bombing, and in particular the relationship between discipline out of the line and in it: 'I guarantee that seven-tenths of men who don't salute and don't dress properly are those who became hysterical when the bombs fell'.[30] Mackay had a reputation among officers for 'carping criticism', but Brigadier Vasey also stated that the campaign revealed deficiencies in Australian training.[31]

On the other hand, the RMO of the 2/4th Battalion noted the confidence of the men even when prospects of getting out of Greece seemed slim. Moreover, he said: 'I have never seen such a large number of people, honestly trying to do something for someone else'.[32] A 2/1st Battalion driver, later killed in Crete, argued after the campaign that the 'only thing [the Germans] couldn't destroy was the spirit of the boys', and this assertion was to be tested in the months ahead.[33] When Mackay made his criticisms in mid-May, his division was widely scattered. Some were in Crete, undergoing their next trial by aerial ordeal, others were regrouping in Palestine, many were in German imprisonment, and still others trying to get back home from Greece.

Photograph 4.18 shows a group of 2/2nd Battalion men who had been unable to rejoin their lines after the fight at Pinios Gorge. They were photographed on 8 May on Euboea Island, which they had reached in separate parties, and from where they were about to travel to Turkey and rejoin the Australian forces. Men like this gave the lie to Mackay's sour comments. Among them were the 2/2nd CO, Lieutenant-Colonel Chilton, fourth from the left among those standing. He was an outstanding commander, as would become especially obvious when he led one of Australia's best brigades. By his side, fifth from left, is Captain Charles Hercules Green, another future CO, who would be killed commanding 3RAR in Korea. On Chilton's other side is Corporal Harry Honeywell. He had revealed

4.18　　　　　　　　　　　　　　　　　　　　　　　　　　AWM 134872

his courage when, in conjunction with Lieutenant Bosgard (third from right), his marksmanship had reportedly helped turn back a tank somewhere in Greece. When warned of danger, it is said that Honeywell often replied: 'The German or Italian has not been born who can kill me'.[34] The Japanese would kill him in Papua. Bosgard would die within days of Honeywell. Corporal James Shanahan (far right at back) would be killed in New Guinea in 1945 as a lieutenant. Captain Buckley, between Shanahan and Bosgard, would become CO of the 2/1st Pioneer Battalion. Three future COs were among other escape parties, who risked all to continue the fight.

As Horner notes, the recriminations between Allies and within the Australian command in Greece demonstrate that generals can find much to criticise in any unsuccessful campaign.[35] The victory in Libya probably made the 6th Division's men unduly confident in their military prowess. Their confidence, at whatever level it sat before the Greek campaign, must have been affected, though their feeling that the odds had been desperately unfair had a solid basis in fact. A seaman aboard a ship that evacuated Australians from Greece to Crete noted: 'They all show signs of their privations but are still able to laugh and crack jokes'.[36] As this suggested, 6th Division men would carry a fighting spirit to Crete and beyond.

CHAPTER 5

CRETE

Map 3a Crete 1941

Some 8500 Australians, predominantly members of the 6th Division, landed in Crete from Greece. In **Photograph 5.1** heavily-laden Australians are arriving at Suda Bay, Crete's main port, in late April 1941. They had to leave their transport and other heavy equipment in mainland Greece, and the two men pictured have saved more equipment than most: the soldier at right is even carrying his slouch hat. Hats were one of many scarce items on Crete. Men rescued from the *Costa Rica* were without arms or equipment, and many had no boots. One disenchanted gunner summed up common problems when he noted: 'We are camping out again and no tucker or blankets not nice prospects'.[1] The pictured soldiers are happy to have arrived, but their smiles would not last.

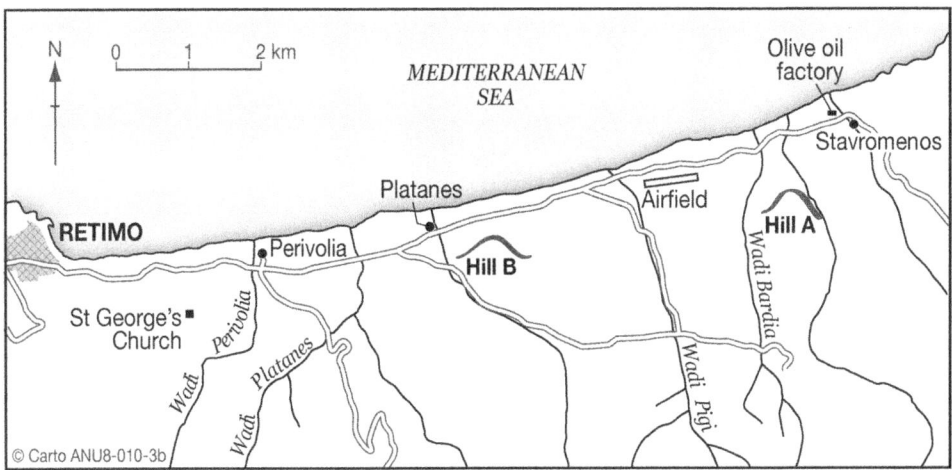

Map 3b Retimo detail

5.1 AWM 007805

On arrival, men were marched away from the harbour, as in **Photograph 5.2**. Bombardier Harold Adeney 'did a forced march of nearly ten miles which left everybody complete[ly] exhausted after our terrific three weeks in Greece'.[2] His regiment marched to Canea, Crete's capital, but others had much longer journeys. The 2/4th Battalion marched for four days before being shipped to Heraklion, where they were warned that a German parachute attack was imminent. By then all had heard the German radio propagandist Lord Haw Haw's warning that Crete was for its garrison an 'Isle of Doom'.

New Zealand general Sir Bernard Freyberg was appointed commander of 'Creforce', as the combined British–Greek defenders were called. General Mackay had flown to Crete on 24 April but was ordered to return to Alexandria on 29 April, leaving Brigadier Vasey as the senior Australian commander. Freyberg is pictured on about 2 May at Suda Bay in **Photograph 5.3**, addressing men of his command, including an Australian (with colour patch) in the foreground. A 2/11th Battalion eyewitness to this or a similar address heard Freyberg refer 'to we Australians as

86   CRETE

5.2   AWM 007623

5.3   AWM 069892

being a tough looking bunch, whom he felt sure could deal very effectively with parachutists. Our reputation with the bayonet should discourage any would be invaders'.[3] An artilleryman noted, however, that the general 'did not fail to stress the inadequacy of our strength to defend the island'.[4]

As Freyberg knew, the key to Crete's defence would be its three airfields. All were in the north: one at Maleme near Canea, in the north-west of Crete, a second 48 kilometres east of Canea at Retimo (as the Australians called Rethymnon) and a third a further 55 kilometres east at Crete's largest town, Heraklion. If German airborne forces captured one or more of these airstrips, air transports could bring in heavy equipment and infantry reinforcements. Freyberg adjusted his dispositions according to his limited means: the artillery pieces and tanks sent from Egypt were inadequate in number and quality. Furthermore, after 19 May he had no aircraft.

5.4   Courtesy Les Bishop and 2/3rd Field Regiment

Enemy air superiority thwarted plans to evacuate the large number of unarmed troops to Egypt. Thus, instead of a reduction of the Australian contingent to 3500, on the eve of the German attack it was still 6500. There were 15 000 British troops, and 7750 New Zealanders. There were also 10 200 Greek troops. Though poorly armed and trained, the Greeks' morale was generally high. So too was the Australians', many of whom were keen for revenge against the Germans. High spirits are apparent among those in **Photograph 5.4**. Major Ian Bessell-Browne (left) and Captain George Killey (bareheaded) of the 2/3rd Field Regiment are sharing a joke with Lieutenant-Colonel Leslie Le Souef (in cap, obscured at right), CO of the 2/7th Field Ambulance. All were Western Australians, all were or would be decorated (Bessell-Browne MBE, Killey MC and Le Souef OBE) and after exerting themselves fully in the campaign, all would be captured in Crete.

Australians figured prominently in Freyberg's defence plan. The 6th Division infantry and artillery units at his disposal and their strengths are shown in Table 4:

Table 4 6th Division infantry and artillery units on Crete, May 1941

Unit	Strength
2/1st Battalion	582 officers and men
2/4th Battalion	553 officers and men
2/7th Battalion	581 officers and men
2/8th Battalion	384 officers and men
2/11th Battalion	645 officers and men
2/2nd Field Regiment	554 officers and men
2/3rd Field Regiment	502 officers and men
16th Brigade Composite Battalion (2/2nd and 2/3rd Battalions)	443 officers and men
17th Brigade Composite Battalion (2/5th and 2/6th Battalions)	387 officers and men

Virtually every unit of the division was represented: there were, for example, 150 men of the 2/8th Field Company. Members of 6th Division Signals feature in **Photograph 5.5**, standing amongst the rubble caused by an air raid on Suda Bay. Signals equipment was in desperately short supply on Crete and lack of adequate communications would heavily influence the coming operations, although 'L' Section of 6th Div Signals used its limited equipment to its utmost and lost most of its personnel in the fighting. In early May, enemy air attacks in Suda Bay made unloading ships so dangerous that only volunteers did it: chiefly from Australian engineer units and the 2/2nd Field Regiment.

On the eve of the German invasion, 6th Division forces had been allotted to three of the island's four main sectors. The exception was the Maleme sector, defended by the New Zealand Division. In the Suda Bay sector, under British General Weston, 2280 Australians and a regiment of Greeks were put under the 2/2nd Field Regiment's CO, Lieutenant-Colonel Cremor, and designated 'Cremor Force'. It included the 2/2nd Field Regiment (fighting as infantry), the understrength and ill-equipped 16th and 17th Australian Composite Battalions, and Groups 'A' and 'B', comprising 600 Australian artillerymen and engineers, respectively.

5.5   AWM P02053.005

In the Retimo sector, under Brigadier Vasey's command, was the 19th Brigade – now comprising the 2/1st and 2/7th, 2/8th and 2/11th Battalions. He stationed the 2/1st and 2/11th at Retimo under Lieutenant-Colonel Ian Campbell of the 2/1st, keeping the other two brigades further west with his own headquarters at Georgioupolis, in anticipation of a German seaborne landing. There was also at Retimo a battery of 2/3rd Field Regiment, armed with 14 diverse guns. **Photograph 5.6** shows 2/11th Battalion men in Crete, perhaps at Retimo in this period. Positioned under olive trees on terraces east of Retimo, the Australian troops were virtually invisible from the air. The 2/1st Battalion was defending the airstrip and Hill A which dominated it, while to their left the 2/11th was on Hill B.

The Heraklion sector was commanded by Brigadier Chappel, whose 14th British Brigade was the core of the defence, but it included the recently reinforced 2/4th Australian Battalion.

On 13 May, the enemy began systematically bombing these sectors. Aircraft were a menace everywhere. A gunner in 2/3rd Field Regiment took **Photograph 5.7**, which indicates just how low they flew. Such attention led one veteran to say even the air attacks in Greece were 'a picnic' compared to those in Crete.[5] On 13 May a Messerschmitt Bf 110 like that pictured was downed by a Lewis gun while circling the Retimo airstrip just 30 metres up; the dead crewmen's map of the Retimo defences was inaccurate.

On 16 May, with the invasion expected daily, Freyberg cabled Wavell that the defenders would 'at least . . . give an excellent account of ourselves'.[6]

5.6

AWM P00129.002

5.7

Courtesy Les Bishop and 2/3rd Field Regiment

5.8   AWM 012571

20 May – Airborne attack

The invasion began on 20 May, and the sight of hundreds of aircraft disgorging thousands of parachutists impressed even those destined to suffer the consequences. The official historian says this sight was for everyone who saw it: 'perhaps the most majestic in their experience'.[7] One private dubbed it 'really a marvellous sight, but one that I do not want to see again all the same'.[8] They realised too how unusual this event was: Bombardier Adeney referred to what followed over the next week as 'the most amazing battle of modern times'.[9] Some fine photographs of the landings were taken late that day at Heraklion. **Photograph 5.8** shows parachutists and a burning aircraft descending in the 2/4th Battalion sector, west of the airfield. Two soldiers later recalled that all nine planes coming towards the 2/4th positions at one point were destroyed by anti-aircraft fire from the aerodrome. The sixth 'dropped its men but was hit and almost crashed on us, passing over our heads with a bare six feet to spare and crashed fifty yards away'.[10]

Lieutenant Cec Chrystal was prosaic in his description of the day at Heraklion:

> Hundreds of aircraft over and about 3000 parachutists were dropped a couple of hours later. We got stuck into them and gave them Hell killing hundreds. Several aircraft full were shot down in flames.[11]

5.9   AWM P02434.005

In **Photographs 5.9** and **5.10**, 2/4th men stand proudly in front of the wreckage of one of more than 240 Junkers Ju 52s that transported the parachutists to Heraklion. Such big, slow, low-flying aircraft made easy targets. Three battalion members like these attacked one transport that crash-landed near their position, killing the occupants with grenades and small arms. This incident epitomised the viciousness of the conflict that was just beginning. As one astute soldier noted, the fact that the defenders had been subjected to two weeks of 'continuous merciless and methodical Aerial blitz' from dawn till dusk led them to extract grim revenge on the paratroops. So did the knowledge that, 'once [paratroops] get a footing you're in bother'.[12] Another 2/4th man explained the 'frightfully bitter' nature of the fighting by the difficulty of guarding and finding room for prisoners.[13] In the background in 5.10 is a hill called 'North Charlie' by the Australians. 'Charlies', Australian slang for breasts, seemed appropriate for the two hills in the 2/4th area.

The German paratroops, or 'brolly men', had made a poor start in the Heraklion sector. Typical was the fate of those who landed near barracks in the 2/4th area: about 90 were killed, as opposed to three Australians. The Germans had greatly underestimated the defenders' strength, and at the end of 20 May were barely holding ground in and east of the town.

At Retimo the story was similar. When the Junkers Ju 52s approached in the afternoon, many were shot down before they could deliver their passengers, and numerous parachutists were killed either while descending or on landing. One

5.10   AWM P02434.007

Western Australian private considered the sight of descending paratroops 'glorious' and likened what followed to shooting ducks in mobs.[14] Like the 2/4th, the 2/11th were apparently ordered not to take prisoners on the first day at Retimo, though not thereafter. One private wrote that the no-prisoners order suited the 2/11th, who 'were out to get square'.[15] In fact, his section finished the day with seven prisoners, his battalion with at least 88.

Photograph 5.11 was taken from Hill A, looking east. The enemy troop carriers, eventually numbering 161, approached the coast between 'Refuge Point', jutting out in the left distance, and Stavromenos, visible on the road just below and to the left of Refuge Point. Flying slowly at about 120 metres, they then turned west. Many paratroops landed on or around Hills A and B. Captain George Killey, seen in Photograph 5.4 and now located in an observation post slit trench on this side of Hill A, shook hands with his signaller as the planes flew over and said: 'We may have five or six minutes to live but we will get a few before we die'.[16] In the next few minutes he killed three Germans with his revolver as they crawled towards him. The paratroops established a foothold on Hill A, but many who landed on low ground below the hills were killed or captured. Testimony to the high morale of the 2/1st Battalion was that even the unit's Transport Section made a bayonet charge, putting an enemy group to flight from a wireless hut near the airstrip. One 2/11th man wrote that 'being right in the drop area we were all in it', another that 'the boys were itching for [a] fight'.[17]

94 CRETE

5.11

AWM 131052

5.12

Courtesy Les Bishop and 2/3rd Field Regiment

When several transports tried to land on the beach, a 100 mm gun like that in **Photograph 5.12** opened fire at them. Ignoring enemy small arms fire, the gunners soon hit the nearest aircraft, which exploded in flames. The four 100 mm guns on Crete were placed on Hills A and B, primarily for indirect fire. Like all guns on Crete, they came without sights and instruments. Their ammunition was unreliable and they were hard to load and fire. Under Bessell-Browne and Killey, the two troops of 100 mm guns and the 75s at Retimo supported various operations over succeeding days.

5.13　　　　　　　　Courtesy Ivor White and 2/5th Battalion

By the end of the first day the Australians had suffered few casualties and still held the airfield. However, Germans controlled most of Hill A, were scattered among the vineyards, and about 500 survivors had drifted out of range to Perivolia village. One soldier's description of his section might have applied to most Australians at Retimo: 'All were as happy as a dog with two tails'.[18] In the Maleme sector on 20 May, the Germans gained footholds close to the airfield. Major Paul Cullen, commanding both the 16th and 17th Composite Battalions, shared his men's disappointment at not being sent immediately to counterattack there, after being warned to prepare. **Photograph 5.13** shows a member of the 17th Composite Battalion striking a martial pose outside his dugout, with Suda Bay in the background. The composite battalions remained in the Suda-Canea area, where the Germans made little ground that day. Nevertheless, the understrength and ill-equipped 2/8th Battalion was brought to support this area. The battle for Crete was in the balance.

MALEME-SUDA-CANEA

On 21 May the Germans consolidated their foothold on Maleme airfield, where transports began landing. Freyberg was determined to recapture the airfield, despite constant air attack and limited communications. He agreed to a night counterattack, which could suffer no enemy aerial interference. He decided to bring an Australian battalion from Georgioupolis in trucks to replace the 20th New Zealand Battalion, which would then use the same vehicles to participate in the counterattack. He also ordered his available artillery, primarily a troop of 2/3rd Field

Regiment, forward from Georgioupolis to shell the airfield. That day he had appointed Lieutenant-Colonel Strutt, the 2/3rd's former CO, to command the New Zealand artillery: a mark of the way Strutt and his regiment had impressed the New Zealanders in Greece.

The 2/7th Battalion was selected to come forward the 29 kilometres from Georgioupolis. Word of its move arrived late in the day. Late too was the transport slated to take it west, and the drivers were nervous of air attack. Vasey had ordered them to leave as close to 5 pm as possible, which the first units did; the last left at 8 pm and the relief of the 20th New Zealand Battalion was completed at about 11.30 pm. The subsequent counter-attack won some ground, but not the airfield. Vasey and the 2/7th's Lieutenant-Colonel Walker considered that the experienced, strong and fresh 2/7th would have been more effective in the counter-attack than the 20th. The 2/3rd Field Regiment's troop of four 75 mm guns under Captain Laybourne Smith made a valuable Australian contribution, hitting at least five and perhaps as many as 17 German aircraft on the airstrip. On the night of 22 May intense German pressure forced Freyberg to withdraw about 4 kilometres east, thus abandoning Maleme airfield.

This effectively ensured German victory in Crete. Reinforced by mountain troops, the Germans continued advancing over the next few days, despite the Australian gunners' disruptive fire. Vasey was allotted an area where he could command the 2/7th and 2/8th Battalions, on a line covering Canea and Suda Bay. By 26 May they were on the right of a new line east of Canea, along a north–south dirt road called '42nd Street'. The Germans were fast approaching. That night Freyberg visited the Australians and found them 'absolutely confident'.[19] His praise of Australian bayonet work would soon be vindicated. The adjacent New Zealanders agreed with Lieutenant-Colonel Walker that should the enemy come to close quarters they would fire and charge. At about 11 am on 27 May some 400 Germans approached the 2/7th positions and raided an abandoned depot. Walker ordered the two forward companies to attack. An eyewitness said this order lifted the previous days' tension. Australians fired and then, in the words of the battalion's Sergeant Thomas:

> Capt St E.D. Nelson with his company ('D') leaped into a bayonet charge. 'C' Coy followed and Maoris on right flew into fray. The onslaught was swift and demoralised the enemy who dropped everything and ran. By 1200 hrs the enemy were over 1 mile back and were running fast . . . A great spectacle to see tired men galvanized into action . . . this cost the enemy 300 killed on our front. 3 prisoners taken . . .[20]

A participant called this charge 'one of the epics of this war', and indeed it was notable in the division's history.[21] The Germans later launched an inquiry into whether Australians killed surrendering men. Rejecting the accusation, the Australians explained that they used not only bayonets but also captured automatic weapons. Ten Australians were killed and 28 wounded, including Sergeant 'Blue' Reiter, who led his platoon despite a head-wound and received a Military Medal for the action. He remembered that in the charge 'All the frustration of months of bombing and strafing was taken out on the Germans'.[22]

That day, Freyberg received orders to evacuate Crete, which he proposed to do by withdrawing over the mountain road to the south coast village of Sfakia. The road was crowded with ill-disciplined troops, while a rearguard including the 2/7th Battalion was formed to hold the rapidly advancing Germans. Between 28 and 31 May nearly 15 000 men assembled near the end of the tarred road, which trailed into a steep goat track down to the beaches. Sergeant-Major Stan O'Brien described the seven-hour journey down the goat track on 28 and 29 April:

> From here to the beach would be about 6 or 7 miles but if you asked anyone who traversed it, the distance they'd unhesitatingly reply 60 or 70. It was pitch dark and you had to keep up . . . I was so tired I wanted to lie down and die. We slipped and slid down boulders and rubble that chipped ankles, elbows and occasionally skulls.[23]

O'Brien was evacuated on 30 May, by which time the final rearguard was in position. Officially the 19th Brigade, it comprised the 2/7th Battalion, 2/8th Battalion, a British battalion and Laybourne Smith's two remaining guns. All had already been part of the rearguard, but this would be their biggest challenge. They ambushed and slaughtered the German advance guards on 30 May. At 9 pm on 31 May the last unit, the 2/7th, was still holding its ground under enemy shelling, despite appalling strain and pitiful rations, when it was ordered to the beach. After several hours of nightmarish marching, they assembled there as best they could among hundreds of hysterical troops.

A naval officer saw the 2/7th 'quiet and orderly in its ranks', but he was on the last barge out of Sfakia.[24] Lieutenant-Colonel Walker told his men that the navy would not return, but to escape if they could. News that they were trapped was 'a terrible blow', wrote one of his officers, for only the men's 'magnificent will-power' and that of their CO had kept them going. Another shock followed, with news of surrender.[25] According to another 2/7th man who later escaped, the commander of their paratroop captors told Walker that 'he considered the 2/7 Bn. the best troops that his men had encountered'.[26] 'Blue' Reiter asserted that everyone who managed to escape was bitter 'and our tolerance of the powers that be, unless they were very bloody good, was never the same'.[27] Lieutenant Marcus Edwards of the 2/2nd Field Regiment wrote in his diary on 1 June: 'Heard of capitulation and refused to believe'.[28] Four years of imprisonment followed. Questions of escape and surrender were also occupying Australian officers elsewhere on Crete.

HERAKLION

On 21 May, Cec Chrystal's diary reads: 'Fighting continued all night and day'.[29] The Germans were on the defensive throughout the Heraklion sector, where some 1250 parachutists' corpses were gathered by 22 May. Afraid of hitting their own men, German aircraft reduced their attacks until 23 May. Some even dropped supplies rather than bombs on the Australians, who used captured code books and flares to deceive the pilots. The 2/4th sustained no casualties from air attack during the Heraklion fighting. On 23 May the meticulous Dougherty sent a standing patrol to occupy the 300-metre high Apex Hill. Though outside the sector perimeter, from it German flanking movements were visible. The Germans were dropping reinforcements. Early on 26 May several hundred approached the Australians on Apex Hill from three sides. A bayonet charge carried them through the fire of at least 50 Germans to safety. The Germans took Apex Hill, but it conferred no decisive advantage.

Early on 28 May, Dougherty was ordered to prepare for immediate evacuation. The news surprised most of the Australians. The Germans dropped more parachutists and many bombs that day, but attempted no advances. That night, three British cruisers and six destroyers evacuated the Commonwealth garrison in a smooth operation, marred for all by the destruction and putrefaction they passed in bomb-torn Heraklion town.

The relief of getting aboard vanished when as many as 100 enemy aircraft at a time attacked for up to eight hours. **Photograph 5.14** shows one of the ships, HMS *Dido*, hit during this bombing. The 2/4th were spread among five ships, but *Dido* contained many. Private Bill Andrews was below decks when the pictured explosions occurred. He recalled:

> ... the P.A. system was beating out a popular tune, 'It's a Hap-hap-happy Day', when a tremendous explosion took place, everything turned red and black, I couldn't breathe.

A mate pulled Andrews on deck, where he recovered. Then:

> We both went back down to help and the scene was shocking. Most of the members of our particular section were dead. Those surviving, with a few exceptions were shockingly burnt.[30]

Another survivor called this the 'worst and longest day I have put in since joining the army'.[31]

5.14   AWM P00090.064

The 600 men killed or captured in the air attacks on the ships included 48 Australians. It was a ghastly farewell to the Heraklion garrison, who had disrupted the whole German plan for Crete. The loss was in part assuaged by the return of 3846 men, now veterans, with this convoy. Brigadier Chappel wrote to Vasey to praise the 2/4th. He noted that 'their behaviour in the pre-blitz period was excellent, and once the show started was outstanding'. He considered Lieutenant-Colonel Dougherty 'a first class C.O.'[32]

Retimo

At dawn on 21 May German troops blocked the roads east and west of Retimo. They also controlled most of Hill A, nearest the airfield. However, Campbell was determined that morning to clear them from Hill A and the low ground between the 2/11th and the coast. The Germans, who had expanded their hold on Hill A overnight, attacked almost simultaneously, and drove back the Australian assault. Captain Boyd Moriarty arrived with his reinforced company and replaced the wounded Captain Channell. When intense German attacks impelled Moriarty to describe the situation as desperate, Campbell brought forward most of another company and at about 7 am ordered Moriarty to attack and capture the hill.

5.15   AWM P04067.001

Moriarty organised his force, scrambling between positions to give them orders, and narrowly avoiding bullets that ricocheted off rocks whenever he became momentarily visible. His force comprised men of all the battalion's companies, including drivers. Their dashing attack succeeded brilliantly, recapturing the hill and leaving only scattered Germans between it and Perivolia. For the rest of the day the Australians mopped up the enemy between Hills A and B. The 2/11th captured Colonel Sturm, commander of the German Retimo force. Sturm was frightened and suspicious of the German-speaking 2/11th CO, Ray Sandover. However, other German prisoners were friendly to the Australians, whose marksmanship and willingness to stand and fight impressed the macho parachutists. They also welcomed the Australians' honourable burial of the German dead. The Australians in turn were impressed by the determination and equipment of the young Fallschirmjäger.

On 22 May Campbell was determined to shift the Germans blocking the roads at Perivolia and the Olive Oil factory at Stavromenos. He sent Moriarty and two companies to attack the Olive Oil factory, but 'the gallant Moriarty' was shot dead while reconnoitring.[33] **Photograph 5.15** shows his original grave, probably where he had been killed as he raised his head to look between the forks of a tree. The attack was aborted. Another assault failed that night. Lack of coordination with Greek units on both flanks hindered progress.

5.16 AWM 131071

Photograph 5.16 depicts crucial ground on the Perivolia flank. With a churchyard protected by a stone wall, St George's Church dominated the area over which the 2/11th had to advance. On 23 May, 2/3rd Field Regiment gunners squeezed a captured 37 mm anti-tank gun into a deserted kitchen in Platanes, east of Perivolia. They scored direct hits with armour-piercing shells on three enemy-occupied windows in the steeple. They later demolished two mortar posts before ducking from sniper fire. The Germans temporarily abandoned the church. A five-hour air attack between Platanes and Perivolia inflicted nearly 40 Australian casualties. However, when the Germans themselves attacked, the Australians 'stood up and shot them like rabbits'.[34]

Two Matilda tanks, including that pictured in **Photograph 5.17**, figured prominently at Retimo. Their British crews were killed or captured when both tanks fell into deep ground on 20 May. After recapturing Hill A, the Australians recovered the tanks undamaged on 24 May. 2/1st Battalion carrier crews got one working, which reconnoitred enemy positions in the east. On 25 May it was used in the west but the appearance overhead of a bomber – British, it transpired – flustered the inexperienced Australian driver, who drove into a creek. It was rescued and on 26 May was accompanying an attack towards St George's Church when its machine gun jammed. The attack was abandoned and the 2/11th suffered 30 casualties that day.

The machine gun was repaired and that morning the tank helped the 2/1st to clear the Olive Oil factory and increase the tally of German prisoners at Retimo to 500. The British crews were rescued, but were too exhausted to resume work. So when later that day the second tank was dug out, it was manned by a volunteer crew from 2/3rd Field Regiment, which also crewed the other vehicle.

5.17   AWM 131042

Lieutenants Lawry of 2/1st Battalion and Bedells of 2/11th Battalion commanded the tanks. On 27 May they supported an attack to gain the Germans' remaining stronghold, at Perivolia. Their 2-pounder guns were now working, and both reached the enemy lines, but these ill-fated vehicles were soon in trouble again. An anti-tank round penetrated Lawry's tank, killing the gunner. The remaining crewmen were badly burned on bailing out. Lieutenant Bedells' tank (photographed in 1945) was moving near the edge of the beach and in the dim light initially fired on friendly troops. A mortar bomb hit the cupola and as Bedells sought to extricate himself, enemy fire cut off several fingers. Australian infantry drove off Germans who tried to capture the tank.

At dark the crewmen, all wounded, escaped.

Captain Honner now wanted to call off the attack, but when misinformed that one platoon had broken into Perivolia, decided he must support them. He sent nine men along a wall from where they could cover the forthcoming advance, only to see each one hit while trying to use the section Bren: only one survived. As one 2/11th soldier wrote, every morning his battalion attacked at Perivolia and got to within 50 yards of the Germans' main trench, but there was 'not a blade of grass, not a

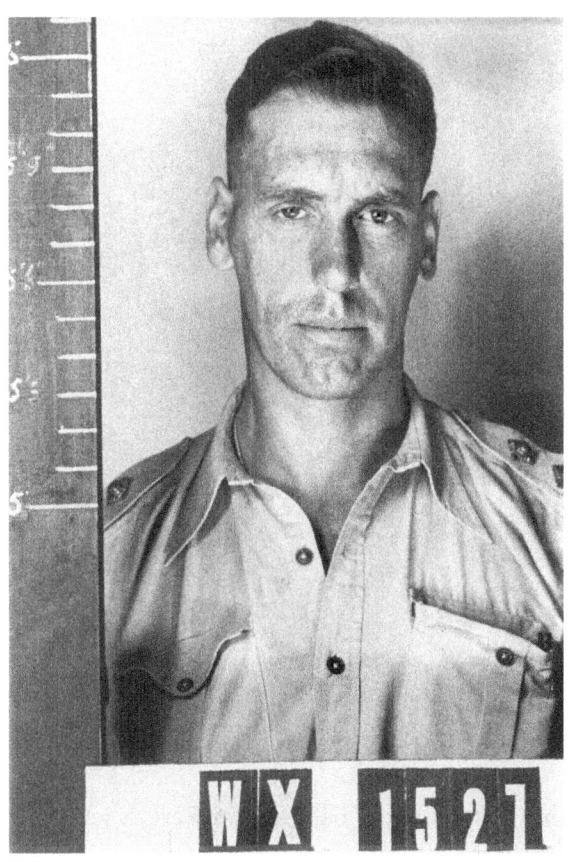

stone or a dip in the ground to give one cover from the wall of lead that Fritz slung on that area'.³⁵ By now the 2/11th was short of ammunition and largely dependent on captured weapons. Among those killed on 28 May was Captain Stanley Wood, a former schoolteacher, pictured in **Photograph 5.18**. He had been wounded in Greece and was now mortally wounded, on his 37th birthday.

Lack of communications kept Campbell ignorant of developments elsewhere on Crete, but on 29 May Greeks brought news that German troops were advancing on Retimo from east and west. When enemy motorcyclists, artillery and tanks appeared, Campbell realised that all was lost. His men had been on half rations for three days and he knew that the Germans were threatening reprisals against civilians who helped the British. Anticipating high casualties among his men and civilians, should his men try to escape, he chose to surrender.

5.18   AWM P02466.263

With enemy fire audible at Perivolia, Campbell telephoned this news to Sandover, who decided to tell his men to destroy their arms and escape through the hills. A brave 2/11th rearguard allowed others precious time to escape: 52 officers and men of the 2/11th reached Egypt, while 16 of the 2/1st did so. The citizen soldier Sandover and the regular Campbell had performed superbly during the battle. Its cost had been 120 Australians killed, with at least 550 Germans dead.

Photograph 5.19 reflects the reversal of fortunes at Retimo. Taken at the airfield which the Australians held throughout, it shows a German motorcyclist with a group of captured men. Looking towards the camera at centre is Captain Cliff Mott, of 6 Battery, 2/3rd Field Regiment. Of this day, he later recalled marching behind 'that grand man', Lieutenant-Colonel Campbell and his quartermaster, who

5.19　　　　　　　　　　　　　　　　　　　　　　　　　　　　　　　　　　AWM 101185

carried the white flag. Wondering how the gunners behind him were reacting to surrender, he nervously turned his head:

> What did I find? Every gunner was in step, every man erect, every man looking his own height and straight to the front. Not a word was spoken, not an eye twitched. Never, I felt, would 6 Battery be defeated. And never, I knew, would 6 Battery be humiliated.[36]

For 6th Battery, one could substitute 6th Division. As early as 23 May Campbell had received from Freyberg the wireless message: 'You have done magnificently'.[37] It summarised the defenders' entire achievement at Retimo and indeed in Crete generally. The battle dealt a death blow to German parachute operations in World War II, but it also severely damaged the 6th Division, which was temporarily unusable. Three entire battalions – the 2/1st, 2/7th and 2/11th – were effectively lost on Crete. It was put to General Mackay that these battalions should not be reconstituted, but he rejected this as 'not to be contemplated'.[38] Those units, and indeed his division, would rise again.

CHAPTER 6

SYRIA

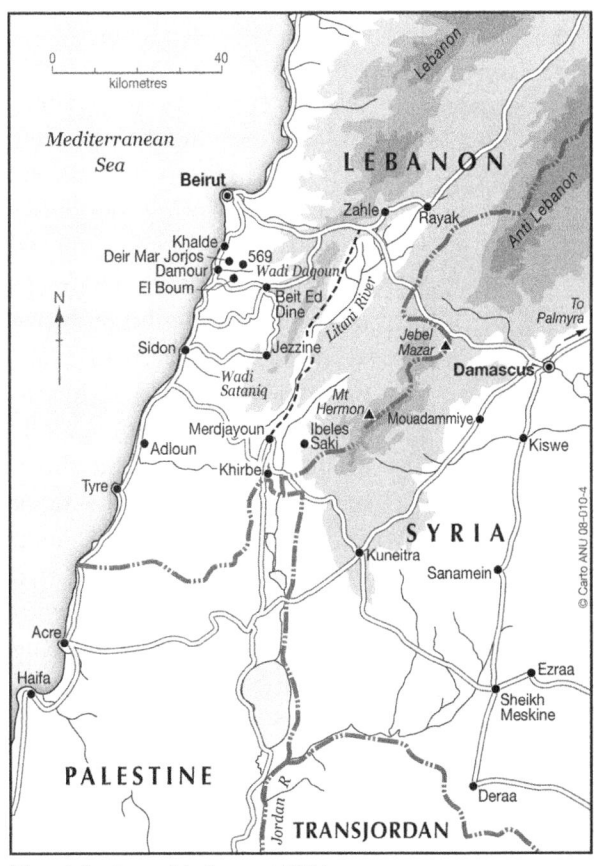

Map 4 Syria and Lebanon 1941

Of the 12 486 men of the 6th Division who had gone to Greece, nearly half – 5600 – were now lost to it forever: killed or captured on the mainland or on Crete. Those who returned needed months for recuperation, while their units required at least some rebuilding. The 2/1st Battalion was typical of the hardest-hit cases. Having suffered more than 700 casualties, in June 1941 it comprised just 70 men in Palestine. To its rebuilding the other two battalions of the 16th Brigade each contributed 100 men. Inevitably some were sad to leave these units, to the point where a number wore a miniature of their old colour patch above the new one. A quota of those transferred were NCOs, while some were original 2/1st officers from other appointments. The remaining 18 officers and 500 men came from the brigade's reinforcement battalion. About one-third of the resulting unit were combat veterans.

While survivors were recuperating and units rebuilding, several units saw more action, in Lebanon and Syria. The campaign occurred in June–July 1941, when British fortunes in the Middle East were at low ebb. The navy and air force had been battered in Greece and Crete, and Wavell was under political pressure to relieve Tobruk and to prevent the Germans from establishing a base in Vichy-held Syria and Lebanon. These two French mandates were together called 'Syria' by Australian forces and we will adopt that usage. Wavell's resources for both tasks were minuscule. One unit employed for both was the 6th Division Cavalry Regiment, which had been spared the Greek ordeal. Fighting its first operation as a regiment, and with a full complement of Vickers light tanks handed over by the 7th Division Cavalry, it first provided reconnaissance for the British 7th Armoured Brigade in the aptly named 'Operation Brevity' in Egypt. **Photograph 6.1** shows one of those tanks with its commander, Corporal Robert Ireland (crouching), and Trooper Ewart Sims. They have good reason to check its tracks, for during the withdrawal near Capuzzo on 16 May their tank, barely keeping up with the column, broke a track. With German tanks driving less than 300 metres away, the Vickers sat immobile all night. Eventually the three-man crew repaired the track and drove off. The fuel pump then broke down. After two days trying to revive it, they abandoned it, eventually being rescued by a passing truck. The tank was salvaged. Ireland would command it again. Sims would drown in a flooding of the Danmap River in 1945. In Operation Brevity, fortunately, the regiment had no

6.1 AWM 008695

face-to-face encounters with German tanks, for the Vickers were slow, presented a high target, had thin armour and were armed only with twin machine guns.

As Operation Brevity reached its unhappy conclusion, the regiment was sent to Palestine for the invasion of Syria. Photograph 6.1 was taken in June, on the eve of the attack. These Vickers light tanks were almost the only armour in the invasion force, the main components of which were the 7th Australian Division's 21st and 25th Brigades, the 5th Indian Brigade and two understrength Free French brigades. The 6th Division's 2/3rd and 2/5th Battalions were also put at the disposal of General Lavarack, GOC 7th Division. Both battalions were well below strength and were not initially committed. Opposing the modest Allied forces were some 35 000 well-equipped and well-prepared Vichy troops holding mountainous terrain. Ominously, their arsenal included medium tanks.

The attackers were allocated three separate routes of advance: one along the coast towards Beirut, a second along a central line to cut the Damascus–Beirut road, and the third further inland directed towards Damascus. Initially the Australian forces took the two routes closest to the sea, and the 6th Division Cavalry provided one squadron for each, with a third squadron in reserve. On the coastal route the 21st Brigade was divided into two columns. The regiment's carriers and some British armoured cars supported one, two troops of tanks the other.

Hopes that the French would welcome rather than fight the attackers quickly evaporated, and tanks and carriers were soon heavily engaged. The French imposed delays by cratering the road, but by the end of 8 June, tanks and carriers had entered the coastal town of Tyre.

In the central sector, the 25th Brigade's forces were also divided into two columns, both supported by the cavalry's tanks. A hidden French 25 mm anti-tank gun ambushed several tanks. Canadian-born Trooper John 'Willie' Wells, pictured in **Photograph 6.2**, was the gunner-operator of the troop leader's tank until a shell pierced the turret and killed the commander beside him. Wells took charge and guided the vehicle back to safety.

6.2 Courtesy John Mole

A second tank, unaware of the ambush, returned from evacuating wounded infantrymen and was hit by another anti-tank shell, before withdrawing with a mortally injured gunner. Wells also returned to the spot, with an artillery observation party, and pinpointed

6.3 AWM 042208

targets for the guns. His 'great courage, initiative and coolness' earned him a Military Medal. In the photograph, taken the following day, Wells is indicating the entry hole in his tank's turret. Apparent here is his Regiment's unique beret, bearing the large 'Rising Sun' badge normally worn on the slouch hat. Other regiments' berets bore the smaller collar badge.

Even the heroics of men like Wells could not penetrate the French line in the central sector that first day. A road demolition, mechanical problems and enemy fire delayed the right-hand column there. In this column as in the others, the cavalry used carriers like that in **Photograph 6.3**. Though more vulnerable than the Vickers tanks, carriers had all-round visibility, more durability and greater versatility in armament: here there are in evidence a Bren gun, an anti-tank rifle, a Vickers machine gun and a Thompson submachine gun! The headgear suggests that this is a relatively safe spot, possibly in camp just before the invasion, but on 10 June a trooper was killed in an ambush seeking to use his TSMG in just this fashion. The greenery shown in the photograph would have been very welcome to the regiment, which had spent more time campaigning in the desert than any other Australian unit. Syria's hills and narrow defiles were not so welcome, however, and severely limited the regiment's role.

When 7th Division infantry forced a crossing of the vital Litani River, the cavalry provided fire support. After that, cavalry carriers bravely led the advance to Adloun. One was destroyed when a 25 mm anti-tank gun opened fire from 20 metres. Machine-gun fire killed two troopers, including the submachine gunner mentioned earlier. Another cavalryman with a TSMG, Lieutenant Tom Mills, who commanded this squadron, went forward on foot on 11 June and with three other carrier men silenced French anti-tank guns, drove off some light tanks and, although his gun jammed, captured 45 Foreign Legionnaires and their plentiful arms. For this, Mills received a bar to the MC he had won in Cyrenaica.

Mills continued to be prominent in the coastal advance to Sidon, though the regiment's tanks were withdrawn when the ground became too difficult. Unfortunately the French medium tanks could still operate. They halted the advance and trapped a group of infantrymen at Wadi Sataniq, near Adloun, on 13 June. Lieutenant Wray led four cavalry carriers as bait to draw them out to where Australian artillery could subdue them while the carriers rescued numerous infantry. The cavalry role on the coast now fell temporarily to 9th Divisional Cavalry.

In the central sector, on 10 June, higher command rather recklessly sent a 6th Cavalry Regiment reconnaissance patrol to check whether Khirbe was still occupied. The loss of four of the five carriers sent into the task confirmed that it was and underlined the courage of their crews. Their squadron, C Squadron, was now withdrawn and replaced by the reserve squadron, which was similarly divided into two columns. They were protecting Australian gun positions when on 15 June the French launched a surprise counter-attack, spearheaded by medium tanks. The Australian cavalrymen remained cool amidst considerable panic, and with anti-tank gunners achieved some local successes against an attacking column.

Here another 6th Division unit began its part in the Syrian campaign. One evening in Palestine 'Jo' Gullett and other 2/6th Battalion officers suddenly heard the 2/5th's pipes and drums and then the rumour that the 2/5th was off to Syria. He recalled:

> We crowded the road as they marched by in full battle order, tall men, their under-strength platoons hard-faced beneath the helmets, marching as the veterans they were, but with the long, easy assured stride which the pipes induce.[1]

On 12 June a 2/5th Battalion company had arrived at Merdjayoun to provide security while the advance progressed north. Expectations of an easy time were

110 SYRIA

6.4 AWM P03034.001

dashed first by heavy enemy shelling, then the approach of strong enemy infantry and armoured forces. Before they could fight, the 2/5th men were ordered to join a general withdrawal south of the town.

The French counter-attack soon lost momentum, and the 2/5th settled into a familiar routine of patrolling while the cavalrymen were widely dispersed to defensive positions where their vehicles functioned largely as signal stations. However, the counter-attack rang alarm bells at headquarters, where reserves were released and forces switched between the three fronts.

One of the most unusual units of the Second AIF now emerged from the ranks of the 6th Division Cavalry. Fighting near Ibeles Saki had brought 32 French cavalry horses into Australian hands, and on 22 June General Berryman, commanding the Merdjayoun sector, ordered the formation of a troop of horse to provide a reconnaissance screen on his eastern flank. Of the 18 original members of the resulting unit, 13 are pictured in **Photograph 6.4**. The unit included many country men, some with experience in light horse regiments. Their French saddles were uncomfortable, and much of their equipment was held together with wire and string. When saddles and packs arrived from Palestine the unit expanded to be nearly 70-strong. Unofficially called the 'Kelly Gang', after Australia's most famous gang of bushrangers, they often had to go on foot in the rough terrain. Fortunately, their French horses seemed untroubled by artillery fire. The Gang gathered much useful intelligence and provided flank protection until called to the coast on 3 July. The remainder of the regiment in the central sector, where two more tanks had been destroyed and two casualties suffered, also moved to the coast on that day.

By then, 6th Division troops had contributed substantially on the third route of advance, to Damascus. On 18 June the 2/3rd Battalion had entrained in Palestine for this front. It left behind one company garrisoning Sidon, and with its recent losses both in action and to the reforming 2/1st Battalion, was under half-strength, with 406 officers and men. Some of these were still recovering from Greece and Crete, and here they were facing another exhausting operation. Their trip to the front, some 8 kilometres south-west of Damascus, was inauspicious, for it included a train crash and a truck journey in which two vehicles overturned. On arrival at Mouadammiye on 20 June the unit was attached to the 5th Indian Brigade and soon came under shellfire. That afternoon British Brigadier Lloyd ordered the 2/3rd's Lieutenant-Colonel Lamb to send one company to cut the Damascus-Beirut road, and the remainder of the battalion to capture steep heights overlooking this road from the south and the Kuneitra road from the west. Seven forts sat atop these heights. The Australians quickly occupied two forts, but a superior French outflanking force recaptured one fort and many soldiers, including Lamb. Then an Indian carrier crew mistook the surrendering Australians for enemy and fired, killing two and wounding Lamb, who was deposited in the Vichy Fort Weygand.

The company sent to cut the Beirut-Damascus road, under Captain Philip Parbury, was soon out of sight of the rest of the battalion. It became involved in a brisk firefight with enemy troops in buildings near the junction of the Kuneitra and Beirut-Damascus roads. Parbury himself scouted ahead, found the Beirut-Damascus road, and called his men forward along it. They cut down two telegraph poles, put them across the road and hid to wait for developments. As French vehicles arrived from Damascus and Beirut they halted in the darkness and were captured, usually without much resistance. Parbury soon had 86 prisoners. Hearing fire from the ridge above, Parbury made a resolution encapsulated in a signal he sent to brigade:

> Water rations and ammo almost depleted and troops becoming exhausted. Enemy on high ground dominate this position from both sides of the road and at dawn position will become untenable. I intend to attack.[2]

This spirit would earn Parbury an MC in this action and propel him to command another 6th Division battalion by war's end. **Photograph 6.5** illustrates the precariousness of Parbury's position. Taken from a position looking west along the Damascus–Beirut road and railway, it shows the position of the 2/3rd roadblock.

6.5　　　　　　　　　　　　　　　　　　　　　　　　　　　　　　　AWM 128439

Parbury left one platoon there and took the rest of his men on a two-hour climb up the cliff. A French armoured car fired on them until the Australians' Bren gun fire scared it off.

Parbury was not aware of the forts on the ridge, and as his men approached Fort Goybet under fire and with 'friendly' shells falling about, they took cover to rest at about 10 am. Captain Ian Hutchison's 2/3rd company now approached the fort from the south-west and captured it after a stiff fight. Simultaneously, an enterprising company quartermaster-sergeant, Carlyle Smith, had led three others with submachine guns to Fort Weygand, where the CO's group was being held. Smith's party shot some sentries and rescued some comrades being held outside the fort. Rescued and rescuers then together captured the fort and freed its prisoners.

On 21 June, the platoon at the roadblock had also been in action. It comprised just nine Australians and three Free French. Lieutenant Murdoch put eight men on the left of the road facing Beirut (in the distance in Photograph 6.5) while he and Sergeant Jim Copeman took up positions on the steep slopes to the right in the picture. Enemy tanks and armoured cars with infantry support tried intermittently for the next 12 hours to break through but somehow Murdoch's band held them off, killing seven, firing at the vehicles' weapon-slits and hurling ineffectual mortar bombs. Indian reinforcements then arrived. The battle for Damascus was already

6.6 AWM 041751

over, however, chiefly because the existence of the roadblock had persuaded the Vichy commander to abandon the city. **Photograph 6.6** shows a Bren carrier of an 'Australian infantry battalion', presumably the 2/3rd, passing through the Beirut–Damascus roadblock after the action had moved further west, which it did almost immediately. The 2/3rd was given one night's rest and then joined the advance attached to the 16th (British) Brigade. A machine-gun bullet hit the battalion's acting CO, Major John Stevenson, in the side, but he continued. The unit came under heavy fire on the Beirut road – they considered it the heaviest they had encountered in three campaigns. Through a combination of their dispersal and haste, one of Parbury's leading platoons avoided all but one casualty, but on taking their hill objective was attacked by two French tanks. The Australians repelled the vehicles with smoke bombs, Very lights, an anti-tank rifle and a Bren.

A major obstacle to the advance was the 490-metre high Jebel Mazar, so British Brigadier Lomax, believing it unoccupied, ordered the 2/3rd to send a company to hold it. Two attacks by the 2/3rd failed, largely because a native guide took them initially to the wrong peak. Lomax ordered a withdrawal to defensive positions, but Stevenson persuaded him to let the 2/3rd attempt the height a third time.

After repulsing a strong French counter-attack, about 140 Australians attacked in darkness and took the height in bloody fighting on 27 June. Unfortunately, blunders on the part of an artillery observer attached to the unit denied the Australians artillery support that would have swept away nearby French forces, and after a day of beating off strong attacks, the Australians withdrew.

Similar frustration applied in the central sector, but General Lavarack, now commanding Syrian operations, made a fateful decision on 26 June. He would replace the Australians at Merdjayoun with British forces and concentrate the 7th Australian Division on the coast. For this operation, part of that division would be the 17th Brigade, temporarily comprising Brigadier Savige's headquarters, the 2/3rd and 2/5th Infantry and the 2/2nd Pioneer Battalions.

Capturing Beirut would probably clinch the campaign, but the next major obstacle to the advance was Damour, a natural defensive position. Savige reconnoitred the ground and contributed to a plan, which the 7th Division commander, General Allen (former commander of 16th Brigade and a friend of Savige), approved. While the 21st Brigade attacked Damour from the south and east, the 17th Brigade would move inland and act like a lid, boxing in Damour's defenders in the north. The 2/3rd and 2/5th were each about 300 strong, with many 2/3rd men suffering from exposure, malnutrition and other ill-effects of the Damascus fighting. Nevertheless, the Australians knew that their opponents were even worse off. As mentioned, 6th Division Cavalry also shifted to the coast, on 3 July, and on that day a machine-gun detachment of the unit supported an attack south-east of Damour.

During the Australian build-up on the coast, 6th Division men were contributing to a little-known action far inland at Palmyra. There a troop of 2/1st Anti-Tank Regiment joined 'Habforce', a British column advancing on the city from Iraq in late June. They faced even heavier air attack than other Allied forces in Syria. A dogged French garrison of 165 held off the attackers for nearly a fortnight. The Australian gunners suffered two killed and nine wounded. **Photograph 6.7** shows the aftermath of the French surrender of 3 July, as Australian gunners pose with a captured French flag, two French helmets and a British sun hat.

Another small 6th Division unit contributing much was 'K' Section Signals, attached to 17th Brigade for the coming operations at Damour. Signalman Tom Neeman and his mates had been 'pleased as punch' on hearing of this job, for 'camp life was beginning to pall. To[o] many guards and red tape to battle with'.[3] The excitement diminished when, soon after arriving in Syria, they learnt that they would be moving not by truck but by foot. Nevertheless, Neeman can still raise a smile at right in **Photograph 6.8**. At left is Signalman Douglas Margetts, at centre a Cypriot muleteer with the mule that will carry their No. 11 Wireless. The area into which they were to accompany the infantry was mountainous – exceeding 500 metres in some areas. Getting food to these advancing troops became

SYRIA 115

6.7   AWM 045077

6.8   Courtesy Douglas Margetts

increasingly difficult, so that when Neeman received a tin of humble bully beef, it 'tasted as sweet as any lamb-chop'.[4] He was less enthusiastic about a subsequent issue of tins of sheep's tongues.

The 21st Brigade attack started on the night of 5/6 July and proceeded well. The 17th Brigade, moving inland from positions some 4.5 kilometres south of Damour, faced a tough march just getting to its start line on the Wadi Daqoun, east of Damour. In places not even mules could negotiate the hills, so the men carried heavy loads. Each battalion carried one No. 11 Wireless set, like that pictured in Photograph 6.8, and the COs kept Savige informed as they moved through El Boum to the Wadi Daqoun start line on 7 July. The 2/5th's Lieutenant-Colonel Roy King wanted to postpone an attack until he could call on artillery support against enemy machine gunners already firing on his troops, while French artillery was soon shelling 2/3rd troops on Qarqafe ridge. Savige, eager to ensure that the attack maintained its momentum, ordered King to begin the scheduled northwards attack that evening, reasoning that 'tired men who had won through were better than dead men killed in occupied positions'.[5] King agreed and the unit slowly crossed the Wadi Daqoun and moved through the 2/3rd positions. **Photograph 6.9** shows 2/5th men, including Lieutenant Alwyn 'Blue' Shilton, advancing in this operation. Shilton's original caption described 'Shelling in progress'. When crossing the deep wadis they moved in single file, resuming formation afterwards. At each halt that night men fell asleep, but they reached their objective, Deir Mar Jorjos, capturing it

6.9   Courtesy Alwyn Shilton and 2/5th Battalion

6.10   Courtesy Douglas Margetts

along with four artillery pieces, eight machine guns, and a Foreign Legion colonel. Savige later reported the 2/5th's 'magnificent acts of gallantry and good soldiering' that night and early morning.[6]

This photograph also evokes the experience of the 2/3rd the following morning. The unit advanced towards heights south-east of Deir Mar Jorjos, including the important Hill 569. In **Photograph 6.10** infantrymen, of 2/3rd or 2/5th Battalion, are facing just such a height in this area. Ignoring pressing thirst, the Australians rushed five heavily defended enemy field gun positions and consolidated the position in several hours of fighting. Neeman was there and wrote: 'our boys have just cleared the enemy off it, absolutely stupendous view'.[7] From the hill, the 2/3rd could probably see Deir Mar Jorjos, where the 2/5th defenders were being mortared. Private John Gower, a recent reinforcement, lost both legs to a mortar bomb. 'Good as gold', he joked as he was carried out. Within an hour he was dead.[8]

The company sent to block the vital Damour–Beirut road spotted Vichy forces gathering under a bridge for a counter-attack. Lieutenant Leask and four heavily armed others pre-empted this assault. Once the dust had cleared, the enemy could be seen fleeing. Colonel King called down artillery fire on other gathering French forces, which also fled. Damour was now pressed from three sides.

6.11 Courtesy John Mole

At this time the 6th Division Cavalry were fighting just south of Damour. Three cavalry troops under three brothers were supporting the 2/2nd Pioneers. Lieutenant Derek Glasgow led a carrier troop, his twin brothers Gordon and Duncan led two troops of captured French Renault R35 tanks. On 7 July Corporal Ferris's tank had narrowly avoided destruction when ambushed by a 75 mm gun at a bend in the road. Sources conflict as to what happened next. The cavalry apparently became annoyed at suggestions they were lagging behind the pioneers. Through some misunderstanding, Sergeant Gordon Glasgow drove his tank round the same bend where the 75 mm had sprung its ambush the previous day; shots quickly destroyed a track and then set his tank alight. The resulting wreck is the subject of **Photograph 6.11**. Only accurate shooting from Ferris in the following tank allowed the crew to escape.

The French began withdrawing that night from Damour and the surrounding positions. The cavalrymen followed hard on the pioneers' heels into Damour on 9 July. The 17th Brigade was now made responsible for the area north of Damour. Cavalry tanks drove nearly 6 kilometres north of the town before reaching a roadblock. The cavalry and the 2/5th Battalion became the spearhead of the advance. On 10 July, the 2/5th, none of its three forward companies stronger than 44 men,

6.12 AWM 042172

moved to Khalde. Savige ordered King to take a ridge overlooking Khalde and to patrol forward to the next French roadblock, about 1200 metres south of a conspicuous wireless mast. French guns that were grouped round this mast fired at the advancing Australians, whose supporting artillery returned the fire with interest. Evading intense artillery, mortar and machine-gun fire, the Australians reached the roadblock that afternoon but became pinned down near an enemy blockhouse. 6th Division Cavalry tanks and carriers came forward, braving this fire and, by expending 15 000 rounds, extricated the infantry. The following day, 2/5th patrols encountered strong opposition. **Photograph 6.12** probably shows one of those patrols advancing on 11 July, or it may be part of the previous day's assault. Shells are exploding in the background. One patrol got within 200 metres of the wireless mast, visible here over the shoulder of the man on the right, before enemy machine-gun and tank fire halted it. King called off the attack. His battalion had suffered 28 casualties at Khalde. The 2/3rd Battalion was fighting that day on isolated ridges further east. That night they received good news by Lucas lamp from Hill 569 – the Vichy French were capitulating.

120   SYRIA

6.13   Courtesy Alwyn Shilton and 2/5th Battalion

The 17th Brigade and 6th Division Cavalry had contributed significantly to victory in Syria. Between them they suffered 168 casualties, some of whom are pictured in **Photograph 6.13**, which shows slightly wounded members of 2/5th Battalion on or after 9 July. Standing at far right is Lieutenant Bill Taylor, who would be killed in New Guinea in 1943. Kneeling in front of him is Corporal 'Bull' Allen, a medical orderly who had shown dedication in Syria and who, as we shall see, became one of the division's best-known soldiers in New Guinea.

Signalman Neeman, who worked alongside both 2/3rd and 2/5th Battalions, wrote a comment that summed up their efforts in Syria well: 'just arrive in time to see the boys preparing for action, no rest straight in. No doubt about them the[y're] wizards'.[9]

Savige was similarly complimentary in his post-campaign report. He stated that his soldiers demonstrated 'a complete disregard for enemy numbers and an assured belief in their own capabilities', skill and cunning, excellent leadership and the ability to rise above exhaustion.[10] This report was probably intended to reflect well on its author, but his conclusions seem incontrovertible. The battalions' experience on high ground would benefit them in their next operations: the 2/3rd on the Kokoda Track, the 2/5th at Wau-Salamaua.

CHAPTER 7

RETURN TO AUSTRALIA

In July 1941 Major-General Mackay wrote a report entitled 'Organisation of an Infantry Division'.[1] He could look back on six months in which his division had fought three campaigns against two enemies, and was just finishing a fourth campaign against a third, in widely divergent terrain and circumstances. He wrote a detailed analysis of the existing form of Commonwealth divisions, and his essential conclusion was that the existing divisional structure was sound. He would surely have been shocked had he known that his division would not fight again as a unified formation for another three years, and that no single component of it would fight again for more than a year.

Mackay himself would not oversee this change, for in late July Prime Minister Menzies suggested, and Blamey concurred, that Mackay should return to Australia and become GOC Home Forces. Within days of the appointment, some 4200 officers and men were mustered to farewell him in a divisional parade on 6 August. **Photograph 7.1** depicts the occasion, as Mackay stands in a Bren carrier in front of the massed ranks in Palestine. As he told the men, his appointment constituted a 'glowing tribute' to the 6th Division's efforts.[2]

Mackay's successor was Edmund Herring, who had hitherto ably commanded the division's artillery. Herring is depicted in **Photograph 7.2** (sitting at left) watching an exercise in November 1941. By then, the units that had fought in Syria had been joined by the remainder of the division, which was now garrisoning and fortifying the area. Herring and Brigadier Vasey, next to him here with pipe, had recently overcome British objections to resiting defences near Baalbek. Like so many 6th Division officers, these two and the other three leaders in the foreground here – from left, brigadiers Boase and Berryman (sitting) and Colonel Roy

7.1

AWM 020043

7.2

AWM 021307

7.3   AWM 021440

Sutherland – were destined for higher appointments. Sutherland, here GSO1 6th Division, would by 1943 be BGS on Herring's I Corps staff, but would die that September in a plane crash. Allan 'Buck' Boase had been given command of the 16th Brigade in August. He features also in **Photograph 7.3**, where he is inspecting splendid-looking veterans of the 2/3rd Battalion at Katana on Armistice Day 1941, before welcoming it back to the brigade from the 17th. A sergeant soon afterwards described Boase as 'a sour faced old bastard, but not as bad as he looks'.[3] With Boase is moustachioed Lieutenant-Colonel Stevenson, who had earned a DSO and two MIDs in Syria. Both men would eventually become generals and would be prominent in the division over the coming year, though Boase would miss out on an opportunity to lead the division in operations and Stevenson would endure the pain of a wound and the loss of 25 kilos on the Kokoda Track.

The return of Mackay and other senior officers to Australia reflected growing concern about the threat of Japan. When it came to fruition, that threat would alter the nature of the war for Australia, and make the 6th Division fight in the disjointed way mentioned above.

7.4 AWM 010375

As some left the Middle East for Australia, other 6th Division men were still making the journey in the opposite direction. **Photograph 7.4** portrays reinforcements to the 2/1st Battalion embarking at Sydney in November 1941. 'Jo' Gullett wrote that after Greece the 6th Division was never quite the same again, for the reinforcements who rebuilt it were:

> generally drawn from a more thoughtful or responsible class of men. Married men who had to guard their lives and watch their pay books. Men with other hostages to fortune. They were there with us because their duty to their country had indicated this course to them.[4]

What motivated the two men in the foreground here, Privates George Leonard (left) and Harold West, we shall never know. Both were Aboriginal soldiers from Goodooga, New South Wales. Full-blooded Aboriginals were legally forbidden to join the AIF, though many were accepted. They included excellent fighters such as Lieutenant Reg Saunders of the 2/7th Battalion. Leonard and West, both in their 30s on enlistment, would die in Papua within about a year of this photograph: Leonard killed in action at Eora Creek in October 1942, West dying of illness in November.

In the winter of 1941, Syria received snowfalls said to be its heaviest for 30 years. **Photograph 7.5**, taken that Christmas, illustrates the conditions. The pictured men are of 2/2nd Battalion and their vehicle sports the divisional sign. The photographer was Sergeant Reginald Blain, who would be killed in very different circumstances as a platoon commander at Templeton's Crossing 10 months later. When this photograph was taken, the chill had been given extra bite by news of Japanese assaults in the Far East and Pacific.

7.5   AWM 130108

On 3 January 1942 the British government suggested that Australia send two divisions to the Netherlands Indies. The Australian government agreed to send the I Corps, based on the 6th and 7th Divisions. In subsequent months the corps' destination would be a topic of disagreement.

The 6th Division, then comprising 18 465 men, moved to Palestine in January and February. The 7th Division left the Middle East early in February. Among 6th Division units, the 19th Brigade sailed first. It was a slow, disrupted journey – the 2/4th Battalion left Tewfik on 12 February, returned that day and left again on 19 February. The Divisional Headquarters left on 18 February in the *Andes*. In the interim, on 13 February, General Lavarack, I Corps commander, wrote from Java to General Sturdee, Chief of the General Staff, that the 6th and 7th Divisions would be unable to prevent Japanese conquest of the Netherlands Indies. The 6th Division would, he argued, probably not be ready for operations in Java until at least mid-April.

Like Lavarack, General Herring had been scheduled to arrive in Java before his division. He had left Palestine by flying boat on 11 February, but by the time he reached India the rapid Japanese advances had forced changes to plans. The issue now was where to send I Corps. The obvious alternatives were Burma, where Japanese invasion seemed imminent, and Australia, threatened by an eventual Japanese assault. Sturdee insisted that the corps return to Australia and Prime Minister Curtin backed him. On 18 February, after the fall of Singapore, Wavell wanted the corps sent to Burma, but by 20 February the 7th Division was considered sufficient. In the political dispute that followed, the 7th returned to Australia and a large part of the 6th Division was diverted elsewhere.

Herring rejoined the Divisional Headquarters at Colombo, Ceylon, on 27 February. He had been ordered to sail on to Australia, and announced this on board the *Andes* just out of Colombo on 4 March. He gave an 'inspiring' speech, calling on those present to be prepared to sacrifice their all in defending their homeland.⁵ At about the same time, the Australian government had decided that most of Herring's division would not yet be following him to that homeland. Ceylon, like Burma, had been preoccupying Churchill's government as a potential Japanese target. At the urging of Sir Earle Page in London, on 2 March the Australian government offered Churchill the 16th and 17th Brigades as a temporary garrison in Ceylon. The British government accepted the offer, which was understood to be for a few weeks before they returned to Australia. Neither brigade offered had by then left Suez, though 19th Brigade was on the water and would reach Fremantle on 20 March. On 10 March, when the *Andes* reached Fremantle, the 16th and 17th Brigades were boarding ships at Suez and by 25 March had reached Colombo. So, instead of returning home to face the Japanese invasion threat, these two brigades were, as one of their diarists put it 'confronted with something entirely different, both as regards country over which we will operate and the methods to be employed'.⁶ The troops had been unaware of the negotiations that had so affected their movements.

The 16th and 17th Brigades were a significant addition to the defences of an island which, if lost, would threaten Allied power in the Indian Ocean. Heavy air raids on 5 and 9 April emphasised the danger. There was considerable tension in anticipation of an invasion, as indicated by the fact that three 2/6th Battalion men were charged with sleeping at their posts and severely punished: the only time this charge was laid in the battalion's history.

Brigadier Boase was promoted to major-general commanding all AIF forces in Ceylon. The brigades were soon moved to the south-west of the island, which seemed most vulnerable to attack. Coconut, tea and rubber plantations, or thick bush, dominated this area. The men spent much time preparing defences, including roadblocks and wire obstacles on beaches. **Photograph 7.6** shows a weapon pit built in a coconut grove. Much time was spent on engineering work, such as widening the narrow roads, developing tracks and strengthening or building bridges. This work was largely done by the 2/1st and 2/8th Field Companies and 2/22nd Field Park Company. While the 2/1st Field Company

7.6   AWM 064673

was attached as usual to the 16th Brigade, of necessity the 2/8th switched from the 19th to the 17th Brigade. This arrangement was to continue into the following New Guinea campaign.

Even more important than their work on installations and defences in Ceylon was the jungle training the 6th Division troops undertook there. Their commanders were keen to prepare for the jungle warfare that lay ahead, and there were plenty of opportunities for training in movement, living on limited rations and physical acclimatisation to jungle conditions. The 17th Brigade even developed a 'Jungle Warfare School'.

Among men keen to go home, frustration inevitably grew as weeks wore into months and pressing questions came from home. In a letter, one lieutenant assured his wife that the rumour that his unit was in Australia was untrue, as was one that 'all the AIF was home except those who volunteered to stay and those kept back by disease'.[7] An anonymous 6th Division poem, 'Remember us Australia', described the men on Ceylon as 'sick and tired of being mucked about on some distant foreign shore'. They longed, it said, to return to Australia 'to fight and die to protect it from a World that's completely insane'.[8]

The brigades eventually sailed from Colombo on 13 July, disembarking at Melbourne between 3 and 8 August.

Many other 6th Division soldiers had by then enjoyed scenes such as that in **Photograph 7.7**. Here soldiers of the Cavalry Regiment are arriving in Sydney Harbour in April after six weeks at sea. Their ship, the *Glen Park*, was one of four that brought the unit home, and it carried many of the cavalry's vehicles. The men were happy to leave their dilapidated tanks behind, but could not have foreseen that they would never use tanks in action again.

The 6th Division troops arriving in Australia since March had been busy in the months before the 16th and 17th Brigades' return. On 27 March, barely a week after landing in Australia, General Herring and some of his staff had flown to Darwin, such was the perceived danger there. The whole area north of Alice Springs had just been put under military control. Herring took command. In April the Divisional Headquarters effectively became Headquarters, Northern Territory Force, and apparently did not officially exist again until August or September.[9] On the day Herring flew to Darwin, the 19th Brigade disembarked at Adelaide. In April its men began a week's home leave, which tended to drift into a second week. The 2/11th Battalion had first been sent to Western Australia and, after reassembling, stayed there for garrison work. The rest of the brigade and the cavalry regiment travelled to the Northern Territory in June, when the supply lines could cater for them.

The 19th Brigade was destined to remain in the Territory for a year. It rapidly became a frustrating time for this superb unit, but initially the Territory was a front-line posting. There the brigade comprised the 2/4th, 2/8th and 23rd/21st

7.7   Courtesy John Mole

Militia Battalions. Based at Adelaide River, some 120 kilometres south of Darwin, the men spent their time on manoeuvres and intensive training. In **Photograph 7.8**, taken in November, some of that training is in progress. Here 2/8th Battalion men, mostly veterans, are receiving instruction on the Boyes anti-tank rifle and the Bren carrier. Both might have been useful had the Japanese invaded the Northern Territory, and the 2/8th found the carrier well suited to service there, but they were obsolete for the jungle warfare that was the only type of fighting that lay ahead for the 6th Division. Its soldiers would only use Bren carriers in action on one more occasion, at Buna. The instructor pointing out the carrier's weaknesses is Corporal Bob Wiltshire, a battalion original who would end the war as a lieutenant in a militia battalion. From April 1942, 6th Division officers of all ranks were sent to lead militia units.

Most of the division's artillery also faced a long period of exasperating inactivity. The demands of national defence and reorganisation of the 6th Division as a 'jungle division' with reduced artillery had disappointing consequences for all four regiments. The 2/1st Field Regiment would remain with the 6th Division

7.8 AWM 027748

in New Guinea, but with the reorganisation of the division was removed from its order of battle in June 1943 and replaced by the 2/3rd Field Regiment as the 6th's one field regiment. The 2/3rd had been unhappily attached to the 5th Division in Queensland since June 1942. The 2/1st then served 'in the wilderness' for 15 months, three of them as wharf-labourers in Queensland, before returning to the division in September 1944. The 2/2nd Field Regiment would only rejoin the division in March 1944 after various assignments. The 2/1st Anti-Tank Regiment, renamed '2/1st Tank Attack Regiment', would be reduced in size and designated a corps unit in 1943, only returning to the division in September 1944.

As mentioned, the 2/11th Battalion was split from the rest of the 19th Brigade and sent to Western Australia. The battalion was given the honour of a parade through Perth on 5 October, and the men can be seen lined up ready to begin in **Photograph 7.9**. The crowd was so enthusiastic that it brought the march to a halt several times. The men are wearing their slouch hats turned down: a 6th Division

7.9 AWM 026921

habit that affronted local provosts. This was not the only tension between the veterans and the local troops, who to the 2/11th seemed rather too casual. Many 2/11th members were given transfers to other units, several to become COs. No fewer than nine COs of other Australian infantry battalions had enlisted in the 2/11th.

In subsequent months the 2/11th undertook amphibious warfare training and in July moved to Geraldton. In May 1943 it moved to Chidlow, east of Perth. As Sandover recalled later: 'The main memories of the long waiting days in the West, are of the constant battle against boredom and the thought that the Battalion might well sit doing nothing for the rest of the war'.[10] Excitement rose in July 1943, when the unit travelled to Queensland to rejoin its sister battalions of 19th Brigade. However, much waiting lay ahead.

By then the other two brigades had been involved in heavy fighting. Within weeks of arriving in Australia from Ceylon in August 1942, the 17th Brigade enjoyed a great parade through Melbourne. The 16th then had one in Sydney.

7.10 AWM 026499

Photograph 7.10 shows the hail of paper and streamers that greeted them on 5 September. The paper was said to be so thick on the ground – up to a foot deep – that it muffled the sound of marching, though the presence of as many as half a million spectators probably contributed too. The 2/2nd Battalion war diary noted that 'a carnival spirit pervaded the whole of the city', with the soldiers' 'marching and demeanour bearing out in every detail their reputation of being the crack Brigade of the A.I.F.'[11] Within four days of this photograph and 36 days after landing in Australia, the men of the 16th Brigade were stunned to hear that they were to move to New Guinea immediately. Their three years away had been followed by just 14 days' home leave.

CHAPTER 8

KOKODA TO THE SEA

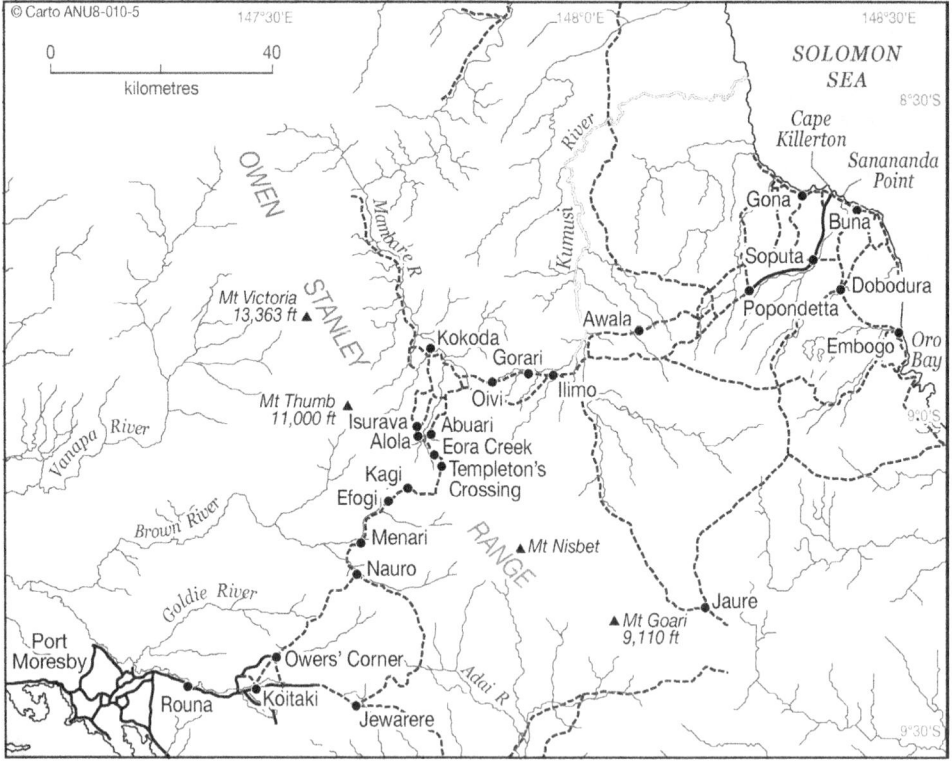

Map 5 Kokoda to Sanananda 1942–3

On 19 September the 6th Division Headquarters opened in Port Moresby. Major-General Boase had expected to command it, but Blamey allocated it instead to Vasey. None of the division's usual major components were present: the 16th Brigade would not arrive until 21 September, the 17th Brigade was sailing to Milne Bay and the 19th was still in the Northern Territory. Instead the '6th Division' temporarily constituted a mixed force of militia and American infantry, AIF and militia artillery, commandos and Bren carriers. This ephemeral agglomeration existed solely to protect Port Moresby. Its existence indicated the anxiety that operations on the Kokoda Track were causing the Allied command. Troops of the classic 6th Division would soon be spearheading those operations. One member described what followed as 'the most bloody, exhausting and telling campaign of the whole series'.[1]

The 16th Brigade landed at Port Moresby after an uncomfortable journey in vessels much less salubrious than the liners that had taken them to and from the Middle East. The Japanese advance had reached its limit at Ioribaiwa. In subsequent days, men under General Allen's 7th Division Headquarters pushed the Japanese back. The 16th Brigade came under Allen's command, but was only called forward from the Moresby defences to join the advance on 17 October. As it began moving up the track on 3 October, **Photograph 8.1** was taken at Owers' Corner. Here American General Douglas MacArthur, Commander-in-Chief of the South-West Pacific Area, and General Blamey are talking to men of the 2/3rd Battalion. The contrast between the generals' khaki and the infantrymen's newly dyed jungle green uniforms is apparent even in a black and white photograph. Major Ian Hutchison (far left) had won an MC at Bardia, been wounded at Tobruk, was outstanding in Syria, and would later command the battalion. Lieutenant Frank Hoddinott, next to Hutchison, had received a DCM in Syria and would win an MC in the approaching campaign. During this fleeting visit from the senior commanders, MacArthur met Brigadier John Lloyd, now commanding 16th Brigade, and told him: 'Lloyd, by some act of God, your brigade has been chosen for this job. The eyes of the western world are upon you. I have every confidence in you and your men. Good luck and don't stop'.[2] Ken Clift says MacArthur thereupon left in his jeep, 'leaving our Brigadier bewildered and stunned by the bullshit'.[3]

Another version has MacArthur and Blamey arriving at the 2/3rd positions with General Allen, who was welcomed as the original 16th Brigade commander. To a group of 2/3rd men sitting in front of him, MacArthur reportedly said: 'I trust you won't run away as your countrymen did'. To this, Private Jack Peppercorn allegedly replied: 'Keep your bastards out of the way and we might have a chance'.[4]

MacArthur's admonition – 'Don't stop' – was to have repercussions for the 16th Brigade.

8.1　　　　　　　　　　　　　　　　　　　　　　　　　　　AWM 013422

The first New Guinea campaign for the 6th Division, which would fight all its remaining campaigns in New Guinea, was about to commence. On 6 October 25th Brigade handed 16th Brigade a Japanese prisoner. The brigade diarist considered this first live Japanese seen by the division 'an unprepossessing specimen'.[5] Yet fighting that enemy would differ utterly from fighting Italians, Germans and Vichy French. The Japanese generally fought to the death, apparently oblivious to hardship. To counter them and cope with New Guinea's extraordinary conditions, the

8.2 AWM 027054

6th Division's men had to change their approach to war in every field from supply to tactics and hygiene.

Photograph 8.2 was taken as the three infantry battalions marched from Nauro to Menari, between 9 and 11 October. In their shorts and shirt sleeves, the pictured men risked mosquito-borne diseases, especially on the lower ground beyond the Owen Stanley mountain range. On their backs are haversacks, which usually contained toilet gear, a change of clothing and a dixie. On the back of his belt each man carries half a blanket rolled in a groundsheet. Carrying half a blanket appears to have been a general instruction, and one that some regretted once they experienced cold nights in the mountains. Others discarded even that, since the regular downpours meant they could not keep it dry.

George Tarlington recalls the 2/2nd Battalion receiving an excellent meal the night before they marched off to Owers' Corner. One man's comment 'fattening us up for the kill' stayed with Tarlington in the weeks ahead. Their meals soon mainly comprised bully beef and biscuits. Already the men were seeing graves and discarded or destroyed equipment. Tarlington was a Bren gunner, like the man second from the rear in Photograph 8.2, and wrote later that it and the other materials they carried 'made the climb and descent well nigh impossible'.[6] Many soldiers considered the descent, as in **Photograph 8.3**, more testing than the ascent,

8.3   AWM 027056

especially when it was muddy. At far right is Private William Kemsley of the 2/1st Battalion, a stretcher-bearer who would soon be Mentioned in Despatches for rescuing a wounded man. Carrying the Bren at far left is Lieutenant George Gidley-King of the 2/3rd Battalion. As was customary for officers in Papua, he has removed all signs of command that might attract enemy snipers. The typical routine was to rise at about 8 am, lunch on biscuits, bully beef and, if there was time to brew it, tea. Rain fell at about 2 pm daily. At 5 pm the march halted and the men bivouacked for the night. By the time the battalions reached Templeton's Crossing, where they took over from the 25th Brigade, the 2/1st diarist reflected that the whole march was 'most arduous'.[7] A private in 2/2nd Battalion was more forthright, declaring:

> For a heartbreaking trail I don't think that Hannibal or Napoleon when they crossed the Alps could have wept the tears of blood that we did . . . How our legs took us over them I am to this day uncertain . . . we were all in bad condition before we met the Jap.[8]

Now it was time for that demanding meeting. Though retreating, the Japanese remained aggressive, and the 16th Brigade war diary summary of instructions on 3 October twice emphasised the need to 'prevent any enemy advance on Port Moresby'.[9] When the brigade began arriving in the forward area on 18–19 October, the Japanese were counter-attacking the troops already there. A 2/2nd Battalion patrol that day was savaged on approaching a Japanese position: the patrol leader, Lieutenant Ryan, was shot in the stomach and barely managed to crawl to safety. Only on 20 October was the position stable enough for Brigadier Lloyd to take over operations. That day, two 2/2nd Battalion companies were sent to outflank the Japanese attacking the 3rd (militia) Battalion beyond the crossing. They trod as quietly as they could on a mouldy uneven carpet that ran through dripping cold bush. One 2/2nd soldier wrote home that the 'gnarled roots, thick ferns and mosses' here gave the scenery a Walt Disney feel: 'In fact we expected to see Snow White at any moment but instead we encountered the Jap'.[10] So well concealed were the Japanese weapon pits that enemy machine-gun fire erupting from them was the Australians' first clue to their existence. The first Australians killed were the commanders of the leading platoons, including Lieutenant Reg Blain. The occupants of these pits were overcome, largely with grenades. By nightfall the two companies had dug in among bullet-riddled trees, the dead of both sides lying grotesquely distorted all around. That night the whole brigade came up to the crossing, in close contact with the enemy. The following morning they found the Japanese gone. Ominously, the Australians had suffered some 24 killed and over 50 wounded in their first fight in New Guinea. For the 2/2nd, with 23 dead, it was even bloodier than the first day at Bardia.

8.4 AWM P02038.144

Like the Australian attackers, the Japanese defenders at Templeton's Crossing found the weather there cold and battle conditions 'extreme'.[11] However, extreme Japanese behaviour at the Crossing widened the gap between the two sides. A burial party sent to find three 2/2nd men killed there found the dead stripped of clothing and with flesh cut from their legs. Evidence of cooked 'fresh meat' in the area suggested cannibalism, which captured Japanese diaries confirmed. **Photograph 8.4** was taken in this vicinity and shows a resting patrol, probably of 2/2nd Battalion. No wonder they look tired and drawn.

Having cleared the track towards the natural defensive position at Eora Creek, 2/2nd Battalion went into reserve, while the 2/1st and 2/3rd led the advance on 21 October. It was nerve-racking work, for where men advanced in single file, the forward scout would usually be hit when the enemy opened fire. The two scouts leading the 2/3rd Battalion advance parallel to the main track were suddenly shot down at about 5 pm. Two Australians advancing along the main track with the 2/1st were killed too, but the survivors planned an attack for 22 October.

No one opposed the advances along and parallel to the track early that morning, and at about 10.30 am the 2/3rd detachment swung in front of the 2/1st and entered Eora Creek village on the eastern bank of the creek. Here they were open to view from high ground on the other side of the creek, and mortar and machine-gun fire soon fell among them. Several wounded men lay in the open all day, until near dusk Sergeant Carson, a stretcher-bearer who had won a DCM in 1917, brought forward members of his pioneer platoon. With stretchers they evacuated the wounded, at the cost of one pioneer dead and one wounded. Carson won a Military Medal for his bravery here.

When Lieutenant-Colonel Cullen, the 2/1st CO, arrived at about 11.30 am he ordered Captain Sanderson's companies across a ford in the creek on a wide flanking movement around the Japanese defences on a spur opposite. As the 16th Brigade mustered on the bare ridge above the village in the early afternoon, the Japanese mountain gun, mortars and machine guns were soon inflicting casualties. Only now did the strength of the Japanese positions become apparent. Late that day, Brigadier Lloyd decided to launch a frontal attack on them, using the two log bridges across the creek north of the village. Cullen and the 2/3rd CO, Stevenson, were unimpressed: while some men adored Lloyd, Cullen later described him as retaining 'a Somme mentality'.[12] Lloyd was mindful of MacArthur's admonition: 'Don't stop'. General Allen was at that time feeling MacArthur's and Blamey's wrath on the pace of his advance, and would be relieved of command on 28 October.

Audacity, tactical acumen and poor Japanese watchfulness allowed Cullen to get most of his attacking company over a bridge in the moonlight before the enemy recognised the threat. Once across, the platoons became separated and trapped in dead-end ground. While they fought for their lives, Captain Sanderson's company approached the Japanese positions from the north-west until it too became trapped by murderous fire from commanding ground. Sanderson was killed, his body surrounded by spent shells from his German machine-pistol. It was daylight when Cullen sent Captain Basil Catterns' two platoons to reach his beleaguered men across the creek. The Japanese covered the obvious approaches, but Catterns got across the second bridge and, because the Japanese on the flat ground over the creek had been pushed back, linked up with some survivors there. Soon his men were digging in to avoid heavy fire from the cliffs. Elements of the 2/3rd were sent to help, but by nightfall on 23 October the 2/1st across the creek were just 30 metres from the enemy, pinned, and unlikely to be able to advance soon.

Indeed on 24 October, the 2/1st had to grit its teeth under close-range mortar fire. So dominant were the Japanese positions that one Australian officer, Lieutenant John Frew, was hit in the foot by a bullet that just missed his head. Only after a second bullet hit him in the other foot was he able to shoot his attacker off his rocky outpost. At Cullen's suggestion, Lloyd sent two 2/3rd Battalion companies round the Japanese left flank. They made progress, capturing two machine guns, but the stalemate persisted till 25 October. At first light that day the mountain gun destroyed a Vickers machine gun just set up by the Australians on the heights opposite. Enemy snipers picked off men making even the smallest fidget. On 26 October the 2/3rd kept moving left in an attempt to outflank the Japanese, thwarting a hefty counter-attack as they did so. The 2/1st, including men previously pinned under the Japanese positions, also moved in this direction. Blamey and Allen exchanged more signals about the lack of progress, but Cullen was also impatient.

The Japanese fell back nearly 500 metres in front of Catterns, but the defence was as resilient as ever and his company's positions as cold, wet and dangerous as before. Driving rain washed away a bridge on 26 October.

Photograph 8.5 depicts a signaller attached to 16th Brigade at Eora Creek at that time. He is probably a member of 'J' Section, which Allen described to Cullen earlier in the advance as the best signallers in the AIF. On 26 October, Signalman Alf Parbery called the last three days his hardest ever. His main problems were keeping equipment and paper dry, and controlling his gastric troubles under fire. The 'sigs' also helped bring up mortar ammunition. Parbery assisted a mortar crewman, who after being hit by an enemy mortar, was 'sobbing and shaking and his teeth chattered'.[13] There was considerable sympathy for those who broke under stress in this campaign.

8.5   AWM P02038.146

A mortar bomb exploded in the barrel, killing three crewmen on 27 October. The same morning the wounded Stevenson handed over battalion command to Major Hutchison, who was determined to 'resolve the situation' with his battalion and an attached company of the 2/2nd.[14] That day's clashes were indecisive, but the next morning fighting bubbled along the rest of the front, with Japanese counter-attacks and grenades contributing to 'a murderous confusion'.[15] The 2/3rd delivered two ferocious hooks around the Japanese right. Vicious fire eliminated the forward scouts but the Australians pushed on, moving from tree to tree. Corporal Pett, 'five feet of dynamite', single-handedly destroyed four machine-gun posts.[16] Then at last the enemy broke, stumbling and squealing down the slope, abandoning posts, weapons and over 50 dead. For the first time, the 16th Brigade saw Japanese running away. The citadel of Eora Creek, with

8.6 AWM P02038.141

machine-gun posts radiating from it in five directions, had fallen once the Australians got above it.

The next morning, 2/1st Battalion patrols found the Japanese gone from the Eora Creek hills to which, in the words of the brigade diary, 'they had clung, limpet-like, for so long'.[17] To Signalman Ken Clift, the Eora Creek victory was evidence that 'these infanteers of ours must be the greatest attacking troops in the world'.[18] By the end of the fight for Eora Creek, the bloodiest battle of the Australian advance through the Owen Stanleys, the 16th Brigade had suffered between 228 and 300 casualties in just nine days.

For the living, hunger was now constant. One soldier complained that 'his guts were flapping against his backbone'.[19] With army rations in short supply, men ate abandoned Japanese rice or local food from deserted villages.

Photograph 8.6 portrays three of those still crossing the Owen Stanleys after Eora Creek. Their jumpers suggest they are still in the mountains. Padre Jack McCabe (right) was the first Salvation Army chaplain to cross the Owen Stanleys. As the 2/2nd Battalion's 'Salvo bloke' he provided numberless cups of tea and invaluable writing material. As a battalion member recalled, 'diarrhoea and dysentery were always with us', with 90 per cent of the men 'uncomfortable'.[20] Malaria became a problem once they entered the plains. McCabe, for example, recalled later that one day there he crossed two rivers, though his temperature reached 105 degrees. Company commander and former Intelligence Officer, Captain Swinton, pictured next to McCabe, was evacuated ill on the eve of the unit's next battle, at Oivi. Next to him is Sergeant-Major Honeywell, one of the 2/2nd's great characters, who we last saw escaping from Greece. The glare and bristling moustache apparent here intimidated many a lieutenant, not to mention soldiers inferior to him in rank. At Bardia he had walked erect through the barrage, in Greece had taken on an enemy tank and would take a leading part in the forthcoming battle. He would not survive the campaign, but on Anzac Day the following year, his CO would say:

> I can't let this opportunity pass without mentioning one man – Harry Honeywell. It is men like him we have to look up to; it is men like him who have made a name for this Unit.[21]

A Great War veteran, at his death Honeywell was thought to have been aged somewhere between 57 and 63.

On 30 October, the 2/1st Battalion occupied Isurava, the 2/2nd Alola. Japanese were seen retreating in the distance. The whole brigade was soon taking the track's right fork through Abuari. General Vasey, now commanding 7th Division with 16th Brigade under command, ordered Lloyd to push on towards Oivi and, beyond that, a bridgehead over the Kumusi River. As they came into a sunnier climate and more open terrain, with local food and some chocolate to supplement their meagre rations, the tired troops' mood improved. Conscious of Vasey's demand that he push on rapidly, Lloyd went so far forward on 3 November that his small party was lucky to escape machine-gun bullets directed at them by the enemy rearguard.

On 4 November the 2/2nd Battalion resumed the advance until halted by machine guns and a mountain gun, which the Japanese withdrew when the Australians started to outflank them. The 2/2nd suffered heavily while trying a larger-scale outflanking move on 5 November. The Japanese held the high ground that commanded the approaches to the small native village of Oivi about a mile away. **Photograph 8.7** illustrates the Japanese defences at Oivi, where the brigade first encountered not just trenches, but bunkers. Log covering was typical. This particular structure held a mountain gun, shell cases for which are visible here. Apart from two of these deadly weapons, the defences included well-sited machine guns, mortars and snipers and extended well behind the front.

Near Oivi, George Tarlington lay on his stomach, firing a Bren gun in continuous bursts without sighting any Japanese. They were there, as he saw a mate shot

8.7　　　　　　　　　　　　　　　　　　　　　　　　　　　　AWM 013639

through the throat and die with a gurgle that haunted Tarlington thereafter. Then it was as if his back had been struck with a hammer. He reached back and felt blood. From a stretcher, Tarlington later saw another mate, Fred Matthews, brought in with blood streaming from a chest wound. A bullet had passed through his body, puncturing a lung. **Photograph 8.8** depicts Matthews at Kokoda, apparently two weeks later, still waiting to be evacuated by air to hospital. The Main Dressing Station set up at Kokoda on 4 November was soon so busy with casualties that some sick men arriving there had to build their own shelters and lie on the ground. Matthews was carried there by 'Fuzzy Wuzzies' like the man giving him a drink here. Though also seriously wounded, Tarlington had to walk to Kokoda.

While the 2/2nd, reinforced by the 2/3rd, fought vainly for the high ground before Oivi, the 2/1st Battalion encountered no opposition in following a parallel path further south. When the main attack turned into bloody stalemate, Vasey resolved to exploit this path. On 7 November he sent the 25th Brigade along that track towards Gorari, with orders to assume command of the resting 2/1st Battalion when they met it.

8.8　　　　　　　　　　　　　AWM 013600

By 7 November the campaign had cost 16th Brigade 386 battle casualties and many more evacuations through sickness. On 9 November the 2/1st advanced behind the 25th Brigade to the main track, and was soon fighting Japanese retreating from that brigade's attack. The 2/1st had cut the main track to Ilimo in the east, and if Vasey's plan to trap the Japanese in the Oivi–Gorari area were to succeed, they would need to hold their ground against Japanese coming from both directions. By defending and attacking day and night on 10–11 November, the 2/1st prevented an enemy breakthrough. They had repulsed the main enemy force retreating from Oivi, which the 2/2nd and 2/3rd Battalions found abandoned on 11 November. That day, Lloyd's tired men rested at Oivi while Brigadier Eather's 25th Brigade pushed on to the Kumusi. Eather, original CO of the 2/1st, relinquished his temporary additional command of 16th Brigade, sending them a farewell message: 'To command such a body of troops is an honour and a privilege'.[22]

Some excellent photographs survive of the 16th Brigade in this period: 11–13 November. **Photograph 8.9** depicts members of the 2/1st Battalion at Gorari.

The official historian uses the term 'rugged' a dozen times for Papua's terrain, but only once for human beings: namely, the men of the 2/1st Battalion.[23] They could be ruthless. One platoon reportedly bayoneted a group of 5–7 captured Japanese left behind by another platoon at Gorari.[24] Others were chastised for removing gold fillings from Japanese dead. Tough as they were, the 608 members of the battalion who had started on the Kokoda Track on 6 October had by 12 November been reduced to 360 all ranks.

The pictured six stand above Japanese helmets used to mark a common grave they have just helped dig. About 600 Japanese were killed at Oivi–Gorari. The only NCO pictured here, 21-year-old Corporal Vic Twomey (second from right), would himself be dead by month's end. Privates Alfred McGoldrick (third from left), Radford Smith (far left) and Vincent Russell (third from right), would be

8.9　　　　　　　　　　　　　　　　　　　　　　　　　　　AWM 151114

wounded in this campaign: all would enter the final campaign with the 2/1st, but Russell would be discharged medically unfit and Smith receive a debilitating calf wound when someone else's Owen gun accidentally discharged. McGoldrick would end the war as a sergeant. All but Vincent Russell had enlisted in the second half of 1940. Russell enlisted in 1941. Originals of the unit castigated such men as 'deep thinkers' – at least until they had proved themselves in action. The service record of Sydney Griffiths (second from left) contains references to Absence Without Leave, detention and breaking out of barracks – he had at least

10 AWLs before this photograph was taken. In 1944 he received a discharge from the army.

Photograph 8.9 was taken soon after the fight, as the men are still bearded and in tattered clothes. Within days that would change. The brigade war diarist talked of men welcoming new boots to replace 'heelless, sodden, shapeless footwear... new shirts and trousers to replace the mud bespattered faded issue which for so long has been our sole wardrobe'. He also praised the fitness and high morale of troops 'so recently emerged from deadly and determined encounters with a much vaunted and tenacious enemy'.[25]

A weapon brandished in such encounters features in **Photograph 8.10**. Here Sergeant Bill Edmonston of the 2/3rd Battalion displays a captured Japanese officer's sword, complete with glistening shark skin handle and gilded hilt, and reportedly used in the close fighting. A 2/1st Battalion corporal shot three charging Japanese from behind a tree and, while reloading his submachine gun, was struck in the head by a samurai sword, which knocked his helmet off. The swordsman then inflicted head wounds, but with his knee and superior strength the corporal subdued the Japanese soldier, whom a second Australian killed. The courageous Edmonston would be a suitably tough RSM to the battalion later in the war.

Photograph 8.11 shows more formidable weapons in the Japanese arsenal at Oivi–Gorari. Unidentified Australians, presumably of 16th Brigade, pose with a 75 mm mountain gun, probably at Gorari village.

8.10 AWM 013643

It may look innocuous, but this weapon had killed and wounded many Australians in preceding weeks. The Japanese had buried a second, dismantled gun, which the Australians found. The other pictured Japanese weapon is a 'Nambu' light machine gun.

On 15 November, the 16th Brigade reassembled and marched to the Kumusi River in high spirits. Reaching the Kumusi marked the end of the Kokoda campaign. Of the three AIF brigades involved – 16th, 21st and 25th – the 21st has since received the most attention, yet its 496 battle casualties

8.11 AWM 013644

barely outnumbered the 16th's 471. The 16th's Papuan ordeal, like the 21st's, was far from over.

The 16th Brigade followed the 25th over the Kumusi on flying foxes and single-log bridges. While the 25th then followed a track branch north to Gona, Vasey ordered Lloyd to take the 16th to Sanananda Point. High humidity and the complete absence of rations on 16 November set the tone. The following day, 57 men of the vanguard battalion, the 2/2nd, fell out on the march but it reached Popondetta on 18 November. As the 2/3rd took over the advance the next day, Brigadier

Lloyd stood alongside. When asked the battalion's objective, he answered: 'The sea!'[26] They encountered only fleeting opposition that day, and on 20 November the 2/1st, now leading, were encouraged by news from Gona and Buna. However, Japanese artillery fire soon fell among the Australians, just kilometres from the coast. The aggressive Cullen sent three companies on outflanking moves to capture the mountain gun responsible. Two companies, comprising 91 men under the outstanding Catterns, came in behind the main Japanese positions and, rather than withdraw, trod as softly as they could into what would certainly be a bloodbath. Just 50 metres from the enemy they were spotted. The Australians broke the silence with a shattering burst of gunfire, then threw themselves forward, hurdling trenches and vines before coming to grips with hundreds of enemy who soon ran screaming through burning huts and scattered corpses. Some 80 Japanese died, but so did many Australians, including five of the battalion's best officers.

On 21 November Catterns' men, now dug in, used their dwindling ammunition to fight off attacks from three sides. By the end of the day, just 23 remained unscathed. Among those killed was Corporal Vic Twomey, who had already been wounded in the thick of the fighting the previous day. The gunfire had transformed the thick surrounding foliage into something like a manicured lawn. The men were close to tears on being relieved that night amidst a thunderstorm. The Japanese had lost ground and had abandoned their mountain gun.

The 'hard-fighting men' of the 16th Brigade now numbered just 1040, all tired and ill.[27] Vasey ordered them to remain where they were until the newly arrived US 126th Regiment took the Soputa–Sanananda–Cape Killerton track junction ahead. The inexperienced Americans made glacially slow progress. Meanwhile, the 16th Brigade continued to hold the front in water-filled pits and to patrol in fierce sunlight. Galling losses included Captain Blamey and one of his men to an errant American mortar bomb on 25 November and five more to another such bomb the following day. In **Photograph 8.12** wounded Allied soldiers receive treatment from the 2/2nd Battalion medical staff in this period. Their 'ambulance' is a car

8.12 AWM 013858

reportedly captured in Singapore by the Japanese, who took it to New Guinea, where Australians recaptured it and cut the back out. The battalion RAP ran a 50-bed hospital at Sanananda, looking after hundreds of Allied troops. The Battalion RMO, Captain 'Mac' McGuiness (probably in helmet), who had won an MC at Eora Creek, and Sergeant Ted Nicholas (probably second from left) were highly efficient.

On 25 November, when the 49th Battalion and the Americans launched attacks, this RAP treated 127 wounded. The 2/2nd Battalion war diary said on 21 November that 'practically everyone was suffering from either fever or dysentery or both'.[28] Continual lack of food had also weakened them. Yet it was a tradition in the 2/2nd that no ill man would leave the line for treatment until his temperature reached 103 degrees (39.4°C). Even then he would have to make an all-day march to Popondetta airstrip. The arrival of battalions of the 30th Brigade heralded the overdue relief of 16th Brigade on 6 December. By that date an astonishing 605 officers and men had been killed or wounded in the campaign, and nearly 1000 evacuated ill. This represented 85 per cent of the strength with which the brigade had set out in October. Its three battalions were now each at company-strength. The relief began with the 2/3rd on 6 December, but elements of all three continued to man the line, and the 130-strong 2/3rd was called back to the front on 9 December. The men of the 2/2nd, as they came out the following day, were too exhausted to carry their automatic weapons, though 'still smiling' according to the brigade war diary.[29] The 2/2nd could muster just 88 soldiers, whereas at Port Moresby in September 1942 it had numbered 670. The 2/1st and 2/3rd were not relieved until 19–20 December. All returned to Port Moresby. At a parade in their mess huts on Christmas Eve, General Blamey impressed the men with the sincerity of his praise for the brigade's work in all its campaigns. He stressed that 'their greatest achievement was their effort in New Guinea'.[30]

While the 16th Brigade's Papuan campaign was coming to a painful end, other 6th Division units were still fighting. On 23 November 'Blackforce', a detachment of 2/1st Field Regiment named after its commander Major Arthur 'Black Tom' Hanson, had flown to a newly established airstrip at Popondetta. Air transport was unprecedented for Australian artillery. By day's end the gunners had moved their two 25-pounders 16 kilometres to Soputa and had brought them into action. They were keen to fire, but more important was the insistence of Brigadier Lloyd, who told Hanson to shoot even before establishing an Observation Post or locating suitable targets: the effect on the morale of his debilitated men would be lifted regardless. The guns fired accordingly on Sanananda village and hit a Japanese headquarters. The sound of the guns was indeed gratifying to men who had been without artillery support since leaving Port Moresby. On first hearing it, some stood up and cheered. Soon afterwards Blackforce had a four-gun troop in

8.13 AWM 013855

operation, supporting the brigade to which they traditionally 'belonged'. **Photograph 8.13** shows one of the Blackforce guns at Soputa. Under 7th Division command, Blackforce contributed substantially to the capture of Gona on 9 December.

Another 2/1st Field Regiment detachment was operating with the Americans at Buna. 'Bullforce', named after Captain Herbert 'Bull' Manning, was flown to Dobodura minutes ahead of Blackforce on 23 November. It too built up a full troop of four guns. Their initial welcome was not as warm as that extended to Blackforce. According to an Australian report, American commanders were not enthusiastic about artillery support, unlike their men who were actually facing the enemy in foxholes.[31]

The American 32nd Division was floundering at Buna. General Eichelberger, newly appointed commander of the sector, planned a major frontal assault with air, artillery and mortar bombardment on 5 December. To spearhead the attack, five Bren carriers were brought forward with great difficulty by boat and barge. Manning them were men of the 17th Brigade, which had landed at Milne Bay in October and which had established a 13-strong carrier platoon. Lieutenant Terence Fergusson was commanding the five Bren carriers. He had served as a trooper in 6th Division Cavalry Regiment when his father was CO, and was now in 2/7th Battalion. Four-man crews from the 2/7th would man four carriers, while the fifth had a 2/5th Battalion crew. Fergusson recognised the dangers of leading carriers against entrenched defenders and the difficulty of the terrain, but believed it possible to negotiate the ground.

Corporal Cec Wilton commanded one of the carriers that went forward after the bombardment that morning. As in all crews, the morale of his men, the first 2/7th troops to tackle the Japanese, was 'extremely high'.[32] After travelling about 100 metres, his carrier, moving like the rest at just 3 kilometres an hour, bellied on a log. Wilton's head jolted as a bullet pierced his helmet but not his skull.

8.14 Courtesy Paul Handel and US National Archives

He reminded himself not to lift his head above the armour plating. On turning off the motor, which drowned out almost all sound, he heard countless bullets pinging off the armour. With three wounded, they abandoned the carrier and withdrew.

Wilton's crew was relatively fortunate. Within 20 minutes of emerging into the open, all five carriers were out of action. The carriers in **Photograph 8.14** are probably those disabled within the Allied lines. Several were hit by anti-tank guns, while crewmen were killed or wounded by bullets, grenades and mortar bombs. Among the six dead were Lieutenant Fergusson, shot while standing up to call to an adjacent carrier, and his second-in-command, Lieutenant Walker, who marched from headquarters to search for the dead and any abandoned weapons. Eleven men were wounded in what Wilton called 'the Buna massacre'. He called it 'one hell of a way to learn that Bren gun carriers are not tanks and cannot be used as such'.[33] They did inflict some damage, especially the lead carrier of Sergeant 'Jock' Taylor, who won a DCM. Fergusson was posthumously awarded an American

8.15 AWM 013856

Distinguished Service Cross. On 14 December, the reinforced Americans took Buna village. The last Japanese ground at Buna only fell in January.

Stubborn Japanese defence continued at Sanananda. **Photograph 8.15** shows a 2/1st Field Regiment officer, Lieutenant 'Jock' Finlay, climbing the 'Big Tree' OP on the Sanananda Track. Finlay's signaller, John Hynes, called this 'a bastard of a location', subject to machine-gun and sniper fire.[34] Obtaining effective observation was difficult in the low-lying beachheads, and FOOs often went forward with patrols to observe targets. Within days of Blackforce's arrival a FOO and

8.16 AWM 014238

his assistant were killed in a patrol clash. Sound ranging and aerial observation helped.

On 28 December, a Japanese raiding party attacked the guns at night, disabling one. The gunners fought back, killing one raider and wounding another. The gun was firing again within 24 hours, continuing the work that made them a priority target for enemy ground and air forces: hence the camouflage in Photograph 8.13. By 31 December both troops had fired some 3000 rounds per gun.

The 2/1st Field Regiment contributed to the final destruction of the Japanese bridgehead in Papua. The CO, Lieutenant-Colonel O'Connell, coordinated all the guns as acting CRA 7th Division. 2nd Battery was moved to the Buna front and an *ad hoc* 'X' Battery was sent to defend Oro Bay. As **Photograph 8.16** suggests, cooperation between American infantry and Australian artillery improved in this period, though the Americans later complained of insufficient guns and ammunition. Here, Lieutenant John 'Snake Eyes' Lewitz (centre) of the 2/1st Field Regiment plans an artillery bombardment with two American officers in January.

Lewitz's left wrist, not visible here, has a plaster cast over an injury he sustained when he hit an escaping Japanese on the helmet with his left fist while shooting a revolver from his right hand. Lewitz received a US Bronze Star for his work in this campaign, which ended when Sanananda fell on 22 January 1943. In the course of the eight-week beachhead campaign, Bullforce's guns fired 17 774 rounds, Blackforce's 16 122. The 2nd Battery added another 593. The regiment lost 12 dead, 14 wounded and 200 evacuated ill.

CHAPTER 9

WAU-SALAMAUA

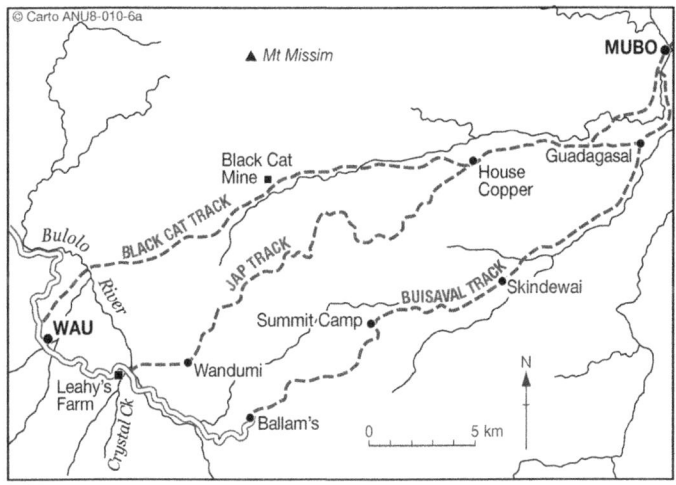

Map 6 Wau 1943

Within days of the Papuan fighting ending at Sanananda, a fierce battle occurred at Wau, in the Mandated Territory of New Guinea. 6th Division troops contributed decisively to its outcome.

Wau (pronounced 'wow') and the Bulolo Valley in which it sat, figured prominently in Allied and Japanese strategic planning in early 1943, for its airstrip could support future offensives for either side. Blamey considered Wau a potential springboard for attacks towards the major Japanese bases at Lae and Salamaua. Holding Wau was also essential to prevent further Japanese attacks towards Port Moresby. Blamey had kept the 17th Brigade intact throughout the previous months' fighting so that he could use the brigade to attack from Wau, or to defend it. When on 7 January the Japanese substantially reinforced Lae, Blamey decided to send the 17th to Wau. There Brigadier Moten, who had commanded the brigade for a year, but not yet in action, would take over 'Kanga Force', the Australian commandos and locally raised militia operating around Wau.

The 17th Brigade had, since October, been a garrison and potential reserve in soggy, pestilential and low-lying Milne Bay. Now it had to travel to an area similarly muddy, rainy and gloomy, but also mountainous.

Travelling to Wau required air transport from Port Moresby. The 2/6th Battalion moved first, beginning to arrive on 14 January. Bad weather, accidents and shortages of aircraft hampered the transfer, but by 19 January most of the battalion had arrived at the Wau airstrip, which sloped up to a range of mountains at its southern end. The troops, many making their first flight, were struck by the beauty of the place. With 563 all ranks, the unit was still some 300 short of its full establishment strength, thanks to the ravages of malaria at Milne Bay.

As the Allied command suspected, the 4000-strong force landed at Lae was earmarked to attack Wau. To safeguard the airstrip – his sole viable lifeline – Moten had to cover two main avenues of potential attack. One was from Lae down the Bulolo Valley. Another was from Salamaua via Komiatum and the forward Japanese base at Mubo. To complicate matters, from Mubo, Moten knew the Japanese could take either of two tracks to Wau: the Buisaval Track or, parallel and to the north, the Black Cat Track. Initially he spread the 2/6th around all these routes until the rest of his brigade arrived.

The Japanese planned to attack Wau through Mubo, not along one of the two main tracks, but along a third one, of which the Australians were as yet ignorant. Movement and communication along the tracks were extremely time-consuming. For example, the 13 kilometres from Wau to the Black Cat Mine, after which one track was named, took a full day's strenuous marching. Once units were committed along a track, switching them to other danger points or returning them to Wau was painfully slow.

So too was the arrival of the balance of 17th Brigade. General Herring, now commanding New Guinea Force, believed the Japanese moves to be purely defensive. However, from 20 January increasing numbers of Japanese were spotted on the Black Cat Track. The 2/5th Battalion began arriving on 24 January, with its main body landing three days later. **Photograph 9.1** depicts some of them after arrival, with a DC-3 in the background. The men sat on the floor of the aircraft, which had been stripped of seats to make way for its human cargo, as well as boxes of grenades, mortar bombs, packs and other supplies. On landing, the 2/5th was sent along the Buisaval Track.

9.1   AWM 014372

By 26 January Moten realised that the main axis of the Japanese advance was on the third track, running between the other two and soon called the 'Jap Track'. However, his limited resources were already committed to the other two tracks. While he was planning to smash the forces on the Black Cat Track, a crisis developed on 28 January when the main Japanese body struck unexpectedly at Wandumi, just a few kilometres and hours from Wau. These first hours of the battle of Wau proved critical, and the 2/6th Battalion's Captain Bill Sherlock, pictured in **Photograph 9.2**, played a pivotal role. Sherlock's A Company had been at Wandumi preparing to attack towards House Copper when the Japanese attacked. His dramatic phone messages to headquarters that day reflected the position. At 7.30 am he said: 'Holding them nicely. Only disadvantage Japs above us'. Later, as his ammunition dwindled and casualties climbed, he noted more enemy forces arriving. At 2.55 pm he called: 'Look like being over-run. Am cut off'. He counted hundreds of them. Fifteen minutes later his signal reflected peril: 'Things very hot. Any help may be too late. One platoon over-run'. Yet his response was typical of the AIF's best traditions: 'Am counter-attacking now'. That counter-attack, a bayonet

9.2   Courtesy Sir David Hay and 2/6th Battalion

charge that Sherlock led, restored the Australian position, but 15 minutes after that message he was 'trying desperately to stop them'.[1]

A brave detachment of 2/8th engineers brought up ammunition to Sherlock's company. Moten sent forward a 2/5th Battalion company that had landed that morning, but its arrival at Wandumi at about 5.30 pm could not change the odds sufficiently. The Australians decided to withdraw. The Brigade Major, Major Muir, came forward, took charge and ordered the troops to halt for the night about one mile from Wandumi in temporary positions designed to allow the 2/7th to assemble at Wau next day, if the weather cleared. No landings occurred in the 24 hours after 9 am on 28 January. Muir estimated the Japanese facing them as 300–500 strong. Some of these soon bypassed Sherlock's group, and at 7 pm a transport driver told Moten that he had seen Japanese marching towards Wau no more than two miles away. That night, amidst the sound of enemy fire and heavy rain, all available men, including walking wounded, were directed to positions in and around the aerodrome. Two 2/5th companies summoned to Wau from Ballam's on the Buisaval Track passed through Japanese pausing astride the road. Neither side recognised each other in the dark, so the Australians reached the aerodrome by 7 am on the 29th.

By then Sherlock was dead. Some time after 3 am he and the two companies west of Wandumi had sought to withdraw as overwhelming forces approached them from the front and flank. While crossing Crystal Creek, Sherlock was killed by machine-gun fire and the rest broke into groups. By dawn, enemy mortar and small arms fire was falling on the south-east of the airstrip. With the issue in the balance, the weather cleared. At 9.15 am an aircraft landed – the first of an unprecedented 60 to do so that day. The 814 men who arrived included the balance of 2/5th Battalion and nearly all of the 2/7th Battalion. Moten positioned these troops around the airfield. After a quick briefing, Major Walker's 2/7th company moved out close to Leahy's Farm, where they killed 15 Japanese and settled for the night. This group felt the wrath of a major Japanese thrust for the airfield before dawn on 30 January. Walker and others were forced back, but those who were able to hold their ground were soon supported by Walker and 2/5th men attacking the Japanese on the flank. When the Japanese tried to outflank the defenders, 2/5th men and commandos cut them down. Walker's force resumed its original position. As a wartime 17th Brigade account says, this was a day that began with Japanese firing from just 60 yards, battles in several places at once, and men everywhere advising: 'Don't give these _____ an inch'.²

That day Moten had an opportunity to start taking the initiative. A section (two guns) of 2/1st Field Regiment arrived that morning. **Photograph 9.3** depicts a gun being unloaded at Wau. The original caption suggests that this was on

9.3   AWM 014376

9.4
AWM 014369

30 January. On that day, the two guns were assembled and in action by 11.15 am. In **Photograph 9.4** a gun is being prepared to fire at Japanese near the aerodrome. The section was immediately put at the disposal of the newly arrived 2/7th Battalion. Captain Wise, commanding the detachment, went out to Walker's positions, established an Observation Post and called down fire. This proved very effective, as well as bringing great relief to every Australian who heard it. A smoke shell fired to assist with ranging landed in an explosives dump near Leahy's Farm, demolishing the farm buildings and killing many Japanese. A group of 400 Japanese spotted marching from Leahy's Farm also came under deadly fire from the guns, from Walker's men and from Beaufighter aircraft. Apart from some feeble counter-attacks, the Japanese now went over to the defensive.

On 31 January 28 survivors of the Wandumi fighting returned to Wau and disclosed the fate of Sherlock and the six other fatalities of his company. As early as 29 January a medical officer at Wau heard that, 'we have been saved by Capt Sherlock of the 2/6th Bn'.[3] Sherlock and his men had gained valuable, perhaps critical, time for the meagre but growing defence of the airfield. Sherlock's name is

9.5   AWM 057859

always coupled with that of Wau, but he was not given the posthumous Victoria Cross that many felt was his due. In attacking Sherlock's position, the enemy battalion lost at least 75 men, including its commander.

By 5 February the Japanese were withdrawing, mainly along the Wandumi to Mubo track. They were harassed by Australian artillery, which by 9 February was at battery strength and had fired more than 3000 rounds. By then too, all Japanese still in the Wau area were dead: about 1200 of the 2500–3000 men who had attacked. In **Photograph 9.5** Corporal Frank McNally of 2/5th Battalion shows a memento of the vicious fights that drove out the Japanese. McNally, an outstanding patroller, captured this samurai sword at Crystal Creek. So many Japanese died in this area – 150 killed by 2/5th Battalion on 9 February alone – that Australians christened it 'the Slaughterhouse'. In the Aitape–Wewak campaign this brave NCO and his section captured a Woodpecker machine gun. It now stands outside the Coonabarabran swimming pool in memory of Bill Wilson, McNally's mate, who was killed in August 1945. A 2/6th Battalion man also clashed with a swordsman,

9.6 AWM P02110.001

on the Black Cat Track. Though wounded in the arm and shoulder, the Australian spoke regretfully of having to 'shoot the poor bastard', whom he thought was a medical officer.[4] The battalion's own CO, Lieutenant-Colonel Wood, received a head wound in the fighting of 9 February during which the 2/6th suffered 16 casualties but inflicted 50–80.

As **Photograph 9.6** suggests, carrying wounded Australians back to Wau was often difficult. Stretcher-bearers from the battalions and from the 2/2nd Field Ambulance were staged on relay posts at intervals of just 300 metres during the battle. This casualty, probably of 2/7th Battalion, is being carried primarily by the indispensable native bearers. The 2/7th employed boat-shaped wire-netting stretchers used by local miners. Casualties had to be strapped in and then half carried, half slid down the steep slopes. A 2/7th Battalion RAP man, Sergeant Bill Russell, would win an MM in April. Just 20 metres from an enemy machine gun, and depending on the light of a cigarette, he successfully stitched the sucking chest wound of a soldier.

At Wau, some men were wounded even before leaving the airfield. They went straight back to Moresby, where one casualty was operated on just five hours after landing at Wau. By 9 February 207 battle casualties and 335 sick had been treated in Kanga Force.

The strange ambulance pictured in **Photograph 9.7** assisted with evacuations to the aircraft. The original caption called it the 'wreck that saves lives'; the defenders of Wau knew it affectionately as the 'Stonkered Taxi Service'. Built from a wrecked car and a salvaged motor van by brigade mechanics of 2/46th LAD, it carried two stretchers on one side, with passengers seated on boards on the other.

Photograph 9.8 depicts a figure of great importance to the 6th Division, who arrived at Wau on 13 February. This was Lieutenant-General Mackay, now

9.7   AWM 014377/21

temporarily commanding New Guinea Force. Here he is talking to Lieutenant-Colonel Starr of the 2/5th Battalion (left) and Brigadier Moten (centre). Mackay visited the 2/5th Battalion and 2/8th Field Company at Crystal Creek and travelled to Bulolo. Though pleased with Moten's performance, he was still anxious about the Japanese threat to Wau and advised Blamey to reinforce the area. Blamey agreed and directed the 3rd Division Headquarters, under another 6th Division veteran, Major-General Savige, to take over at Wau.

In fact, the Japanese would not return. By 1 March they had retreated to the Guadagasal–Mubo area, where their ill-fated drive on Wau had begun. The subsequent Australian advance halted in the Guadagasal–Waipali area for lack of supplies. Moten sent patrols towards the Japanese base at Mubo. He replaced Starr, reportedly because he believed his patrols were too slow to provide the required intelligence, but the men of the 2/5th were sad to lose their esteemed CO. Moten was capable, but he was considered remote, literally as well as figuratively. His geographical remoteness was even celebrated in verse. Indeed, he and General Savige had a disagreement about the location of Moten's headquarters, after which Moten moved the HQ forward from Wau to Skindewai in May.

9.8 AWM 044258

While working at 17th Brigade Headquarters in April, Major Harry Dunkley, an original of 2/7th Battalion, described his quarters as 'a refuge for the incorrigibly frivolous '39ers – a proud but vanishing race'. Old friends would enter Dunkley's tent, throw their hats and guns on his bed, call him an old bastard and, over a cup of tea, discuss in bawdy detail their recently arrived superior officers.[5] From Moten down, these recently arrived leaders, many brought in to replace officers transferred to militia units, were expected to prove themselves. One reinforcement fighting his first campaign was Lieutenant Alexander Robertson. This former primary school teacher wrote to his wife on 8 February: 'I can count myself a soldier now, as I have killed at least one man – a Jap machine-gunner. And I don't feel the least bit remorseful'.[6]

The other ranks that did most of the killing were now largely late arrivals too: for example, replacements for about 200 officers and men who had left the 2/6th Battalion in Australia in 1941–2. The men in **Photograph 9.9** are a case in point: the four pictured 17th Brigade men all enlisted in 1941 or 1942. These tired but happy patrollers are reaching the end of an arduous 10-day patrol, probably on 17 April 1943. Apart from the bandaged man, a commando of 2/3rd Independent Company, all four uniformed men are 2/5th Battalion members. They left Observation Hill on 8 April and patrolled to Bobdubi Ridge, from which they reportedly saw Salamaua. On the return trek they rendezvoused with commandos, who brought along the pictured 'cargo boy' and two American pilots eager for a ground-level tour. One of the Americans took this photograph and after the war gave it to patrol leader Private John Vincent, third from left. A 2/5th Battalion report stated that the numerous patrols in this period affected this company's stamina in the gruelling

WAU-SALAMAUA 165

9.9

9.10 AWM 054752

operations ahead. During those operations, Private John Friend (second from left) would earn an MM when, armed with his Tommy gun, he and a Bren gunner together held off Japanese attackers for 20 minutes at Mount Tambu.

On 23 April, Major-General Savige's 3rd Division assumed responsibility for defending Wau, although a second attack was unlikely after the Battle of the Bismarck Sea destroyed Japanese reinforcements in March. The 17th Brigade came under Savige's command, and apart from a militia battalion, an independent company and a mountain gun section, comprised the main part of the 'division'. In the months ahead, militia reinforcements arrived but the 17th Brigade remained Savige's 'spearhead and clenched fist'.[7]

From December 1942, the army sought to improve north–south communications and New Guinea's supply-lines by creating a jeep track running north from Bulldog to Wau. The Japanese attack on Wau and the manifest difficulty of supplying an advance towards Salamaua gave the project extra impetus, and it was made possible by the expertise and efforts of the 2/1st Field Company and the pioneer platoon of 2/7th Battalion. **Photograph 9.10** shows some of the challenges of this project of creating a road more than 100 kilometres long and in places nearly 3000 metres high. Here 2/1st Field Company sappers are making a track along the cliff face at Fox Gap. Lacking mechanical equipment, they are undertaking the task by hand. Even when equipment was available, it was less efficient at high

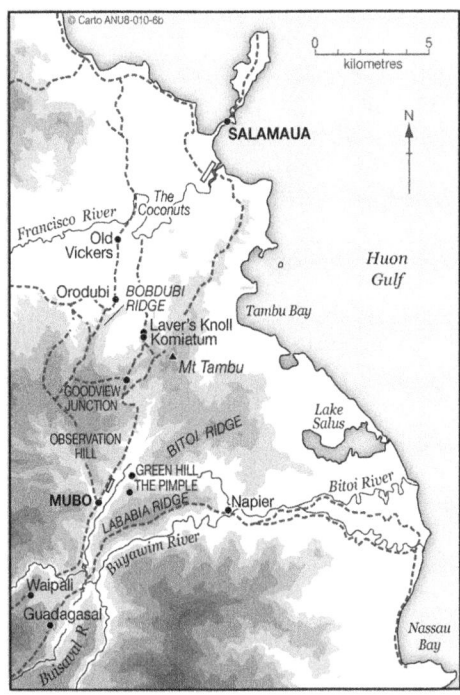

Map 7 Salamaua 1943

altitudes, and landslides were a constant danger. A landslide in this area killed Lance-Corporal William Aytoun of this company. The road opened in August 1943, but Australian advances soon reduced its value and it was closed in mid-1944. As the engineers' historian says, 'none of the men who worked on the road would have looked back on their time there with anything but distaste'.[8] Nonetheless, enthusiasm seems to have remained high among 2/8th Field Company engineers and infantrymen who extended the jeep track, again with limited tools and in high and obstacle-ridden terrain, east from Wau to Summit.

In the forward area east of Wau the Australians could maintain only a small force: by late April this comprised the 2/7th Battalion and the independent company. From Lababia Ridge the 2/7th made several abortive and at this stage 'pointless' attempts to seize two features, called The Pimple and Green Hill, astride the main track east of Mubo.[9] On 9 May Japanese forces surrounded a 2/7th company forward of Lababia Ridge, but the Australians held off eight attacks until relieved two days later. Even the cooks volunteered to be part of the relief force.

The 17th Brigade was about to become involved in new Allied strategic initiatives. On 6 May MacArthur had ordered Blamey to seize Salamaua and Lae. The primary target, Lae, was to be taken after an amphibious landing, but this meant first securing a shore base for landing craft within 100 kilometres of Lae. Savige was ordered to secure Nassau Bay for this purpose. This would also allow the Australians at Mubo some supply from the sea. An American force would then land and assist the 17th Brigade in attacking Mubo and Komiatum. Savige was also to push the Japanese north of the Francisco River, which entered the sea a few kilometres south of Salamaua. Blamey planned to draw Japanese forces towards Salamaua and away from Lae.

Photograph 9.11, taken near Mount Tambu, suggests why the offensive towards Salamaua was to be physically arduous and nerve-wracking. The dripping vegetation was claustrophobically close, well-suited to ambush from enemies who were seldom seen but often present around the all-important tracks.

9.11 AWM 056762

9.12　　　　　　　　　　AWM 015380

The depressing conditions imposed deprivation and disease. There were terrible challenges for every arm and service, from engineers, signallers and service corps to infantrymen. All were eternally wet, their clothes and boots rotting after weeks of constant wear. By the end few had underclothes or socks, though ironically water was often scarce on the crucial hilltops.

According to a war correspondent, Australian wounded returning from the front in April and May talked of Komiatum, one of the closer targets of the forthcoming operations, as though it were Tokyo, so distant did it seem. **Photograph 9.12**, taken near Mubo, epitomises the exhaustion of the coming operations. A wartime publication talked of 'nightmare trails between Wau and Salamaua' and quoted soldiers grimly saying: 'You can't get any place in this blanky country without going on your flat feet'.[10] The ground was rarely flat, and indeed the campaign that followed was called 'The Battle of the Ridges'. Some even cried with pain from the jarring of repeatedly descending these heights.[11] The pictured soldier, Private Herbert Escreet, would in 1945 win the MM for supporting his platoon with a Bren gun in open ground despite being wounded. A 17th Brigade publication labelled this photograph: 'The Waipali track. Any other track would seem easy after that nightmare'.[12]

In late May 2/6th Battalion relieved the 2/7th and by 9 June had found a route from Lababia Ridge to Nassau Bay. From 20 to 23 June the 2/6th's forward company, reinforced halfway through by a second company, defied a sustained attack by two Japanese battalions comprising some 1500 men. **Photograph 9.13** shows four men of the forward company in this Lababia action, which the unit history calls 'one of the most important in which troops of the Battalion took part'.[13] The soldier at far right, Private George Lamont, was wounded at Lababia

9.13   AWM 055633

and would be killed seven days after being photographed. His older brother had died of wounds in February 1942. A 3-inch mortar, such as the 2/6th one depicted in **Photograph 9.14**, proved critical in breaking up the attacks on Lababia Ridge.

American troops landed at Nassau Bay on 30 June. A covering force from the 2/6th Battalion helped them ashore and into defensive positions. After a few skirmishes the 2/6th cleared the path to Napier for the inexperienced and timid Americans.

By advancing subsequently to Bitoi Ridge the Americans threatened to encircle the Japanese at Mubo. In that area on 7 July the 2/6th Battalion assaulted Observation Hill. In this campaign, 6th Division troops probably received the best air support of any of their campaigns thus far, and this assault was well supported by Allied aircraft and artillery. By 13 July the Japanese had abandoned the Mubo area.

The Japanese line blocking the way to Salamaua now ran through an arc from Bobdubi Ridge to Tambu Bay and included Goodview Junction and Mount Tambu. The recently arrived 15th Brigade advanced towards Bobdubi Ridge. On 16 July a 2/5th Battalion company captured important high ground at the southern end of

9.14   AWM 055632

Mount Tambu. Sergeant Bill Tiller, pictured at left a week later in **Photograph 9.15**, single-handedly wiped out a Japanese machine-gun crew and then helped his men kill 20 Japanese in hand-to-hand fighting that gave his men a valuable knoll. Another platoon took a second knoll, but that night the enemy launched eight attacks to recapture this ground. Mortar, mountain gun and machine-gun fire accompanied attacks launched from just 10 to 15 metres away, but the Australians held on and countered the Japanese fire and taunts with their own. Tiller was again prominent, encouraging his men and leading by deadly example. Tiller would not see his well-deserved DCM, for the day after this photograph was taken he was killed while acting as a forward scout.

The Australians' mortar fire and excellent marksmanship reduced enemy numbers on 17 July and helped one platoon hold off 200 Japanese. When, on 18 July, the Australians gained another 80 metres, Lance-Corporal James Jackson (centre in Photograph 9.15) destroyed an enemy machine gun with three grenades, and the occupants of another pillbox with his Tommy gun. His DCM citation said Jackson personally inflicted some 30 enemy casualties. On 19 July the Japanese finally withdrew. They had suffered at least 350 casualties, the two Australian companies just 39.

The captured Japanese weapon pit in **Photograph 9.16** was almost certainly one of those from which the attacks of 19 July were repulsed. It was photographed just 50 metres from the Japanese lines, on 23 July. Quickly consolidating captured ground was imperative, for the Japanese invariably counter-attacked. Battalions often formed a series of company and platoon perimeters, each ideally comprising well-stocked two-man slit trenches in mutually supporting positions and with fire lanes cleared and booby traps laid. Small groups, rarely larger than one company, now decided the fate of key positions. Cooks, batmen, orderlies and

9.15 AWM 056760

9.16 AWM 056767

9.17   AWM 056768

battalion headquarters personnel gave critical assistance, toiling forward with precious ammunition, water and food, then back with the wounded. The day following this photograph the Bren gunner, Corporal Edward Thompson, would be wounded and the Thompson submachine gunner, Corporal Bob Jones, killed. According to a recent letter to his mother, Jones had 'had enough of this Island of Paradise, [where] it never stops raining and there are too many hills'.[14]

The vegetation restricted aerial reconnaissance, so the 2/5th was still sending patrols to and beyond enemy lines. **Photograph 9.17** allegedly depicts a forward scout in an attack, though its official date of 23 July suggests either that he was on a patrol or that the photograph is posed. A Japanese soldier lies dead on the right. A 2/5th Battalion officer summed up the attitude of 'the whole division' towards Japanese thus: 'they were despised as one despises a mad dog, a sadist or a killer of children.'[15] The Australian pictured, Private Fred McVicar, would himself be killed the following day.

Supplying the forward troops was extremely problematic. Early in the campaign, supplies were flown to Wau then carried to the troops, mainly by native carriers. However, lengthening supply lines necessitated air dropping. Then loads were prepared and carried forward. Natives worked magnificently carrying food,

9.18 AWM 054508

ammunition and wounded, as did many 17th Brigade soldiers. **Photograph 9.18** epitomises some of the problems. Grim-faced signallers of 17th Brigade and 6th Division Signals are forming a food line to carry supplies from the air dropping area on Guadagasal Ridge to their cookhouse. Further forward there were no steps like these, and there was a constant danger of the enemy interrupting. Partly to improve the supply arrangements, Herring, again commanding New Guinea Force, now decided to occupy Tambu Bay. From there Savige's troops could receive supplies by sea and by air. Moreover, whereas artillery at Wau could not be moved within range, from Tambu Bay additional artillery could support the 3rd Division. American forces landed accordingly and by 27 July some 26 Allied guns were demoralising Japanese forces.

On 24 July the 2/5th Battalion attacked the Japanese holding Mount Tambu. In **Photograph 9.19** troops under Captain Lin Cameron (far left) wait tensely for zero hour. Cameron had only learnt the day before that his 59-strong company would be attacking. Before dawn on 24 July he had crept to within 15 metres of the seven pillboxes blocking their advance and determined that he had no alternative to a frontal assault. Cameron had won a Military Cross at Crystal Creek, and would win another in 1945. Intense and ascetic in his single-minded dedication to war-making, in battle he was efficient and without emotion. He drove his men hard, but was said to cry over their losses after action. He would have reason to weep following the forthcoming attack.

Supporting artillery and mortar fire did not eliminate the pillboxes, which poured fire into the attackers. Cameron was wounded, three of his men killed and 12 others wounded. The wounded included Corporal John Smith, pictured in **Photograph 9.20** just after receiving the MM for an action in which he had used a Bren and a TSMG to clear enemy posts blocking the advance at Khalde

9.19 AWM 056769

9.20 AWM 023145

in Syria. Now with three other men, including two Americans, Smith reached the crest of Mount Tambu in an extraordinary charge that the Japanese halted with hand grenades, mortar bombs and bullets. Though only semi-conscious, Smith had to be dragged out of the fight: he later died of more than 40 wounds he had sustained. This frontal attack on formidable defences effectively had no prospect of success.

On 30 July an American company tried the same approach, with identical results. Corporal 'Bull' Allen of the 2/5th Battalion now came to the fore. **Photograph 9.21**, a justly famous image of the archetypal Australian stretcher bearer, depicts Allen rescuing an

9.21 AWM 015515

American knocked unconscious by a mortar bomb. Under fire, Allen saved this and 11 other casualties that day. Allen, who we last saw in Syria, had won an MM at Crystal Creek when he had carried at least three wounded men out of danger, one of them 200 metres. For his courage at Mount Tambu he received a US Silver Star.

Many wounded were taken on arduous journeys to the tent depicted in **Photograph 9.22**. This is the operating theatre of the 2/2nd Field Ambulance in July, days after it had been erected at Buigap. Until May, this unit's 191 soldiers had provided all Kanga Force's medical services, operating from a remarkable 22 locations in New Guinea. By the time of the photograph, another field

9.22 AWM 056751

9.23 AWM 015378

ambulance and a mobile operating unit were also present. They were kept busy by wounds and disease, especially malaria. The first operation was in progress here just three hours after the surgical equipment arrived. A surgeon, Captain William Stening of 2/5th Australian General Hospital (second from left in Photograph 9.2), is talking here to Captain Owen Williams of 2/2nd Field Ambulance. As we shall see, in the 6th Division's next campaign in 1944, Williams would be 'an outstanding R.M.O.' for the 2/4th Battalion.[16] The quality of the 2/2nd Field Ambulance's response to the extraordinary demands of the Wau–Salamaua campaign was reflected in the OBEs awarded to its two COs, Lieutenant-Colonels Refshauge and Smibert, and the 13 MIDs received by other members.

The medical personnel's courage and fortitude were well matched to those of their patients, such as the 2/5th walking wounded from Mount Tambu pictured in **Photograph 9.23**. Major Dunkley's description of 2/7th Battalion could have applied to many:

> Met a brace of my show . . . yesterday one with a broken shin where a bullet met him, one with a nicked lung. Both very perky . . . Bloke with shin . . . lay out for three nights with Japs passing ten yards away, before the boys got him out.[17]

The stalemate at Mount Tambu led Moten to decide to encircle the enemy there. A means was discovered when 2/6th Battalion patrols found a path through exceptionally difficult country to Laver's Knoll, near Komiatum. **Photograph 9.24** shows preparations for a 2/6th Battalion patrol in that region. Crouching at right is Captain Harold Laver, after whom Laver's Knoll was named. He would win an MC in the week ahead. There were other formidable men in the pictured group: Private Leonard McGrath (far right) and Sergeant 'Smoky' Hedderman (crouching with

9.24 AWM 055635

slouch hat) each won an MM at Lababia in June. Hedderman would add a DCM in 1945. Knowing their calibre, Moten had specifically asked that Laver's company be selected to find a way around the enemy positions. Hedderman's patrol had done it by 7 August, just three days before this photograph was taken.

Photograph 9.25 was also taken on 10 August, when General Savige and Brigadier Moten had come forward to visit. From left to right are Hedderman, Laver, Lieutenant-Colonel Wood, Moten and Savige, all looking at Japanese positions. 'Top brass' were often far from welcome among their subordinates in forward areas. After a general and three brigadiers visited 2/7th Battalion in June, Major Harry Dunkley wrote: 'My blokes were so stunned at the flash of scarlet and gold [on the senior officers' uniforms] that they were inclined to jump and salute when a stick broke near them for hours after'.[18] Captain Cam Bennett found himself accompanied by not only Moten but also General Berryman, Deputy Chief of the General Staff, at the forefront of an advance in August. The general asked many questions and eventually the exasperated captain replied: 'How the Christ do I know, Sir? I wish to God you would go to buggery and take the brigadier with you'.[19] Berryman followed this advice. Despite differing temperaments, the

9.25 AWM 055638

senior officers pictured in Photograph 9.25, Moten and Savige, were now working harmoniously. With the help of all ranks below him, Savige was achieving his task of attracting and holding many Japanese at Salamaua. Parts of all three Japanese divisions in New Guinea were by late July around the 'Salamaua magnet'.

Meanwhile, on 2–4 August A Company of the 2/7th Battalion, which had been supporting 15th Brigade, held off 14 frontal attacks on the Old Vickers position. **Photograph 9.26** depicts two leaders of the battalion as it moved forward from Goodview Junction to prepare for an attack on The Coconuts, at the northern end of Bobdubi Ridge. They are Lieutenant Keith Pritchard (left) and WOII Roy Doran. Briefings before attacks had to be especially thorough in this campaign, as giving the usual visual signs was often impractical in the dense bush. Firing was frequently from the hip. Doran has an Owen gun, which after positive reports from forward sections trying it in May was replacing the Thompson in the 17th Brigade. The 2/7th War Diary in July talked of the 'strangeness' of this new weapon to the men.[20] The attack on The Coconuts began on 14 August after a heavy aerial bombardment that destroyed the so-called Centre Coconuts. Among the 2/7th attackers were some 57 men of Bena Force, which from January to July had been

9.26 AWM 055618

defending and patrolling the Bena Bena area in the Central Highlands. Severe fighting captured North Coconuts, but South Coconuts had been largely unharmed and the attackers had to withdraw after suffering 27 casualties. The Japanese eventually abandoned the position on 17 August.

The 2/6th had captured Laver's Knoll the previous day and then held on against the inevitable ferocious counter-attacks. Komiatum Ridge was soon in Australian hands. Facing encirclement, the Japanese abandoned Mount Tambu and Goodview Junction on 19 August. That day a 2/7th Battalion company captured Orodubi. The battalion war diary reported on 20 August: 'It was learned with deep regret that Lieut Pritchard and CSM Doran had both been killed during the Coys attack on Orodubi'.[21] This indicated the high regard in which these two 32-year-olds were held. Pritchard was a grazier from New South Wales, Doran a driver from Melbourne. Doran was a popular 2/7th original who had gone from storeman to company sergeant-major. They exemplify the sacrifice of the 2/7th, which had the highest losses of the three battalions in the drive on Salamaua.

The 17th Brigade advance halted on the last ridge line before Salamaua. On 21 August the 29th Brigade began relieving the 17th, which had been fighting since January. Even then, the 2/7th Battalion remained with the 15th Brigade. Part of the battalion crossed the Francisco River that day and the unit kept fighting and advancing, doing a 'magnificent job' according to a wartime publication, until 13 September.[22] The 17th Brigade had contributed massively to achieving the objectives set out for 3rd Division Headquarters in May. Indeed, on 20 September, after militia troops occupied Salamaua, Herring sent a message for Moten to promulgate to all ranks:

> I want the 17 Aust Inf Bde to know that it is primarily their triumph. It was the 17th who saved WAU and kept the Jap at bay in the MUBO area. It was the 17th who won the battle of MUBO and finally it was the 17th who drove the Jap from the MT TAMBU-KOMIATUM area – an achievement of the highest order.[23]

Even Tokyo Radio acknowledged that in this campaign: 'The Japanese fought against the most experienced brigade in the Australian army'.[24]

On 23 September 1943, after exactly 50 weeks overseas, 17th Brigade came under command of the 6th Division again, on the Atherton Tableland. Its achievements, in some of the worst conditions faced by the proud 6th, were undeniable. 'Jo' Gullett caught the spirit of the campaign:

> My memory of those days is of gaunt-faced men, yellow with Atebrin [the anti-malarial drug], many shivering with fever, standing round a dismal smoking fire because there was no place to sit. But we were winning.[25]

CHAPTER 10

THE LONGEST WAIT: AUSTRALIA 1943-4

All three AIF infantry divisions experienced a long, dull, trying hiatus before the final campaigns, but the 6th Division waited longest. One brigade, the 19th, waited three and a half years. The shortest break, for the 17th, was more than a year. Frustration and disappointment resound through the contemporary writings and memoirs of all who endured 1943 and 1944 in camps in Queensland's Atherton Tableland.

Between July and September 1943 the 16th and 19th Brigades believed they were about to move to New Guinea, and indeed while undertaking amphibious training were warned to prepare for movement overseas. However, in late September the divisions already in New Guinea were making such progress that the move was deferred. There were some diversions in the way of sport and, from mid-1944, a 6th Division Other Ranks' Club, the 'Kangaroo Club' was established and well patronised in the Wondecla area, where the division was based. However, in their none-too-salubrious camps, 6th Division men tended to feel isolated and neglected by the civilian community. One's own family circle was of course an exception, and men still hankered after personal leave.

Public parades also brought attention. On 18 November 1943, the 17th Brigade marched past huge crowds in Melbourne, which endorsed the message shown on the banner in **Photograph 10.1**: 'Well Done the 17th'. This march signalled the end of the brigade's leave. **Photograph 10.2** symbolises what the soldiers left behind when they went back to camp, as here a beautiful blonde attaches herself to one of the marching men. Naturally the presence of wives, girlfriends and other loved ones made leave the most enjoyable feature of this period for 6th Division members.

10.1   AWM 059974

10.2   AWM 139992

Photograph 10.3 evokes the more serious loss that the division's service entailed, as casualties from the brigade look on at those fit enough to march.[1]

There was a memorable parade for the rest of the division, too, at Herberton Racecourse in November. **Photograph 10.4** shows General Blamey being driven in a clearly marked 6th Division carrier to this parade on 5 November. He spoke warmly to the formation, which been his first command in the war and which he called 'the good old Sixth'. He promised that it would soon be reunited in 'the same grand old division that no formation anywhere in this war will surpass'.[2]

184 THE LONGEST WAIT

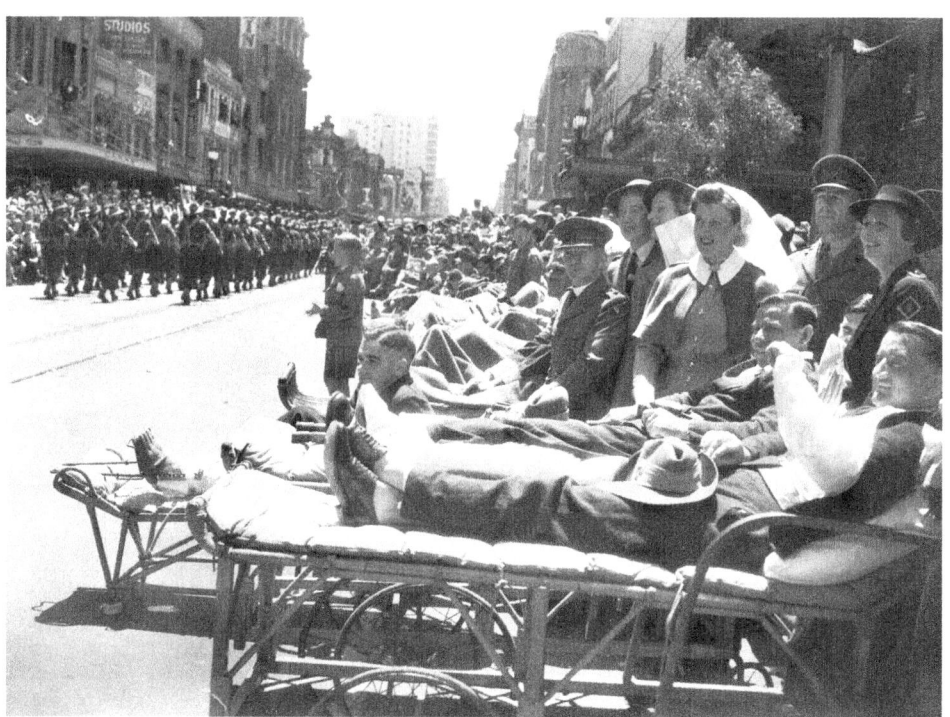

10.3 AWM 140031

10.4 AWM 059936

While the units were reuniting, many of their individual members were departing. The 2/6th Battalion history describes the unit's 'dispirited' feeling as it reassembled at Wondecla in late November. The unit had lost more than 100 members through medical downgrading, often through tropical illness or transfers in the previous six weeks. About the same number had still not returned to the battalion. Roughly half were not back in January. The other brigades nursed similar disappointments.

Photograph 10.5 is instructive. A 2/11th Battalion mortar team is competing at a 6th Division gymkhana held at Wondecla in October 1943. Of the four crewmen who can be identified all but the soldier at far left, Private Fred Yeo, had left the unit within a year of the photograph. Such transfers could be illustrated with almost any unit photograph of the period. They accorded with a reduction in the size of the army and a widespread desire to escape the monotony of isolated camps. Also typical is that all four pictured men had enlisted in 1941. There were now very few originals in the battalions.

By November 1944 the 2/6th, for example, had 78 originals. In the 2/1st Battalion, by July 1943 there were only 41. Moreover, of the 200 members of the 2/2nd and 2/3rd battalions who had joined the 2/1st after it was decimated in Crete, just 24 remained. Nevertheless, because it had absorbed large contingents from the disbanded 30th Brigade's battalions, it contained a relatively high number of men with experience of New Guinea.

Even among officers, though many or even most had been in the division since 1939, there were many reinforcements: three-quarters of the rifle platoon commanders in the 2/6th Battalion had not seen action on the eve of the unit's next campaign. This followed partly from the promotion of 6th Division officers to other less experienced units.

Highly capable men were still rising through the ranks of the division. **Photograph 10.6** depicts two of them marching at a graduation ceremony at Seymour, Victoria in November 1944. At the far end of the line is Lieutenant Timothy Donoghue, who as an expert Bren gunner had won the MM with the 2/3rd Battalion at Damascus. He would soon add to that an MC with the 2/2nd Battalion in New Guinea, where he would be wounded leading a charge. Second from right, wearing his 2/7th Battalion colour patch, is Lieutenant Reg Saunders, the first Australian Aborigine to receive a commission. As this suggests, he had fought with distinction after joining the unit in Libya. Unlike Donoghue and most newly commissioned officers, he would return to his unit. To Saunders' indignation the new CO did not realise this, but instead told him of the 2/7th's traditions, which he admonished Saunders to uphold. This gaffe was later smoothed over, but it emphasised the change in this unit, where most of Saunders' friends had been killed or transferred.

186 THE LONGEST WAIT

10.5　　　　　　　　　　　　　　　　　　　　　　　　　　　　　AWM 058252

10.6　　　　　　　　　　　　　　　　　　　　　　　　　　　　　AWM 083167

10.7　　　　　　　　　　AWM 064777

A higher proportion of senior officers had stayed in the division, but as **Photograph 10.7** suggests, there had been considerable change in that area too. Here the divisional commander, Major-General 'Jackie' or 'Ocker' Stevens (centre) poses with his senior officers at Wondecla in March 1944. They are, from left, Brigadier John Reddish (CRA 6th Division), Brigadier Roy King (16th Brigade), Brigadier James Martin (19th Brigade) and Brigadier Murray Moten (17th Brigade). None of these four had been in his current post at the outset of the war and a glance at Table 3 (in the Introduction) will show that the same applied to every command position listed there. More surprisingly, even this late in the war only one of the pictured commanders, Moten, had fought the Japanese. The others' most recent action had been in 1941, Stevens commanding 21st Brigade, the others commanding battalions. They typify the fact that opportunities for advancement existed in the Australian Army throughout the war. Most of the army's senior commanders on the eve of the final campaigns were formerly in the 6th Division. For example, the commander-in-chief, the two corps commanders and 13 of the 21 brigadiers about to go into action had sailed for the Middle East with the 6th Division's original 12 battalions. Of the 59 battalion commanders, 31 were originals or early reinforcements of the 6th.

Stevens had been appointed to command the division in April 1943. A subaltern in the First AIF, he had been the original commander of 6th Division Signals. He oversaw the training of the division to a high level and took the opportunity to train the whole formation, even using it in a corps exercise with 7th and 9th Divisions in July 1943. **Photograph 10.8** depicts a group of 2/6th Battalion privates training in Queensland in April 1944. Training involved its own dangers: a Japanese anti-tank bomb exploded during a demonstration to the 2/6th Cavalry (Commando)

10.8   AWM 066131

Regiment in September, killing two and wounding 55. Private Douglas Hocking (far right) is using an Owen gun modified to take two magazines. Private John Davie (far left), would be killed in action almost exactly a year after this photograph was taken.

When the 2/6th Battalion moved to New Guinea, more than 55 per cent of its men were entering their first campaign with the unit. However, the battalion historian says they had been 'fully absorbed' into the unit through nearly a year's training.[3] The 2/7th Battalion historian describes the reinforcements' infectious enthusiasm, asserting that the veterans passed off their own renewed eagerness for action with such comments as, 'someone has to look after the bloody idiots'.[4]

By mid-1944 the division's personnel were largely inexperienced, but as eager and well-trained as ever, and better equipped. Some of that equipment is visible in **Photograph 10.9**, as the 2/1st Battalion prepares to embark from Cairns in late 1944. The long white bags are evidently new camp stretchers issued in this campaign. Men also carried half-tent shelters, which could be combined into tents. 'What luxuries!!' wrote one veteran during the forthcoming campaign, as he compared these sleeping arrangements to the Owen Stanleys campaign, when the sky

10.9   Courtesy Jan Donohue

was their roof.⁵ Men now also carried more tools such as small shovels, short picks and machetes.

More new equipment is visible in **Photograph 10.10**. Here a 'Short' 25-pounder and jeep of 2/2nd or 2/3rd Field Regiment are participating in a divisional parade in July 1944. The standard 25-pounder had not disappeared, but the Short was intended to complement it, arming one of each regiment's three batteries. The officer commanding the 2/41st Light Aid Detachment described the process of replacing eight standard guns with the unreliable Shorts in the 2/3rd Field Regiment

10.10　　　　　　　　　　　　　　　　　　　　　　　　　　　　　　AWM 067318

as replacing 'my old loves' with 'little horrors'.[6] The parade was a much more enjoyable affair. A 2/3rd Field Regiment man recalled:

> I saw the Parade from the best possible position, and what a magnificent sight it was. Left and right, to the ends of the oval, extended the jungle green clad 6 Division tightly packed ranks ... It was the only time in six years that 6 Division ever paraded together, three brigades and support troops. The General Salute was as spinechilling as it was thrilling. All those .303s moved as one and bayonets glinted in the sun and *Old Tom* [Blamey] shone like the sun itself. The memory of that mass of men, the finest fighting force Australia has ever had, will remain with me forever.[7]

Even that late in the war, one of the division's original field regiments was missing from this unprecedented parade. Under the reorganisation of the 6th into a 'jungle division' in 1943, the 2/3rd Field Regiment had become the formation's one allotted field regiment. In March 1944 the 2/2nd Field Regiment rejoined, but only in September did corps headquarters inform 6th Division that a third field regiment would be added to the division's order of battle. Divisional HQ immediately requested 2/1st Field Regiment, which happily arrived with 2/1st

10.11 AWM 082052

Anti-Tank Regiment before month's end.⁸ Of the four artillery regiments, only the 2/1st had seen action against the Japanese.

In July 1944, General MacArthur informed Blamey that Australian forces would be required to relieve American units in the New Guinea area, to free them for operations elsewhere. Against Blamey's advice, he insisted that four Australian divisions be employed. This necessitated the use of one of the AIF divisions. Only the 6th Division would be ready by 15 October, the date stipulated by MacArthur for the relief of Aitape, in northern New Guinea. With 16 951 men it was virtually at full strength in July, unlike the 7th and 9th. Thus, the latter two divisions would be held as a corps for use in later operations further north. The 6th might also be used in such operations, for in September 1944, MacArthur told Berryman that he expected to bring the 6th Division to the Philippines in March 1945 for the final drive on Manila.

In **Photograph 10.11** Privates Stanley Brown (right, with stretcher) and Tom Watson of the 2/4th Battalion are boarding the transport USS *Mexico* on 28 October for departure to New Guinea. Much smaller than the *Strathnaver*, which had taken the battalion to the Middle East, it was crowded, but the few veterans who remembered that were content that there was now no room for parades, training or exercises, just sunbaking and resting. They look happy that their lengthy wait is at last over. The battalion history says that when during the voyage the destination was revealed as the Aitape area of New Guinea, men felt insulted at this sending of 'men on a boy's errand', but that it was at least preferable to 'everlasting training'.⁹ This, its final campaign, would be the first time since Greece that the whole division had served together. There was, however, a bitter twist in its tail for one of these two: Private Brown would be killed while acting as a forward scout in a night patrol on 6 May, aged 24. Whether the division should even have been sent to New Guinea was controversial then and has remained so ever since.

CHAPTER 11

AITAPE–WEWAK

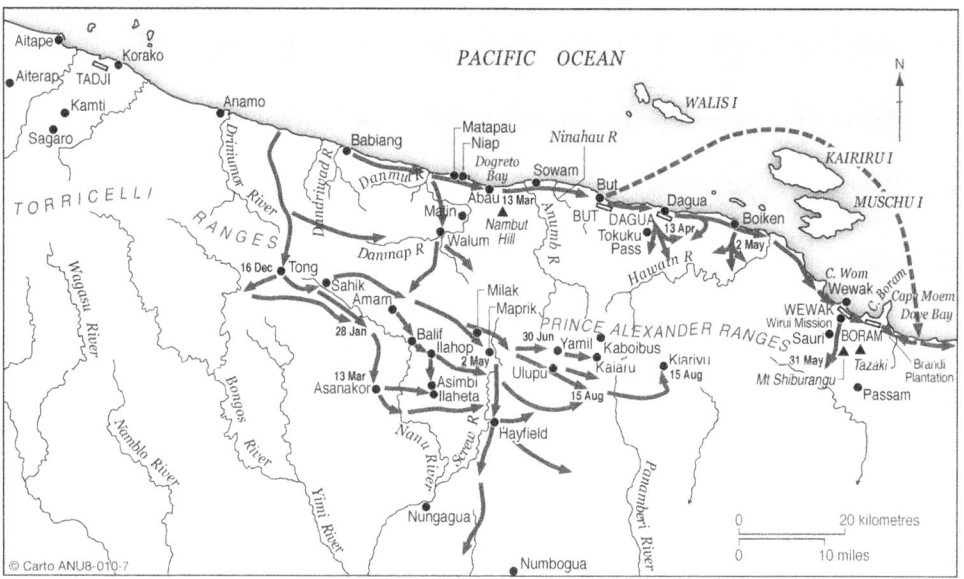

Map 8 Aitape–Wewak 1944–5

As the core of the Australian force in northern New Guinea in 1944–5 the 6th Division is rightly identified with the operations generally known as the Aitape–Wewak campaign.

The Americans, from whom the Australians took over at Aitape in September–November 1944, had stayed within a small perimeter, rarely interfering with the Japanese. General Blamey believed Australian troops were too inherently aggressive

11.1　　　　　　　　　　　　AWM 083558

to follow a policy of allowing the enemy to 'wither on the vine'. He was also eager to assign the 6th Division a task after its long inactivity. Consequently, Lieutenant-General Sturdee, Commander of First Army, transmitted three roles to Major-General Stevens: protect the airfield and radar installations around Aitape; support Australian New Guinea Administrative Unit (ANGAU) and Allied Intelligence Bureau (AIB) units in establishing patrol bases, intelligence-gathering, and protecting the native population; and, most aggressively, destroy Japanese forces in the area while preventing them from advancing westwards.

The division arrived at a trickle between October and December, thanks to shortages of shipping and unloading equipment. In **Photograph 11.1** soldiers disembark from a landing barge in November. This man's gear includes Australian innovations in the Owen gun, the Owen magazine pouch and a large basic pouch. The war-time caption identifies him as Corporal M Gill of 2/7th Battalion. The pictured men are not wearing or carrying helmets, which were no longer on issue. Many would have agreed with another, unnamed 2/7th Battalion soldier, who wrote on first seeing Aitape: 'What a god-forsaken cow of a place it looks . . . What a bastard of a place to fight a war!'[1]

The first fighting unit to arrive was the 2/6th Cavalry (Commando) Regiment, which had been remodelled in January 1944 and now comprised three Commando Squadrons: the 2/7th (formed from the experienced 2/7th Independent Company), 2/9th and 2/10th. On arrival the unit, now much bigger than ever, was ordered to increase the scant available information on Japanese strength in the coastal area. Then on 2 November a patrol was ordered to clear the coastal strip as far

11.2 AWM 083069

as the Danmap River, some 80 kilometres east of Aitape, and to make a base there. This expansion beyond the American perimeter represented a new stage. In **Photograph 11.2** a patrol from 2/10th Commando Squadron are crossing the Dandriwad River at the eastern end of that perimeter on 7 November. Leading is Lieutenant Ian Ewing, who would be Mentioned in Despatches for his 'exceptional service' in this campaign. Immediately behind him is 20-year-old Lance-Corporal Charles McFeeters, who would die of wounds received in an ambush seven months later. Marching in this campaign was generally not quite as strenuous as in the Owen Stanleys or Wau–Salamaua, but numerous soldiers wrote of being exhausted by the many hours of trudging. While carrying his home on his back the typical footslogger had once again to endure heat, rain, hills and disease.

The Japanese the cavalrymen met in November seemed preoccupied with finding food, and there was evidence of cannibalism among them. Here and in the Torricelli Mountains, which overlook the narrow coastal strip, the cavalrymen encountered small groups of disorganised Japanese, and at a cost of one Australian killed and one wounded had by 30 November killed 73, captured 7 and cleared a large area.

11.3 AWM 083404

In **Photograph 11.3**, two of their prisoners are pictured with Sergeant Francis Lea. The prisoners are also sergeants, but their physique and weakened condition are in marked contrast to Lea's. For Lea there was a contrast too between fighting on foot at Aitape and commanding a tank, as he had, in Syria.

The Japanese the 6th Division would face in the months ahead were short of supplies and weapons, and without air or naval support. Nevertheless, the 35 000 Japanese of the XVIII Army, commanded by Lieutenant-General Adachi from his headquarters near Wewak, outnumbered the Australians. Indeed, one soldier arriving in December reported that the departing Americans thought 'the Japs will have a lash to retake this place with only a div. to defend it'.[2] He felt that the Australians would fight hard with their backs to the sea, but this never proved necessary. The 6th Division was far better supplied and equipped, generally enjoying the best food of any campaign, dehydrated or tinned though it was. They also had some naval support, and substantial air support from the RAAF. Nevertheless, Allied Headquarters did not consider this campaign a high priority for supplies or shipping.

Uncertainty about the future deployment of the 6th Division limited planning for a long time. As late as February 1945, for example, MacArthur wanted it sent to Borneo, but at Blamey's insistence the government refused. As it gradually became apparent that the 6th would not be needed elsewhere, the goal became the capture of Wewak by means of parallel advances along the coast and the Torricelli Mountains.

On 26 November 1944 the relief of the Americans was completed and Stevens assumed command. He considered the two advances complementary, for unless the mountains were secured the Japanese on the coast could simply retreat to their garden areas in the highlands where they were cultivating food or, further south, to the Sepik River valley. He was already planning and soon got approval for a limited offensive to cut the enemy's forward line of communications and destroy Japanese forces east of the Danmap.

In early December the 19th Brigade took over the coastal advance from the cavalry, which sent the 2/7th Commando Squadron inland to establish a patrol base at Tong. In **Photograph 11.4**, 2/4th Battalion officers are returning from

11.4 AWM 084216

a day patrolling the Danmap River area on 6 December 'in search of Japanese forces'. That phrase from the original caption epitomises patrolling in this period. The unit destroyed the scattered groups they found west of the Danmap. The photographed officers are, from right to left, Lieutenant Jim Brown, Lieutenant-Colonel Nevis Farrell (CO), Captain Owen Williams (RMO) and Captain Dick Bawden, Adjutant. Williams, who we last saw on the track to Salamaua, wrote home that jungle patrols were 'pretty grim work'.[3] In July 1945 Brown would be leading a patrol when a man was hit. Williams would rush forward to his aid, only to be shot and mortally wounded. A private collection at the Australian War Memorial contains his last letter home, in which he talked about this photograph. It also contains numerous letters from men inside and outside the 2/4th, of high and low rank, testifying to Williams' courage and integrity. Further evidence of his standing was the MBE he received for service in the 'Danmap River and Aitape areas'.

On 17 December the 2/4th Battalion crossed the Danmap. By 22 December, when the 2/11th relieved it, the 2/4th had pushed the Japanese back some six kilometres and killed 28 in a single ambush. Lieutenant 'Mac' Wilson, who had been a private in Libya and Crete, was well satisfied with the recent campaigning, but acknowledged that the unit had learnt much. Jungle warfare, he admitted: 'is very nerve wracking [sic], and you can't relax for a minute'. He referred to the ambush where 28 were 'slaughtered', but noted that the Japanese rarely left thick jungle. He pinpointed a feature of this campaign often mentioned by participants:

> The night is the worst, it is pitch dark from 6 till 5 in the morning, and you can imagine how time drags . . . one lad says he only hopes his marriage night is as long as these seem to be.[4]

The 2/4th's Private Reg Dove wrote starkly of this period: 'One of my best mates was killed and eat [sic] by the Japs'.[5]

While the coastal advance proceeded, the inland front was witnessing progress. After establishing their patrol base at Tong, the intrepid commandos clashed with enemy patrols and secured a wide area. With Tong as a launchpad for further advances, Stevens ordered the 2/5th Battalion into the area. The Bren gunner pictured in **Photograph 11.5**, Private 'Corny' Pye (left), was on a patrol from Tong, when he called: 'Me gun's jammed'. From Pye, who 'treated that gun like a mother would her firstborn', this was amazing.[6] He was told he had 10 minutes, or another platoon would do the patrol. Later in the campaign this might have been welcomed, but Pye rushed, gasped 'she's under control', and the men were soon on their way. In late December, the battalion approached the enemy's main defences in the Torricellis.

11.5 Courtesy Ivor White

One veteran of the 2/11th, now leading the coastal advance, recalled the patrol work as 'mainly hide and seek', struggling through the jungle for hours without contact, but always alert. In the last days of December two patrols struck a pocket of resistance near Matapau. Headquarters planned an attack for 2 January, backed by air and artillery support. **Photograph 11.6** depicts 2/3rd Field Regiment gunners preparing for this attack by digging in their Short 25-pounder on New Year's Day 1945. This was a sad day for the unit, which the previous day had suffered its first battle casualties since Crete: one gunner killed and another badly wounded in an ambush. With well-founded rumours of cannibalism circulating, they were especially worried that the gunner's body had not been recovered. Their worst fears were realised some days later.

The enemy spoiled Australian plans for 2 January by sending 30–35 men to attack a company perimeter. The artillery had zoned in their guns for such a possibility and, together with the infantry's small arms fire, drove back the attackers. The 2/11th immediately took the initiative, pushing another company across the Wakip River with a FOO in order to achieve the day's original objective. **Photograph 11.7** depicts part of that movement. Crossing water obstacles was in fact almost continuous in this campaign: between Aitape and this area alone there were some 40 rivers and creeks. They were places of danger – both of drowning and of being ambushed – but they also gave some relief from the humidity and

AITAPE–WEWAK 199

11.6   AWM 078071

11.7   AWM 078055

smell of sweat. The caption says the men are moving under fire, and a subsequent photograph shows the soldier at left being treated for wounds. The men were fired upon from 'Razor Spur' and, after felling one sniper, returned to the west bank and allowed artillery to blast the 20-metre high position. The Australians then occupied Razor Spur, from which they called down gunfire on the enemy pocket. At least 14 Japanese were killed. The 2/11th lost two dead: a devoted family man killed lying on his stretcher bed that morning and a veteran shot through the head. There was some cathartic laughter about a soldier who in the ambush mistook the latrine for a firing pit. The 2/11th advance resumed and, with artillery, tank and air support, had by 20 January taken Niap, Dogreto Point and Abau.

While the 2/4th and 2/11th advanced on the coast, their sister battalion, the 2/8th, had been moving on an inland route through the foothills of the Torricellis. Though a shortage of native carriers delayed its progress, by 8 January it occupied the village of Malin, south of Niap. A large Japanese force trying to recapture Malin was driven off in sharp fights around the upper Danmap. The terrain was so rugged that carrier pigeons had to be used to get written signals to brigade headquarters.

The 19th Brigade had killed 434 Japanese for the loss of 36 dead by the time the 16th Brigade was ordered to take over. As it did so, on 21 January the flooded Danmap River destroyed a bridge that Australian engineers had been constructing. In **Photograph 11.8** a member of the 2/2nd Field Regiment is using a small caterpillar tractor to haul a standard 25-pounder gun across a shallow section of the Danmap on 26 January. Over the next 24 hours, torrential rains would flood the river, which trapped many soldiers and uprooted giant trees. Lieutenant Tim Fearnside of the 2/3rd Battalion, a veteran of Tobruk and Alamein, described being stranded at night on a tiny island in the river as the 'most terrifying experience of my life'.[7] At the height of the floods:

> . . . our island was engulfed and we were flung pell-mell into the torrent, or some were. Some were killed outright in that mad onslaught of frenzied water and green timber; others were swirled beneath the press of timber and drowned; others were knocked unconscious and their bodies snatched and sent racing downstream and turned over and over, like otters . . .[8]

Eleven Australians drowned. Seven of the 46 bridges between the Danmap and Aitape were washed away. These floods temporarily halted the coastal advance.

In the Torricellis, the 2/5th Battalion made steady progress and by the end of January had driven the more numerous enemy from an area some 20 kilometres (west to east) by 13 kilometres. RAAF bombers made useful airstrikes in front of the Australian positions almost daily, guided by radio telephone and mortar smoke. Air supply was not so plentiful, with only one transport aircraft to support

11.8 AWM 078815

the inland advance. Supplies were dropped by parachute and then carried to the forward troops by native carriers.

Equipment shortages also hamstrung progress on the coast: here it was lack of heavy equipment such as bulldozers, tip trucks and graders. Stevens warned Sturdee early in January that without more 'maintenance facilities and air support' his advance would halt in February. Hoping that these would be provided, Stevens offered plans for advances to Wewak and, in the mountains, Maprik.

In January, Stevens and his division became involved in a controversy relating to the strange-looking routine pictured in **Photograph 11.9**. Malaria precautions, including taking suppressive Atebrin tablets and using insect repellent ('Mary'), were routine in units before they reached New Guinea, but the incidence of the disease reached alarming heights in December and January. On 29 January Stevens ordered that the Atebrin dose be doubled to two tablets per day for the entire division. He laid down a daily Atebrin drill for all units not in contact with the enemy, including some measures visible in this photograph of cavalrymen in July: an officer must 'place the Atebrin tablets one at a time into each man's mouth'.[9] Each man had to take a container of water other than a bottle, must take a

11.9   AWM 094177

mouthful of water after each tablet, and after the second one drink all his water, call his name and show the officer that his mouth contained no tablets. The officer would then mark the names in a roll book and sign. Officers and men found these parades degrading and insulting. Moreover, despite these measures, there was a malaria epidemic in April. It later emerged that a malaria strain relatively resistant to Atebrin was prevalent in the area. This discovery came too late to enable victory over malaria, though it did diminish in July and August, and did not prevent military victories before that. The discovery of the new strain showed that lack of discipline was not the major cause of the epidemic in the 6th Division.

   One positive development at the end of January was the provision of landing craft to carry supplies, including heavy items like trucks, from Aitape to Dogreto Bay. On 30 January Japanese troops attacked a platoon of the 2/1st Battalion, which was now leading the coastal advance. The platoon, under Lieutenant Haydon, occupied 'Haydon Knoll', on the western end of Nambut Hill, which overlooked an unusually narrow coastal strip cut by several creeks. For five hours that night 30 Japanese tried to drive the Australians back with small arms,

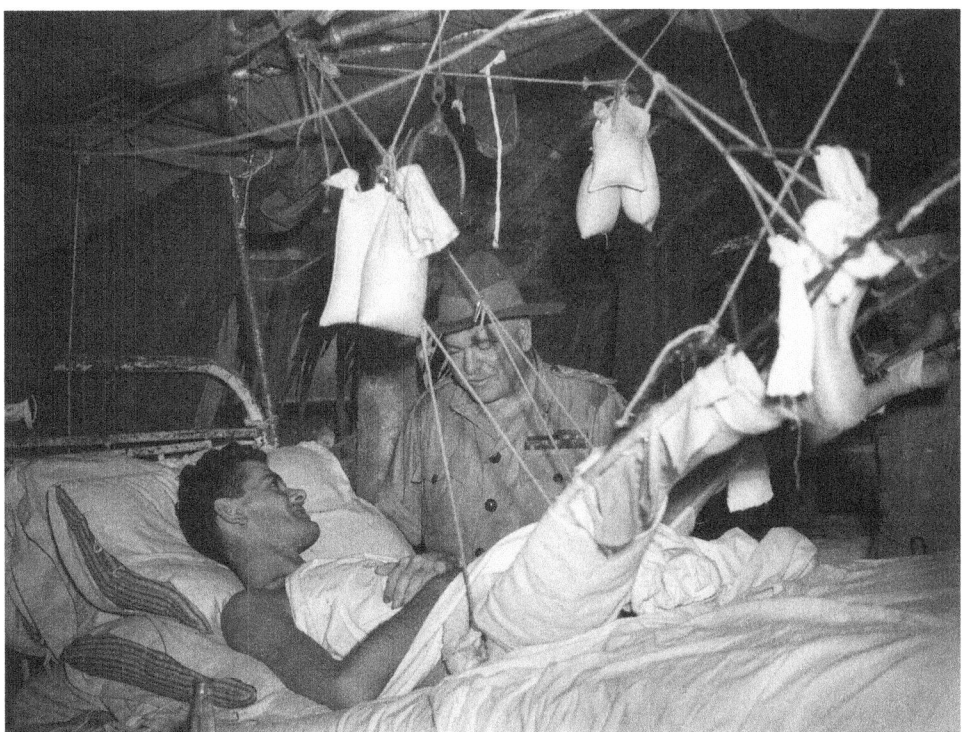

11.10 AWM 090114

grenades and gelignite. They were the vanguard of a battalion sent from Wewak with the impossible task of forcing the Australians across the Danmap.

Nambut Hill symbolises the strangeness of the 6th Division's early role in this campaign, for although Lieutenant-Colonel Cullen was eager to occupy the whole ridge, he was denied permission because the division was forbidden by First Australian Army to advance east beyond a grid line running through that feature. Cullen patrolled aggressively along the ridge. Stevens eventually gave him permission to take the hill, which courageous infantry, well supported by artillery and aircraft, took on 18 February. In **Photograph 11.10**, a casualty of this fighting is chatting with General Blamey at hospital at Aitape. Hit in the thigh during an attack on the ridge, Private Henry Murphy was one of 27 wounded in 22 days of fighting there. The unit also lost 24 killed, while the enemy lost at least 75 killed, and in Nambut Hill a pivotal section of their defences. A platoon subsequently became isolated near a feature called The Pimple, but the Japanese were soon pushed off. In **Photograph 11.11**, 2/1st Battalion men are passing one of 26 damaged trucks found in a nearby dump, together with 14 machine guns and much equipment.

11.11   Courtesy Jan Donohue

Photograph 11.12 depicts a patrol crossing the Anumb River between 23 and 28 February. The man in the foreground has strapped a medical satchel above his haversack. This is unusual: men generally 'diced', or discarded, every possible extra ounce of weight. On 27 February a patrol crossed the river mouth in a jeep trailer and entered Sowom Village, from which an enemy field gun had been firing on the unit. The 2/1st patrol killed four Japanese. On 28 February the 2/2nd Battalion relieved the 2/1st. Meanwhile, the 2/3rd Battalion, on the inland coastal route, had won a series of sharp fights on Long Ridge.

Stevens had sanctioned the Nambut Hill attack and subsequent advance because on 10 February Sturdee ordered the 6th Division to continue its drive on Wewak. It must, however, do this 'within the limit of its own resources and without becoming involved in a major engagement'. In short, Stevens would have to make do with even longer supply lines. Nevertheless, he informed his brigadiers that he intended to take But, Dagua and Wewak on the coast. In the mountains he would capture Maprik, then push eastwards. He told Sturdee that 'administratively the operation was a complete gamble'. This was most apparent in the inland advance, where

11.12 Courtesy Jan Donohue

supply difficulties restricted Moten to employing just one battalion plus one company and two commando squadrons. The coastal advance was hampered, too, by uncertain weather and lack of shipping at Aitape.

In February the 2/5th Battalion advanced through the Torricellis. After capturing Balif village, the Australians cleared a light airstrip, from which casualties could travel by air rather than endure a six-day carry through the mountains. At the same time, specially picked men – all rugby players – of the 2/1st Field Regiment carried two heavy mortars to Balif, whence they fired on dug-in Japanese. The 2/5th Battalion and 2/10th Commando Squadron drove off counter-attacks. When the 2/5th was relieved by the 2/7th it had, in its two-month stint, lost seven killed, while counting 376 enemy dead and taking 12 prisoners.

The Australian advance through the Torricellis was driving up to 2000 Japanese further south, where they could sustain themselves in garden areas. To minimise any consequent threat to his flank, Moten sent a 2/6th Battalion company under Major David Hay ('Hayforce') to sweep through the area, slightly ahead of the main advance, and to drive the Japanese east.

11.13 Courtesy Keith Johnston and 6th Div Cav Regt

In late February to early March, the Japanese in the area were reinforced, and became more aggressive in patrols and ambushes. After 'B' Troop of 2/10th Commando Squadron occupied Milak, a village two days from the nearest Australians but close to the Japanese base at Maprik, 150 Japanese surrounded them on 13 March. The 40 Australians were on relatively open ground, measuring 45 by 65 metres and circled irregularly by palms. **Photograph 11.13**, taken that month, shows three men crucial to the battle that followed. Corporal Tony Gannan (far left), of 2/7th Battalion, commanded a 3-inch mortar detachment. He is sitting beside the mortar pit they dug on arriving at Milak. Two men could stand upright in it under cover and ammunition was dug into the parapet. They fired their first round conventionally, from above ground, and knocked out a Japanese machine gun. However, when the Japanese attacked in earnest, especially at night, Gannan's crew put into practice a method they had perfected in Queensland, whereby they could fire at ranges as short as 30 metres. This required firing without bipod or baseplate. Holding the barrel in his hands and using the treetops for alignment, Gannan fired just 10–15 metres beyond the Australian slit trenches, cutting a swathe through Japanese ascending the sloping ground around the village. By the second day the Australians had instituted a means of communication via parachute cord lines running from the mortar pit, and also encouraged men to call directions such as 'seven o'clock' from their pits. Wireless communication with the outside world was maintained from the hut pictured here. Aircraft provided vital aid, too, dropping bombs as close as 15 metres from the defenders, and also food and supplies of mortar bombs and other dwindling ammunition. Material falling beyond the perimeter had to be fought for. The enemy brought up a big mortar, too, but after just two rounds it was spotted and knocked out by Gannan's skilled crew.

At right, hatless, is Lieutenant Neil Redmond, who celebrated his 23rd birthday as the troop occupied Milak. He would be killed in July. Commanding the Australians at Milak during the intense five-day siege was Lieutenant Ken Perkins (centre), who received an MC for his 'conspicuous gallantry and courage'. He had risen through the ranks and sustained his men, who saw him as a mate. On 18 March the mauled Japanese finally halted their attacks. The exhausted Australians counted 45 enemy dead, though more were later found, and estimated at least as many wounded. As the regimental history says, Milak 'was a small action, unknown outside 6th Division, but it was as courageous as any in Australia's history'.[10]

In mid-March, the 2/10th Commando Squadron were relieved on the northern flank of the mountain advance, where the 2/6th Battalion joined the 2/7th and Hayforce. By the beginning of April they were poised for the drive to Maprik.

On the coastal sector, the 16th Brigade, with 2/9th Commando Squadron under command, was also pushing forward with aggressive patrols. When Brigadier King established that no Japanese were defending the approaches to the But airfield, he ordered a 2/2nd Battalion company to dash ahead and seize it and its jetty as a potential base. After overcoming a complex of bunkers and foxholes astride the coastal track, by 17 March the whole battalion was established round But. **Photograph 11.14** depicts several members of a 2/2nd rifle company resting before crossing the Ninahau River. Corporal Robert Smith (centre) maintains radio contact. Private James Isedale, who was wounded in the Papuan campaign, looks on. On the ground is Staff-Sergeant John Gurr, who later this day would be killed by supplies air-dropped to the unit. In **Photograph 11.15** a man with a more conventional wound is helped to a jeep-ambulance, probably of 2/7th Field Ambulance, on the same day. Private John Parkes has been shot in the face. Helping him at left is Sergeant Harold Martin of the 2/2nd Battalion RAP, who dealt with the administrative and physical challenges of the work with remarkable cheerfulness. Heavy rains often hampered evacuation by road.

So rapid was the Australian advance that day that the confused enemy was still firing artillery shells several kilometres behind the foremost Australians, who in the next few days destroyed four field guns.

11.14   AWM 079800

11.15   AWM 018290

From 19 March barges began arriving at But, which, as King had anticipated, became a thriving base. An important arrival that day was General Blamey, who approved plans for an advance over the remaining 30 kilometres to Wewak. Soon afterward, Stevens was pleased to learn that he would be allotted 10 additional landing craft (LCTs), four RAN warships, six motor launches and more aircraft. Stevens' desire to make an amphibious landing beyond Wewak could now be fulfilled.

The enemy soon retreated to well-prepared positions in the steep hills south of But. The 2/2nd Battalion had the important task of clearing these Japanese, who threatened the flank of the advance on Wewak. Some of the campaign's toughest fighting ensued, especially around the Tokuku Pass. On 25 March the leading platoon advancing on one narrow ridge near Dagua was pinned down. Lieutenant Bert Chowne, pictured in **Photograph 11.16**, was commanding the reserve platoon and now took action. Running up the steep track, he threw grenades that knocked out two machine guns. Then, firing his submachine gun from the hip, he led his platoon in a charge that took the feature and, after he had killed two more Japanese, cost him his life. Chowne was posthumously awarded the Victoria Cross, the first for the 6th Division. That the award came so late reflected not lack of valour in the division's men, but excessive parsimony in their senior officers.

11.16 AWM 134484

Tough fighting followed Chowne's action. On 27 March the 2/2nd lost three killed and 14 wounded. Exhausted stretcher bearers are carrying one of the latter in **Photograph 11.17**. In a report on the battalion's medical activities that month, the RMO, Captain McLennan, described the stretcher bearers as 'excellent' in their

11.17 AWM 090150

work and knowledge, as well as 'courageous and quick to go forward'. They were kept busy, for that month the unit suffered 98 casualties.

The Japanese were losing men, too, as well as ground and equipment. In **Photograph 11.18**, 2/2nd Battalion troops are looking over a captured 20 mm Japanese dual-purpose gun. Private Aubrey Pritchard, at left, would later be wounded. Many Japanese guns found on the coast were neglected and unserviceable, though a gun like this had recently engaged Australian artillery. The 2/2nd Field Regiment's guns had been firing about 300 rounds a day during the 16th Brigade advance, but in late March they moved away from the restricted coastal stretches to the But airstrip, where the more open terrain and arrival of more ammunition allowed them to fire many more rounds. In **Photograph 11.19** an F Troop gun is firing one of 1520 rounds the troop fired that night at Tokuku Pass. A further 2500 rounds were fired in the next few days, and on 5 April the Tokuku Pass fell to 2/2nd and 2/3rd Battalion troops attacking from both sides.

On 2 April, a two-company patrol of 2/3rd Battalion ambushed a Japanese headquarters, killing about 28 of some 40 Japanese present, for the loss of two of

11.18   AWM 018307

11.19   AWM 090228

11.20 AWM 090442

their own. **Photograph 11.20** was taken after the return of one of the battalion's many patrols in this period. Private Ken Warmington is enjoying perhaps the most desired pleasure on campaign: mail. When he replies, the sword and flag apparent here suggest that he will have plenty to tell, although as flags and swords feature in several photographs from this period, it appears that they were relatively easy to find. Another battalion member wrote home at the time that the enemy in this campaign was 'not in the same class' as the Marines the unit had encountered in the Owen Stanleys.[11] On the day of this photograph the unit killed six Japanese for the loss of one dead. On the coast, men not only received mail, but also metropolitan newspapers only a day old.

On the inland front on 3 April, Moten issued orders for the capture of Maprik. An essential preliminary was to establish an airstrip. A site had been identified in January about 13 kilometres south of Maprik. Hayforce captured it on 12 April, after which the 2/7th Battalion's pioneers and about 200 natives began creating the strip. **Photograph 11.21** shows some of the Australians involved. This improvised roller made from bush timber and dragged there by natives was the most sophisticated equipment available.

The 2/7th Battalion had the task of taking Maprik itself and opened their attack on 15 April. Determined and well-ensconced Japanese had to be evicted by manoeuvre, firepower, air support and great courage from leaders such as Lieutenants Reg Saunders and Jim Bowden. In his first campaign as a platoon commander, Saunders led a successful outflanking movement outside Maprik on 19 April. The following day Bowden ignored a wound in leading a patrol to the summit of the enemy defences in the area, at House Tamboran. Maprik fell on 22 April.

11.21   AWM 112652

Much fighting in the mountains remained, but the arrival of the first Douglas aircraft on Hayfield on 14 May signalled that the 17th Brigade would henceforth be better equipped to do it. Virtually all troops were now brought in or out by air, as was heavy equipment such as field guns, tractors and jeeps. A road was constructed to Maprik and continued east behind the advancing troops. **Photograph 11.22** was taken during the advance, probably in May. Here 2/6th Battalion men are offering succour to a wounded New Guinean, probably a 'native sentry'. Natives often guided patrols in the mountains, where they could better detect enemy presence. Sergeant Jack Daniel, second from left in the background, had carried the native through enemy sniper fire to help near Maprik. For 'outstanding courage, initiative and leadership' at Maprik, Daniel won a DCM in June to add to a MM won at Nassau Bay. In April, another 2/6th Battalion NCO, Corporal Fred Quinn, wrote of a native sentry boy stopping a Japanese bullet that was intended for him. It was a miracle, said Quinn, that this was the only casualty of a patrol in which Japanese ambushers opened fire from just 10–15 metres.[12]

Stiff fighting had continued on the coast. The 2/3rd Battalion attacked Boiken Plantation on Anzac Day and 26 April. Two Matilda tanks of 2/4th Armoured Regiment gave invaluable support, and in **Photograph 11.23** three members of the 2/3rd and a tank crew are admiring souvenirs of the action. Matildas had fought alongside Australians in their first campaign and were now with them in their last. Beyond the Bren gun, everything else in this photograph looks very different from that

11.22   AWM 018695

11.23   AWM 091261

earlier campaign. The 2/2nd Battalion and a squadron of tanks crossed the Hawain River the following day, 27 April.

The 16th Brigade had by now advanced 56 kilometres, killed 909 and captured 27 Japanese for the loss of five killed and 192 wounded. Its men were exhausted. Indeed the official historian, Gavin Long, states that in the period February to April Australian troops were increasingly convinced that this campaign 'was not worth their blood and sweat'.[13] This conviction, he says, was strongest among the veterans, who tended to be the most likely to take risks and thus be killed in close jungle fighting. Long states that the malaria controversy and the lack of air and sea transport or heavy engineering equipment provided to Aitape–Wewak reinforced this attitude. There is a good deal to this argument, though his contention that troops on Bougainville and New Britain were less likely to harbour this feeling is debatable. The 6th Division fought its final campaign, including the concluding stages, with as much spirit as ever, and Long elsewhere acknowledged that in each attack veterans and young soldiers 'performed deeds of fine gallantry'.[14] Moreover, as the 2/6th Battalion historian says, most originals were now in 'specialist positions', while the 'cutting edge' of the unit comprised younger men.[15] In **Photograph 11.24** such members of the 2/1st Battalion are seen posing with a Japanese naval gun at But.

11.24 Courtesy Jan Donohue

11.25   AWM 091718

The battalion was now in reserve, but patrolling, working and coping with malaria continued, at least for those not medically downgraded and removed from the unit.

The 19th Brigade took over the coastal advance from the 16th. From 3 May it was to thrust to Cape Wom, and from there attack Wewak from the west. The Cavalry (Commando) Regiment and other detachments would simultaneously land some 15 kilometres east of Wewak. Nearly all the division's artillery was brought forward to support the 19th Brigade's advance. **Photograph 11.25** depicts one of forty-four 25-pounder guns in the Cape Wom area, as its 2/1st Field Regiment crew sit at mess during a lull in the firing on about 7 May. That day the 2/4th Battalion reached the outskirts of Wewak, having faced no organised opposition. However, the pictured men, and all Australians on Cape Wom, underwent a shocking ordeal. American Lightning aircraft mistook that cape for the Japanese-held Wewak Point and attacked the unsuspecting Australians. Eleven were killed, including six men of 2/1st Field Regiment, its only fatalities for the campaign. Fifteen of the 21 wounded were of the same regiment, including WAJ Sullivan, third from left with elbow on knee in the photograph. Warrant Officer Kenneth Kell had jumped into a pit and would probably have been killed had someone else not jumped in above

11.26   AWM 091714

him and been hit. He recalled the Americans later sending a message that the raid was 'unforgivable' and 'unforgettable'.[16]

The real enemies were on Wewak Point, which the 2/4th Battalion attacked on 10 May with five batteries of artillery and two troops of tanks in support. **Photograph 11.26** depicts one of the huge 155 mm 'Long Tom' guns of the 2/3rd Field Regiment firing on Wewak. As the regiment's historian put it: 'Night was turned into day when the "Long Toms" were fired'.[17] This was one of two guns brought in secrecy to the Naugub–Welubi area in March. On 8 May every 6th Division artillery piece fired one round to recognise the end of the war in Europe. This goal, for which so many 6th Division men had suffered, seems to have aroused little emotion, let alone ecstasy, among men preoccupied with jungle warfare.

The artillery contributed valuably in the fight for Wewak, but as eyewitness Captain Owen Williams wrote, the work of the infantry in the battle on 10 May was 'magnificent'. Even Long's sober official history calls the Australians' work 'brilliant'.[18] **Photograph 11.27** shows some of those brave men going into action with tank support that day. The tanks were available because 19 sappers of 2/2nd Field Company had the night before silently built a 30-metre bridge across Minga Creek, without moonlight or artificial light and within 450 metres of the enemy.

Wewak Point fell quickly, but then bunkers, caves and tunnels had to be cleared. In **Photograph 11.28** an infantry weapon new to the division, a flame-thrower, is seen in action that day, employed by Private Arthur Willett of the 2/8th Battalion. The 2/8th Battalion's flame-throwers were detached to the 2/4th Battalion, which needed them and sappers with blast bombs to clear the well-defended caves. One flame-thrower operator was badly wounded. This work must have been exceptionally hot in conditions where men were generally lathered in sweat anyway. In the fight for Wewak the Japanese lost more than 100 dead, the Australians just two. There were, Williams said, 'plenty of machine guns and shelling but they just moved straight thru' it all and their very courage, discipline and training carried them on to their objectives'.[19] In **Photograph 11.29** one of those machine guns is at the feet of a group of 2/4th Battalion men on 10 May. Wewak harbour is in the background. Of the pictured men, only one, Private Abraham Sargent (standing with Owen gun, second from left), would be wounded in this campaign. Yet he remained in the army, serving in postwar Japan.

The Australians took the airfield on 11 May, killing another 80 Japanese in the process. Further south the 2/11th Battalion, which was seeking to block the Japanese retreat from Wewak, captured the 710 Feature (so named for its height) in an intense struggle.

The planned amphibious landing of 'Farida Force' at Dove Bay, east of Wewak, occurred on 11 May. This force comprised 2/9th and 2/10th Commando Squadrons, a detachment of 2/1st Anti-Tank Regiment, a 2/3rd Machine-Gun Battalion company and three mortar detachments of 16th Brigade. Two of the latter had their weapons mounted on barges to support the landing. On 11 May ships transported the troops to a point nearly 10 000 metres off Wewak, where the soldiers were transferred to landing craft. General Stevens appeared on the rail of HMAS *Colac* to farewell one group: 'There's Ocker!' shouted one trooper, followed by a chorus of 'Hooroo, you old bastard!' Stevens smiled and waved. In **Photograph 11.30** a landing craft is disgorging alert troops at Dove Bay that morning or in the following days. The naval bombardment, including 700 rounds from the barge mortars, as well as impressive air support, negated the desultory enemy resistance, and those ashore were soon looking to advance to link up with the troops further west. Enemy resistance continued to be fragmentary and quickly overcome. In **Photograph 11.31** three Australians are looking at a Japanese soldier killed in Brandi Plantation, west of the landing area on about 15 May. Standing is Captain Stan McDonald, of 2/9th Squadron, who on the day of the landing killed several Japanese. He had been wounded in March by 'friendly' bombing. The man next to him, Sergeant Douglas Parkin, was a member of 2/3rd Machine-Gun Battalion, a corps unit attached to the division in this campaign. He

11.28 AWM 091749

11.29 AWM 091760

11.30   AWM 018501

would be killed in June, just as his brother Roy, of 2/11th Battalion, had been in Greece in 1941. The commandos' historian says that at this time 'the division's war was whimpering anaemically away', but there was still much blood to be shed.[20]

Further west, 19th Brigade troops were embroiled in hard fighting at Wirui Mission, a steep hill nearly 100 metres high, covered in thick kunai grass and overlooking the airfield. With tank support, the 2/4th Battalion captured its eastern slopes and summit on 14 May, but the Japanese kept firing from bunkers on the north-western slopes. The next day, as a 2/4th Battalion company sought to eliminate these bunkers, several men were hit and its leading section became pinned down. Private Ted Kenna, who was with the supporting section just 50 metres from the bunkers, stood up in the kunai grass, in full view of enemy machine gunners, and fired his own light machine gun at them. The duel was inconclusive, so Kenna called for a rifle, with which he was a crack shot. With four bullets he silenced the enemy post. Then, taking the Bren again, he eliminated a second post about 65 metres away. **Photograph 11.32** shows one of the

11.31　　　　　　　　　　　　　　　　　　　　　　　　　　　　　　　AWM 018502

posts, its Japanese .5-inch machine gun still in position. Two dead Japanese were also found there, one of whom had been shot between the eyes. A tank knocked out the third and last post, thus allowing a meeting of the 2/4th and 2/11th. Kenna received the Victoria Cross for his contribution to the victory at Wirui Mission, by which the Australians secured the Wewak coastal plain. While attacking another knoll on 5 June, Kenna was wounded in the face and back at close range. He is still recovering from his wounds in **Photograph 11.33**, taken in Melbourne after the war in September 1945. General Stevens is congratulating him enthusiastically.

After Wirui Mission fell, the 2/8th Battalion took up the advance, capturing Boram village and airfield and, on 22 May, linking up with Farida Force. The work of engineers like those pictured in **Photograph 11.34** was essential to this and other advances in the campaign. With the aid of personnel of 2/2nd Field Company and

11.32 AWM 096199

11.33 AWM 114771

2/8th Battalion a bulldozer is being used to clear debris in preparation for bridging a creek on 30 May. The unnamed bulldozer driver is a member of 2/22nd Field Park Company, a 6th Division unit that had also served in Libya, Greece and Crete and varied in size from 163 to 204 sappers. In **Photograph 11.35** the fruits of such hard work are apparent as a 25-pounder gun of 2/2nd Field Regiment is towed across a bridge built by 2/8th Field Company in mid-May. Many bridges were named after significant places in the division's history, such as Larissa and Sollum.

At the end of May the campaign entered its final stage. The Japanese had lost all their bases on the coast and retreated inland to the mountains. To their west was the 17th Brigade, forward of Maprik. To their north were the rest of the 6th Division. Nevertheless, the Japanese were still organised, determined, relatively well fed and armed, and located in positions well-suited to defence. As Lieutenant Wilson said, 'The hills appear to be never ending ... and the Jap sits on all the highest of them'.[21] One Japanese party that had not fought to the finish like so many others is pictured in **Photograph 11.36**. Here Lieutenant Cyril Miles (who had

11.34 AWM 092708

11.35 AWM 092013

11.36 AWM 128796

won an MC near Mubo) and his *ad hoc* platoon of 2/5th Battalion pose in front of 42 Japanese who surrendered to them at Kubriwat, about 20 kilometres south of Tong. Commanded by a lieutenant-colonel, the Japanese had reportedly been moving on Aitape, but after Miles' party intercepted and attacked them, they had capitulated. The Australians gathered many souvenirs from this group, but the arrival of a generous food drop left their captives overjoyed. These Japanese were reportedly very docile. Private Ivor White even sang a duet with one of them. Private Cornie Pye, whom we saw with his Bren in Photograph 11.5, and whose brother was a POW, was furious to see White with his arm around this Japanese prisoner. Here the prisoners are at Maprik, about to be flown to Aitape.

Air support had been invaluable to the division, but from the end of May to 9 July there was an acute shortage of bombs. In June a soldier in the mountains complained bitterly that a shortage of mortar and aerial bombs meant 'five good men killed because sufficient metal couldn't be had to saturate the objective they had to take'.[22] The division was also acutely short of reinforcements. Nevertheless, the supply advantages won by the establishment of Hayfield benefited the 17th Brigade as it approached the enemy's elaborate mountain defences. Supported by artillery, aircraft and the 2nd New Guinea Battalion in the south, the 17th Brigade eventually drove the Japanese from successive features. Support of another kind is apparent in **Photograph 11.37**. Private Wallin of the 2/5th Battalion wrote in June of bagpipes being played for 20 minutes some 450 yards from enemy positions. There was a piper attached to each company of this unit, with its strong connections to the Victorian Scottish Regiment. Wallin sounded a bit sceptical as he wrote: 'whether their purpose is to supply music keep up the moral[e] or frighten

11.37   AWM 018760

the Nips I don't know'.[23] The piper is Private Andrew Masterson, playing at Yamil No. 3 on 10 July. The 2/5th was meeting stiff resistance, but the previous day had broken the enemy's main defences in the Ulupu area. One eyewitness reported: 'Our men are all over the hilltop now firing down into pillboxes and heaving grenades down'. Soon afterwards a patrol returned, reporting finding, 'twenty five Nips killed arms heads blown off, the bodies were being dragged out of the pillboxes, a heavy machine gun, six swords twenty watches and documents were found'.[24] Corporal Jack 'Trout' Reynolds (centre in Photograph 11.37), who had already been wounded in this campaign, had joined the AIF almost exactly five years earlier. Four days later he was recovering from an insect bite at the RAP when his platoon went on patrol. At the last minute he joined the patrol, only to be killed by a random shot. Another five-year veteran, Private Ivor White (at right in Photograph 11.37), would replace his mate Reynolds as section leader and be shot in the chest a fortnight later. He became a postwar President of the 6th Division Association in Victoria.

Guns like that pictured in **Photograph 11.38** played a valuable direct-fire role in the 17th Brigade advance. This is a 75 mm pack-howitzer gun of 2/1st Anti-Tank Regiment. Sergeant Gordon McGovern (foreground) is using a paralleloscope to make an adjustment as Gunner Arthur Green prepares the gun for firing. Both men had been in the AIF since 1940, but their unit had seen no action since 1941. Here they are supporting the 2/7th Battalion near Kiarivu in August. There were just two of these guns inland, and another two on the coast, sometimes manned by 2/1st Field Regiment gunners. The anti-tank regiment's men were used as infantry, near Wewak, but also protected Hayfield and patrolled well south of it. They provided FOOs and manned 4.2-inch mortars. In all, the regiment suffered 33 casualties in this campaign.

11.38   AWM 095164

To maintain some initiative, Japanese troops made night raids, often individually. The 2/5th talked of 'Charlie the bomb thrower', the 2/7th of 'Dynamite Dan', intrepid Japanese who roamed through Australian positions, removing Australian booby traps and throwing picric bombs, landmines and grenades. Night picket was stressful anyway, for the jungle always seemed alive with sinister noise and crawling shapes. Private Wallin described a typical raid: 'A hell of a row black smoke everywhere as I reared up out of a dead sleep grabbed the rifle and made for the weapon pit – for three and a half hours we sat there waiting for more to be thrown and to add to the discomfort it poured rain'.[25] In

Photograph 11.39 two members of 2/7th Battalion are examining one such bomb that failed to explode when thrown into a company perimeter. It comprises six sticks of picric acid bound with cane around a Japanese grenade. These generally had a length of rope fuse that could be ignited and were tied to a stick that could be thrown.

By 8 August the 17th Brigade had secured a base at Kiarivu, which Stevens had set as a major objective. The Japanese strength in the ranges, it was later discovered, was twice that of the Australians who were attacking them so effectively.

The main body of the 6th Division had also been heavily engaged in mountain fighting, south of Wewak. Stevens assigned to the 19th Brigade the capture of two crucial heights, Mount Tazaki and Mount Shiburangu. The 2/4th Battalion took Mount Tazaki with little resistance, though Japanese continued to fight around it. **Photograph 11.40** was taken on 11 June, during the 2/8th Battalion's fight for Hill One, on the way to Shiburangu. Private William Bassula is examining a dead Japanese, probably one of five killed in the supporting artillery bombardment. Bassula's company killed a further 15 Japanese, and he earned an MM for

11.39 AWM 095429

'conspicuous gallantry and leadership' in this action. His company suffered 11 wounded that day, while he himself would be wounded in July. The pictured Japanese was dressed in Australian uniform and using an Australian rifle. The enemy were also found to be using Australian grenades, manufactured in 1943.

In **Photograph 11.41** stretcher bearers strain to bring a wounded man to safety in the successful five-hour battle for Hill Two, on 16 June. The unidentified bearer in the centre is holding the hand of the casualty, Private Francis Hewett, who was beyond help and died just two days short of his 25th birthday. Troops were always determined to bring back to their own lines not only the wounded but also the dead, for fear of Japanese cannibalism. This could be difficult for small patrols, especially as evacuating a casualty often required four or more men.

The 2/8th Battalion assaulted Shiburangu on 27 June. The 2/1st and 2/3rd Field Regiments fired 3000 shells in support, and there was a powerful aerial bombardment. The infantry spearheading the attack showed great skill and courage.

Lieutenant Jim Trethowan, the cool and experienced officer at left in **Photograph 11.42**, played a key role. His platoon climbed 100 metres up an exposed 60-degree slope before taking the surprised enemy from behind. Supported by Vickers gunners, they captured this 'Juki' machine-gun before it fired a shot. Four Japanese bullets that were fired at Trethowan passed through his clothing, including one through his hat. On Shiburangu up to 50 bunkers were captured, with four machine-guns. The 2/8th suffered three killed, the enemy 67. The courageous and popular Trethowan, who won the MC in this campaign, was nicknamed 'The Blot', after a comic-strip character. The battalion also applied that name to a height nearly 1 kilometre south and which was found to be still higher than Shiburangu. It too had to be taken. In **Photograph 11.43** a member of the

AITAPE–WEWAK 229

11.40　　　　　　　　　　　　　　　　　　　　　　　　　　　　AWM 093054

11.41　　　　　　　　　　　　　　　　　　　　　　　　　　　　AWM 093156

11.42 AWM 093475

11.43 AWM 094021

2/8th is just visible on 'The Blot' on 14 July, the day it was captured. This area had been heavily wooded before the 2/1st and 2/3rd Field Regiments poured up to 4500 rounds on to it. Mortars and Vickers guns also eased the way for the infantry, who advanced nearly 1 kilometre to reach it.

The battalions of the 6th Division were now generally at only about half strength in riflemen. Some also lacked officers to command even half their rifle platoons. The division was more than 2000 officers and men short of its establishment. Disease and Japanese resistance, including foraging raids on the coastal plain, continued to take casualties. Stevens relieved the 19th Brigade with the 16th in the last week of July. Stevens himself was not in charge when the campaign came to an end in August. Against his wishes he had been given a senior public service appointment. This had nearly happened in March, when only the accidental death of his appointed replacement, General Vasey, had prevented Stevens from making a similar enforced move. Major-General 'Red Robbie' Robertson was appointed the new divisional commander, but when the war ended, Brigadier King was in temporary command. The imminent end of hostilities was announced on 15 August. The divisional war diary commented drily on the surrender: 'After a long wait and many false alarms the news caused no exuberant expression of feelings'.[26] There was more enthusiasm at the front, though danger persisted. Blast bombs like that photographed on 15 August in Photograph 11.39, continued to be thrown, killing several Australians on 17 and 18 August. Like soldiers everywhere, 6th Division men remembered those who had not survived. Many wondered how they themselves had emerged from the dark days of 1941 and 1942.

The Aitape–Wewak campaign was a strange chapter in the division's history. The 6th could undoubtedly have excelled in more demanding operations, such as those in the Philippines. Its opponents were the weakest it faced in all but its first campaign. However, this physically demanding, stressful and dangerous campaign was not easy. It was the division's longest, with its troops in contact with the enemy for longer than in all its Middle East campaigns combined. With 442 killed, it was also the division's costliest in casualties sustained. Every veteran of the formation's fighting units lost friends.

Another 1141 Australians were wounded and more than 16 000 were admitted to hospital because of sickness. The Japanese lost about 9000 killed and 269 captured, the highest total inflicted in any 6th Division campaign. It meant an astonishing ratio of more than 20 Japanese killed for every Australian fatality. The Japanese also lost 7700 square kilometres to the Australians, who advanced more than 110 kilometres along the coast and more than 70 kilometres inland. Sixth Division soldiers and their military and political masters doubted the political and strategic necessity of the campaign even as it was being fought, but this only heightens the admiration due to the division's troops for the professional and determined way they achieved their advance over dreadful terrain against a stubborn enemy.

11.44　　　　　　　　　　　　　　　　　　　　　　　　　　　　　AWM 090443

Looking back on this campaign, the 2/3rd Battalion's Lieutenant Jim Copeman paid a great tribute to 6th Division men who fought it. Copeman is at left in **Photograph 11.44**, just days after he earned an MC to add to the MM he had won in Syria. Next to him, also recovering after an April patrol, is Private Ken Colbert, who would later win a DCM. Copeman, a 25-year-old original, made a point of praising reinforcements who had joined the unit on the Tablelands. There was, he wrote:

> . . . no glory in this campaign, not like the Western Desert or Greece or Syria when we were really the only ones fighting for freedom; here in the jungle we were virtually forgotten men . . . Borneo, American exploits in the Pacific filled the papers back home, our action was of no importance to the world in general. To the soldiers involved, however, it was a different story. A burst of enemy fire is just as exciting in the backblocks of the war as in the most important campaign. I doffs me lid to the men of Danmap, Wonginara, Boiken and Wewak, to those that fell and those that still survive, courageous, loyal, unselfish, brave.[27]

CHAPTER 12

Conclusion

When the news of the Japanese government's surrender offer reached the 2/6th Battalion, part of the unit was still in contact with the enemy. The battalion war diary said the news 'aroused very great interest', while the acting CO wrote of 'much joy about the camp'.[1] However, on 16 August an angry sergeant in the battalion wrote bitterly about what he considered the 'sickening riotousness and frivolity with which Australia is celebrating the end of the war'. He felt such frivolity was unjustified until the 'treacherous' Japanese laid down their arms – something that did not seem likely where he was.[2] He could hear firing and he knew that Australians were being hit.

Perhaps more depressing for the sergeant was his conviction that, once the tumult died down and the Australians returned home: 'We will not be welcome – not sincerely anyhow. We return to claim the fair deal for which we have been fighting so long. The rotten animals who stayed at home . . . will do their damndest to see we don't get it'.[3]

How typical were such feelings? An officer in the 2/4th Battalion virtually replicated these sentiments in a letter home. He wrote that in his unit there was 'much sarcastic talk about the peace celebration'.[4]

The sergeant's misapprehension about civilian life seems more extreme than most, but the lieutenant also said: 'Few expect to get any help in their future life from the Government, and in fact Australia stands pretty low in their estimation'.[5] Soldiers' letters during and after the campaign reflected annoyance, suspicion and contempt for Australian politicians. The troops were angry at shortages of supplies and reinforcements and then, in the campaign's aftermath, cynical and frustrated by the delays involved in getting them home.

234 CONCLUSION

The 6th Division arguably had more than its share of reasons to be cynical about the 'higher-ups'. Its commitment to Greece had been a strategic error with terrible consequences, as had flaws in the preparation and senior command of the battle for Crete. And if the 7th Division grumbled justifiably about the 'silent' treatment of its hard fighting in Syria, the elements of the 6th committed to that tough campaign could make the same complaint. Moreover, the brigade of the 6th Division committed to the Kokoda campaign probably received less publicity than any other brigade involved in that vital operation, even though its casualty totals were similar. The division's final campaign also received poor publicity: not until March 1945 were the public told that the 6th Division was in the Aitape–Wewak area.

The formal surrender of the XVIII Japanese Army in New Guinea occurred in September, despite Australian attempts to hasten it. In **Photograph 12.1** Lieutenant-General Adachi, commander of XVIII Army, is handing over his sword to Major-General Robertson as part of that ceremony. This took place at Cape Wom airstrip on the morning of 13 September. In the background are some of the

12.1   AWM 019296

3000 Australian soldiers drawn from various units of the division to witness this historic event. One of the men opposite the surrender table was Lieutenant Bruce Flude, of 2/8th Battalion, who reported:

> 'Red Robbie' had the Japanese general debus from the jeep at the far end of the airstrip and march through the ranks of 6 Div while the parade was 'at ease'. [Robertson] was rubbing his hands with glee and positively gloating as Adachi approached.[6]

Robertson was due some glee with the division, for his command had not been entirely smooth. He had arrived at Cape Wom on 1 August, assumed command on 2 August, but the same day had flown to Australia to visit his sick wife. The plane ditched in the sea off Lae, and though rescued, Robertson did not return to the division until 29 August. A series of strange mishaps had then plagued him, as the CRE reported: 'The Marsden mat . . . on the bridge tore the exhaust pipe off his car. His special lavatory is not working, the blind in his residence fell on his head'.[7]

Robertson had other reasons for a headache, as his increasingly restless troops waited to depart for civilian life. In mid-October he reported to General Sturdee that the men were blaming shipping shortages on strikes and other labour disputes in Australia. Such strikes had been a bugbear of 6th Division men since the Middle East. Thus Major Bevan French of the 2/6th Battalion wrote in his diary in October: 'From where I write this I can see a cemetary [sic] with many white crosses in it. I wonder what they would say if they were to come back to life. They died getting 6-/ a day. I wonder what the wharfe [sic] labourers are getting'.[8] A sense that the campaign victory had not been worth the cost in lives angered men.

Robertson nominated as another factor in the 6th Division's restlessness, 'the feeling prevalent formerly that this was forgotten div and tendency to fall back into that frame of mind'.[9]

As elsewhere, men were not released in formations or units, but as groups who had qualified under a points system rewarding long service, or on compassionate or essential services grounds. Fortunately, numbers dwindled rapidly in the subsequent two months.

Photograph 12.2 depicts some 6th Division men doing valuable work in November 1945. Sergeant Ron Bader (second from left) of 2/7th Field Ambulance and Corporal John Dyce (second from right) of 2/3rd Battalion are among Australians and Indian troops assisting at an identification parade of suspected Japanese war criminals arranged by the War Crimes Commission. The Indians were keen to ensure justice for some 2800 of their compatriots who had died in Japanese captivity in the area. From December 1944 Australian troops had been helping escaped Indian POWs. An officer who had seen a group of Sikhs and

12.2 AWM 098714

Punjabis come into the Australian lines in May had called them 'a great race . . . great in adversity'. He considered their ennobling spirit of service something 'sadly lacking in so much of our country at present'.[10]

The admiration had proved mutual. When in January 1946 one of the Sikh officers, Jemadar Chint Singh, was departing New Guinea, he composed a 'Farewell to the Aust. 6th Div'. He recalled that in imprisonment, 'we were suffering from terrible diseases and there was no hope of life'. But 'at this hour of our calamity, the Division worked as Angels for us'. They were cared for in hospitals and camps. 'The sympathy, care and affection shown by . . . every individual of the Div will always be with us'.[11]

More than 5000 members of the 6th Division had been POWs too, and the end of the war in Europe brought the release they had longed for since 1941, or even 1940. The first member of the division, and indeed the AIF, to be captured had been taken at Giarabub in December 1940. The first Australian captured by the Germans had also been of 6th Division, in February 1941. Nearly all were returned to Australia between May and August 1945. In **Photograph 12.3** Private Thomas

12.3 AWM 109558

Manns, who had been captured with the 2/1st Battalion at Retimo in 1941, is receiving a leave pass before obtaining his pay in Sydney in June 1945. He would be discharged in August.

The return of participants in the division's last campaign is the subject of **Photograph 12.4**. Members of the 2/4th Battalion are holding a Japanese flag captured at Tazaki and turned into an honour roll for C Company men in this campaign. None of the pictured men who can be identified were in the 2/4th Battalion when it had fought its previous campaign, on Crete. Here they have just arrived in Sydney in December 1945. The division's units were winding down, and its war diary halted in January 1946. Its last entry for 1945 was a scathing description of Wallgrove camp, to which up to 2000 6th Division men were sent: personnel spent their first night there in pouring rain without shelter of any kind, including tents or blankets. There must have been many echoes of the earlier complaints about Australia's ingratitude. The last entry in the diary, for 6 January, said of Ingleburn camp, 'Arrangements there were good'.[12] This was a phrase that all too rarely could have been used about provision for the men during their campaigns.

12.4

AWM 121352

As General Robertson said in an address following Adachi's surrender at Cape Wom, the 6th Division had been the first AIF division in action, and had still been fighting when the war ended. Both campaigns had been victories. And while the division's troops had been caught up in defeats, they could not have averted those disasters. Indeed, the feats of arms of 6th Division troops at Brallos Pass, 42nd Street, Retimo and Heraklion were as noteworthy as any others. In every campaign there had been extraordinary efforts and names like Post 11, Derna, Tempe Gorge, Hill A, the Beirut-Damascus roadblock, Eora Creek, Wandumi, Mount Tambu, and Wewak Point could be readily multiplied. Like men of all the other AIF divisions, those of the 6th had fought magnificently. Although for a long period the formation did not fight together, its first two and its last campaign were as a united formation. Why had it been so good? The reasons varied over time and between sub-units, and as usual in good formations the ingredients included background, training, leadership, esprit de corps and comradeship.

There was a uniquely adventurous spirit in its first incarnation. One should not ignore either a sense of duty – to nation, or empire – and this was undoubtedly a factor in the air of superiority among 'Thirty-Niners'. There was also a sense of being pioneers, as the first division of the Second AIF to see action. This spurred men on in Libya, and was a source of pride that never left the various units even after most of their members had left. Of all the divisions, the 6th was probably the one in which reinforcements received the most 'old-soldiering' from originals or early recruits.

Esprit de corps was arguably more important in this division than in any other. That spirit always owes much to leaders, and the 6th Division was the nursery, or perhaps hothouse of AIF leadership. Nearly every famous officer of the Second AIF had a role in the 6th Division in its early days. In 1945, for example, 13 of the 21 brigadiers in the infantry and armoured brigades had sailed with the 6th Division, as had both corps commanders. Indeed, original officers of the 2/2nd Battalion alone had provided one divisional commander (Wootten), three brigadiers (Chilton, Dougherty and Edgar), three battalion COs and seven senior staff officers. Several young battalion commanders at Bardia, who had reached that rank despite all the neglect of the military in the interwar years, proved outstanding wartime commanders: Dougherty, Eather, Chilton, Walker and Porter. While these leaders had a reputation for strictness, their men had one for roughness. Some of the rough men failed in battle, as did some of the leaders, but generally the combination was successful. Captain Bill Sherlock epitomised leaders in the battalion: another fine 6th Division officer, Lieutenant-Colonel Bill Dexter, described him at an Anzac Day address at their alma mater, Geelong Grammar, as 'the embodiment of all that is good and decent, scrupulously fair, brave, loved and respected by his troops'.[13] Moreover, many of the other ranks showed leadership ability that allowed them to rise to positions of command.

As he finished his diary for the war, Major Bevan French wrote of 'friends that one will always remember'.[14] Some were dead, others would continue to muster and talk, like the men pictured in **Photograph 12.5**. Here a group of recently released members of the 2/5th Battalion tease a mate who is still in uniform. The latter is Frank Pirois, who had joined the 2/5th Battalion in November 1939 and chose to remain in the postwar army. The men around him include prominent members of the unit. Holding Pirois' right hand is Dick McAuley, an iconic battalion 'character'. Between McAuley and Pirois is Fred McCormack, whose outstanding work as a sergeant and platoon commander at Mount Tambu won him an MM. The same award had gone to Bob Beddome, the big ex-sergeant with his hand on Pirois' right arm. Posed the photograph may be, but the laughter and fellowship were real features of such meetings.

They had been characteristic of all the 6th Division campaigns too. None had been easy, and the men had accepted terrible trials – climates hot and cold, wet and dry; terrain requiring jarring ascents and descents, crossing rivers and gullies in

12.5 Courtesy Ivor White

jungle and desert; supply shortages; tropical diseases; insufficient air support; allies who, while often magnificent, could be overbearing and inept; enemies ranging from the incompetent to the overwhelmingly strong, cunning and brutal – all with the typical resigned, grumbling amusement of Australian troops intent on getting their jobs done and looking out for each other. Whether they were sappers or cooks, gunners or stretcher-bearers, signallers or riflemen, all demonstrated adaptability, determination and skill to win renown for 'the good old Sixth Divvy'. Paul Cullen said of his 2/1st Battalion in 1945 that it was 'a marvellous team to be captain of'.[15] Such sporting analogies come easily to Australians, and should not be pushed too far in an endeavour where savagery, inhumanity and horror are everyday occurrences. Yet the 6th Division was in some ways like a champion sports team of veterans and young recruits, and clearly one of the best ever to leave Australia. While tragedy is a cliché in sport, it is a reality in war, and the 6th Division's reputation was built on its skill and fortitude in the necessary tasks of facing and inflicting pain and death.

APPENDIX I

6TH DIVISION CASUALTIES

No two sources on 6th Division units or campaigns seem to agree entirely on casualty figures. For example, the 2/11th Battalion history provides two casualty tables and explains that the differences in them cannot be resolved. Consequently, the following tables can readily be challenged. They should be viewed with that warning in mind. Most or all figures should be accurate within a few per cent, but the tables are intended only as a guide to the numbers of casualties suffered by the division in its various campaigns, in its various units, and overall. Here DOAS (Died on Active Service) figures include only those who died during or immediately after campaigns. Almost every unit also lost a small number of men to illness or accident between campaigns and in captivity. WIA (Wounded in Action) does not include died of wounds or accidentally wounded, where these can be identified. Men wounded twice are counted as two wounded.[1]

APPENDIX 1: CASUALTIES

Table 5 Casualty totals in all 6th Division units – by unit

	KIA	DOW	DOAS	WIA	POW	TOTAL	Members*
2/1st Battalion	191	31	7	414	567	1210	3491
2/2nd Battalion	134	33	11	410	167	755	2851
2/3rd Battalion	120	35	26	432	112	725	3303
2/5th Battalion	149	39	5	401	115	709	2967
2/6th Battalion	116	21	12	337	351	837	2965
2/7th Battalion	143	36	14	472	499	1164	3155
2/4th Battalion	62	25	7	243	195	532	2624
2/8th Battalion	55	16	6	248	203	528	2793
2/11th Battalion	108	24	7	297	460	896	2939
6 Div Cav Regt	40	12	5	141	6	204	2051
6th Div Engineers	30	2	9	46+	149	190+	NA
2/1st Field Regt	21	3	2	77	71	174	c.2000
2/2nd Field Regt	17	4	5	NA	NA	NA	NA
2/3rd Field Regt	25	6	5	49	130	215	1887

* 'Members' refers to the total number of men who passed through the unit

Table 6 Casualty totals – Libya

	KIA	DOW	DOAS	WIA	POW	TOTAL
2/1st Battalion	16	5	1	81	7	103
2/2nd Battalion	23	8	1	96	0	128
2/3rd Battalion	22	5	1	90	0	118
2/5th Battalion	26	6	0	60	0	92
2/6th Battalion	21	1	2	75	0	97
2/7th Battalion	15	2	3	75	1	96
2/4th Battalion	6	4	0	48	7	65
2/8th Battalion	17	10	0	88	0	115
2/11th Battalion	6	3	2	46	0	57
6 Div Cav Regt	6	1	0	6+	6	19+
6th Div Engineers	10	1	2	NA	NA	NA
2/1st Field Regt	2	1	0	12	7	22
2/2nd Field Regt	1	0	1	NA	NA	NA
2/3rd Field Regt	0	0	0	2	0	2

APPENDIX I: CASUALTIES   243

Table 7 Casualty totals – Greece

	KIA	DOW	DOAS	WIA	POW	TOTAL
2/1st Battalion	10	7	0	17	51	85
2/2nd Battalion	11	4	0	46	119	180
2/3rd Battalion	8	5	1	31	62	107
2/5th Battalion	18	2	0	28	55	103
2/6th Battalion	23	5	0	43	217	288
2/7th Battalion	5	3	0	7	65	80
2/4th Battalion	21	5	3	35	165	229
2/8th Battalion	20	1	1	40	106	168
2/11th Battalion	14	6	3	32	37	92
6th Div Engineers	14	1	1	34	31	81
2/1st AT Regt	12	6	0	16	79	113
2/1st Field Regt	3	2	0	7	64	76
2/2nd Field Regt	8	3	1	10	23	45
2/3rd Field Regt	4	4	0	18	1	27

Table 8 Casualty totals – Crete

	KIA	DOW	DOAS	WIA	POW	TOTAL
2/1st Battalion	40	2	0	80	516	638
2/2nd Battalion	2	0	0	6	49	57
2/3rd Battalion	2	0	0	1	50	53
2/5th Battalion	2	1	0	3	58	64
2/6th Battalion	2	0	0	11	136	149
2/7th Battalion	27	0	1	70	433	531
2/4th Battalion	18	4	0	34	23	79
2/8th Battalion	7	3	2	32	97	141
2/11th Battalion	48	6	0	126	423	603
6th Div Engineers	3	0	0	12	118	133
2/2nd Field Regt	7	0	1	23	56	87
2/3rd Field Regt	18	1	1	13	129	162

Table 9 Casualty totals – Syria

	KIA	DOW	DOAS	WIA	POW	TOTAL
2/3rd Battalion	12	4	1	77	0	94
2/5th Battalion	9	5	0	28	2	44
6 Div Cav Regt	5	2	1	25	0	33

Table 10 Casualty totals – Papua (Kokoda to the sea)

	KIA	DOW	DOAS	WIA	POW	TOTAL
2/1st Battalion	92	13	6	171	0	282
2/2nd Battalion	56	13	2	136	0	207
2/3rd Battalion	43	17	9	103+	0	172+
2/6th Battalion	0	0	0	0	0	0
2/7th Battalion	5	1	0	4	0	10
2/1st Field Regt	9	0	1	15	0	25

Table 11 Casualty totals – Wau–Salamaua

	KIA	DOW	DOAS	WIA	POW	TOTAL
2/5th Battalion	77	15	2	165	0	259
2/6th Battalion	43	11	5	133	0	192
2/7th Battalion	69	19	5	221	0	314
6th Div Engineers	3	0	1	NA	0	NA
2/1st Field Regt	1	0	1	8	0	10

Table 12 Casualty totals – Aitape–Wewak

	KIA	DOW	DOAS	WIA	POW	TOTAL
2/1st Battalion	33	4	0	65	0	102
2/2nd Battalion	42	8	8	126	0	184
2/3rd Battalion	33	4	14	76	0	127
2/5th Battalion	27	10	2	116	0	155
2/6th Battalion	27	5	5	85	0	122
2/7th Battalion	22	11	5	95	0	133
2/4th Battalion	17	10	3	126	0	156
2/8th Battalion	11	2	3	88	0	104
2/11th Battalion	40	9	2	93	0	144
2/6 Cav Cdo Regt	29	9	4	99	0	141
6th Div Engineers	0	0	5	NA	0	NA
2/1st AT Regt	14	1	2	16	0	33
2/1st Field Regt	6	0	0	24	0	30
2/2nd Field Regt	1	0	1	NA	0	NA
2/3rd Field Regt	3	1	4	15	0	23

The words of caution apply with extra force to the figures in Table 13, which are estimates, based mainly on the official histories, of the numbers of men from original 6th Division units killed, wounded and captured in its various campaigns. Most figures should be accurate to within a few per cent.

Table 13 Casualty totals in all 6th Division units – by campaign

Campaign	Killed*	Wounded	Captured	Total
Libya	241	790	21	1052
Greece	320	494	2030	2844
Crete	274	507	3102	3883
Syria	39	129	0	168
Papua	207	397	0	604
Wau–Salamaua	240	520	0	760
Aitape–Wewak	442	1141	0	1583
Total	**1763**	**3978**	**5153**	**10 894**

* Includes those who died of wounds

In short, the division suffered over 5700 men killed or wounded in World War II. A rough guess as to the number of men who passed through the division is 40 000, so those killed or wounded probably constituted about 14 per cent. If you add those captured to the figure, approximately a quarter of the 6th Division's men were killed, wounded or captured.

APPENDIX 2

6TH DIVISION HONOURS AND AWARDS

The system of awarding medals for bravery was notoriously uneven in application. Every combat veteran recalls someone who missed out unfairly on a 'gong'. Some also have grievances about cases where individuals did win medals. There were quotas of medals set for campaigns and units, and there was great scope for personal prejudice and luck in the process of recommendation. Moreover, those with the power to give awards in the 6th Division seem to have taken perverse satisfaction in being parsimonious about it. For example, a wartime publication of the 2/2nd Battalion boasted that where decorations were concerned the unit had imposed standards that were 'rigid to the degree of harshness'.[1] The unit subsequently received one of the division's only two VCs: there should have been more. A similar example comes from the 2/5th Battalion. Private John Vincent, pictured in Photograph 9.9, took a leading role in a 10-day patrol in April 1943. After the war when he met his company commander, the latter reportedly told Vincent: 'Sorry about the M.I.D. recommendation [for this patrol] – the Colonel didn't believe in decorations. He thought it was "One in All in"'.[2]

Most of the division's awards for distinguished or gallant service or conduct are listed in Table 14. It is based mainly on the unit histories, the AWM Honours and Awards Database and the Australian Military Units section of the AWM website. It has at times been impossible to find conclusive figures.

The C-in-C Card figure includes Commander in Chief's Card and Commander in Chief's Commendation Card. Where they can be distinguished, awards won by POWs are not included here. As in my other divisional histories, where an individual receives two awards of a medal (a 'bar'), this is counted as two awards in the unit total.

APPENDIX 2: HONOURS AND AWARDS   247

Table 14 Honours and awards to 6th Division units

	DSO	OBE	MBE	VC	MC	DCM	MM	BEM	MID	C-IN-C CARD	Other
2/1st Battalion	4				15	7	28	1	68		
2/2nd Battalion	4		2	1	10	4	24	1	79	1	1
2/3rd Battalion	4				16	12	30	1	50		
2/5th Battalion	2	1	3		14	6	20		56		1
2/6th Battalion	5		1		14	5	33		51	2	
2/7th Battalion	6		4		12	4	25		44		2
2/4th Battalion	2		4	1	9	6	11	1	47	2	2
2/8th Battalion	1	1			11	6	15		53		
2/11th Battalion	2	1	3		6	4	20		66		
6 Div Cav Regt	3				9	1	12		57		
2/1st Field Regt	3	1			4		4	1	29		10
2/2nd Field Regt	2	2	1		6	1	3	1	6+	1	1 GM
2/3rd Field Regt	1	3			4	2	1		43	5	

Notes

Introduction
1 Pte J Butler, 2/23 Bn, diary 13 Jan 1941, 3DRL 3825, AWM.

Chapter 1 Origins and Early Days
1 16 Inf Bde War Diary, 13 Oct 1939, AWM52, 8/2/16, AWM.
2 Quoted in DM Horner's introduction in Long, *To Benghazi*, p. xx.
3 Lt KA Carroll, 2/6 Bn, diary 24 Oct 1939, 3DRL 1003, AWM.
4 Ron Phillips, quoted in Hay, *Nothing Over Us*, p. 8.
5 Long, *To Benghazi*, p. 64.
6 16 Inf Bde War Diary, 4 Nov 1939.
7 Gullett, *Not as a Duty Only*, p. 67.
8 16 Inf Bde War Diary, 14 Nov 1939.
9 Pte AJ Ulrick, 2/2 Bn, letter 7 Jan 1940, PR82/177, AWM.
10 Long, *To Benghazi*, p. 67.
11 16 Inf Bde War Diary, 12 Dec 1939.
12 Maj SHWC Porter, 2/5 Bn, letter 2 Feb 1940, MS11477, SLV.
13 Sig TR Neeman, 17 Bde Sigs, letter 24 Jan 1940, MJC.
14 Maj SHWC Porter, 2/5 Bn, letter 23 Apr 1940.
15 Maj SHWC Porter, 2/5 Bn, letter 1 Jan 1940.
16 Wavell, *Speaking Generally*, p. 1.
17 Quoted in Horner, *General Vasey's War*, p. 56. The *Bulletin* was a journal that traditionally emphasised the distinctively Australian. The conservative, nationalist and populist *Smith's Weekly* was directed towards ex-soldiers.
18 2/4 Battalion War Diary, 27 Mar 1940, AWM52, 8/3/4, AWM.
19 Lt C Chrystal, 2/4 Bn, diary 15 Jul 1940, MJC.
20 Bdr HW Adeney, 2/2 Fd Regt, letter 23 Nov 1940, MS 10868, SLV.

Chapter 2 Bardia
1 Bdr HW Adeney, 2/2 Fd Regt, letter 31 Dec 1941, MS10868, SLV.
2 Spr RC Beilby, 2/1 Fd Coy, diary 20–22 Dec 1940, MS10019, SLV.
3 16 Inf Bde War Diary, Jan 1941, p. 8, AWM52, 8/2/16, AWM.
4 16 Inf Bde War Diary, 17 Nov 1939.
5 Clift, *The Saga of a Sig*, p. 148.
6 Bdr HW Adeney, 2/2 Fd Regt, letter 29 Dec 1940.
7 Bdr HW Adeney, 2/2 Fd Regt, letter 31 Dec 1940.
8 Spr E Loubet, 2/1 Fd Coy, diary 3 Jan 1941, PR01676, AWM.
9 16 Inf Bde War Diary, 2 Jan 1941.
10 Long, *To Benghazi*, p. 164.

11 Ritchie, 'The Yeomen of Old England', quoted in Rankin, *Lest We Forget*, pp. 54–5.
12 Philip Hurst, 'My Army Days', p. 32, MSS1656, AWM. He advanced with 2/7 Bn later in the day.
13 Sig TR Neeman, 17 Bde Sigs, letter Jan 1941, MJC.
14 Spr RC Beilby, 2/1 Fd Coy, diary 3 Jan 1941.
15 16 Inf Bde War Diary, Jan-Feb 1941, p. 64.
16 Quoted in Wick, *Purple over Green*, p. 59.
17 Spr RC Beilby, 2/1 Fd Coy, diary 3 Jan 1941.
18 Chapman, *Iven G Mackay*, p. 184. Each brigade had its own anti-tank company, though only the 16th had a full complement of 2-pounder guns.
19 Philip Hurst, 'My Army Days', p. 33.
20 Philip Hurst, 'My Army Days', p. 33.
21 Lt C Chrystal, 2/4 Bn, diary 4 Jan 1941, MJC.
22 Pte A Hackshaw, 2/11 Bn, diary Jan 1941, 3DRL 6398, AWM.
23 Pte E MacLeod, 2/11 Bn, letter 6 Apr 1941, MJC.
24 Pte AJ Ulrick, 2/2 Bn, letter 12 Jan 1941, PR82/177, AWM.
25 Quoted in Forty, *The First Victory*, p. 148.
26 Fulton, *No Turning Back*, p. 107.
27 Pte JK Atock, 2/7 Bn, letter 11 Jan 1941, 3DRL 6372.
28 16 Inf Bde War Diary, 10 Jan 1941.
29 Cpl A Parsons, 2/3 Fd Coy, wartime reminiscence, 3DRL 3908, AWM.
30 Ross (ed.), *The Seventeenth Australian Infantry Brigade*, p. 12.
31 Pte AE Wallin, 2/2 AGH, diary 7 Jan 1941, MS10172, SLV.

Chapter 3 Tobruk to Benghazi
1 Capt CW Golding, 2/1 Bn, letter 6 Feb 1941, MJC.
2 Spr E Loubet, 2/1 Fd Coy, diary 21 Jan 1941, PR01676, AWM.
3 Capt G Laybourne Smith, 2/3 Fd Regt, letter 25 Jan 1941, MJC.
4 Pte JK Atock, 2/7 Bn, letter 28 Jan 1941, 3DRL 6372, AWM.
5 Capt G Laybourne Smith, 2/3 Fd Regt, letter 25 Jan 1941.
6 Spr E Loubet, 2/1 Fd Coy, diary 21 Jan 1941.
7 Gnr F James, 2/2 Fd Regt, diary c. 22 Jan 1941, PR00607, AWM.
8 Sgt RJW da Fonte, 2/8 Bn, diary 21 Jan 1941, MJC.
9 O'Leary, *To the Green Fields Beyond*, p. 60.
10 Wilmot, *Tobruk 1941*, p. 45.
11 Gnr G Clark, 2/1 Fd Regt, diary 21 Jan 1941, PR01035, AWM.
12 Spr E Loubet, 2/1 Fd Coy, diary 22 Jan 1941.
13 Lt ER Wilmoth, 2/8 Bn, letter 7 Mar 1941, PR86/370, AWM.
14 Pte MJ Wilson, 2/4 Bn, letter 10 Feb 1941, PR01343, AWM.
15 Pte E MacLeod, 2/11 Bn, letter 6 Apr 1941, MJC.
16 Gnr G Clark, 2/1 Fd Regt, diary 25 Jan 1941.
17 Ken Kell, 'The Early Years', p. 28.
18 Sgt RJW da Fonte, diary 27 Jan 1941.
19 Gnr G Clark, 2/1 Fd Regt, diary 30 Jan 1941.
20 Sig TR Neeman, 17 Bde Sigs, letter 3 Feb 1941, MJC.
21 Ken Kell, 'The Early Years', p. 30.
22 L/Cpl RK Turner, 2/11 Bn, letter 8 Mar 1941, PR83/42, AWM.
23 Bdr HW Adeney, 2/2 Fd Regt, letter 6 Feb 1941, MS10868, SLV.

Chapter 4 Greece
1. McDonald, *Damien Parer's War*, p. 110.
2. Max Cook, diary, quoted in Bishop, *The Thunder of the Guns!*, p. 183.
3. Capt DA Crawford, 2/1 AT Regt, quoted in *The Thunder of the Guns!*, p. 189.
4. Capt G Laybourne Smith, quoted in *The Thunder of the Guns!*, p. 189.
5. Quoted in Unit History Editorial Committee, *White Over Green*, p. 115.
6. Long, *The Six Years War*, p. 70.
7. Bishop, *The Thunder of the Guns!*, p. 198.
8. Sergeant R da Fonte, 2/8 Bn, diary 11–12 Apr 1941, MJC.
9. Griffiths-Marsh, *Sixpenny Soldier*, p. 168.
10. G Laybourne Smith, 2/3 Fd Regt, letter 7 May 1941, MJC.
11. Capt G Laybourne Smith, 2/3 Fd Regt, letter 7 May 1941.
12. Lt J Harkness, 2/2 Bn, letter 11 May 1941, PR88/89, AWM.
13. Long, *Greece, Crete and Syria*, p. 121.
14. Capt G Laybourne Smith, 2/3 Fd Regt, letter 7 May 1941.
15. Bishop, *The Thunder of the Guns!*, p. 212.
16. Lindsay, *Equal to the Task*, p. 241.
17. Sig TR Neeman, 6 Div Sigs, letter 1 May 1941, MJC.
18. Spr PM Barrett, 2/8 Fd Coy, letter 7 May 1941, MJC.
19. Gnr G Clark, 2/1 Fd Regt, diary 20 Apr 1941, PR01035, AWM.
20. Quoted in Long, *Greece, Crete, and Syria*, p. 143. Vasey's brigade major translated this order as: 'The 19th Brigade will hold its present defensive positions come what may'.
21. Gnr L Howard, 2/2 Fd Regt, letter 20 Jul 1941, PR00428, AWM.
22. Haywood, *Six Years in Support*, p. 88.
23. Spr JL Wilson, 2/2 Fd Coy, diary 25 Apr 1941, MS10169, SLV.
24. Capt G Laybourne Smith, 2/3 Fd Regt, letter 8 May 1941.
25. Pte J Browning, 2/4 Bn, letter 17 Jun 1941, PR03192, AWM.
26. Ken Kell, 'The Early Years', p. 41.
27. 2/4 Bn War Diary, Apr 1941, p. 3, AWM52, 8/3/4, AWM.
28. Bennett, *Rough Infantry*, p. 79.
29. Long, *Greece, Crete, and Syria*, p. 196.
30. Quoted in Chapman, *Iven G Mackay*, p. 238.
31. Green, *The Name's Still Charlie*, p. 79.
32. 2/4 Bn War Diary, Apr 1941, AWM52, 8/3/4, AWM.
33. Pte RF Cameron, 2/1 Bn, letter 3 May 1941, 3DRL 506, AWM.
34. Cpl N Shoemark, 'War Dog' quoted in Marshall (ed.) *Nulli Secundus Log*, p. 99.
35. Horner, *High Command*, p. 98.
36. JKE Nelson, diary, quoted in Hadjipateras & Fafalios (eds) *Crete 1941 Eyewitnessed*, p. 31.

Chapter 5 Crete
1. Gnr AS Cobb, 2/1 AT Regt, diary 27 Apr 1941, MS10131, SLV.
2. Bdr HW Adeney, 2/2 Fd Regt, letter 6 May 1941, MS10868, SLV.
3. 'Report of WX953 Pte Carroll, S.L.' in papers of Brigadier TS Louch, 3DRL 6045, AWM.
4. Lind, *Escape from Crete*, p. 9.
5. Lt KR Walker, 2/7 Bn, letter c. Jun 1941, PR00178, AWM.
6. Quoted in Long, *Greece, Crete, and Syria*, p. 220.
7. Long, *Greece, Crete, and Syria*, p. 221.
8. Pte MJ Wilson, 2/4 Bn, letter 5 Jun 1941, PR01343, AWM.

9   Bdr HW Adeney, 2/2 Fd Rgt, letter 31 May 1941.
10 Norm Johnstone and Dick Parry, quoted in *White Over Green*, p. 157.
11 Lt C Chrystal, 2/4 Bn, diary 20 May 1941, MJC.
12 A/WOII S O'Brien, 2/7 Fd Amb, letter Jul 1941, Backhouse Papers, MS10616, SLV.
13 Johnstone, *Dearest Geraldine*, p. 82. Similar in Pte J Browning, 2/4 Bn, letter 17 Jun 1941, PR03192, AWM.
14 Pte LF Williams, 2/11 Bn, letter 3 Nov 1941, MJC. The same parallel occurred to Thornton, 2/11 Bn, quoted in Hadjipateras & Fafalios (eds) *Crete 1941 Eyewitnessed*, p. 111.
15 Pte LF Williams, 2/11 Bn, letter 3 Nov 1941. On no prisoners, see also Pte A Hackshaw, 2/11 Bn, diary 20–21 May 1941, 3DRL 6398, AWM.
16 Quoted in Hadjipateras & Fafalios (eds) *Crete 1941 Eyewitnessed*, p. 112. See also Bishop, *The Thunder of the Guns!*, p. 314.
17 Pte A Hackshaw, 2/11 Bn, diary 20 May, 1941. Pte LF Williams, 2/11 Bn, letter 3 Nov 1941.
18 Pte LF Williams, 2/11 Bn, letter 3 Nov 1941.
19 Quoted in Long, *Greece, Crete, and Syria*, p. 251.
20 Sgt HW Thomas, 2/7 Bn, diary 26 May 1941, AWM 54, Item No. 253/1/10, AWM.
21 Pte C Kelly, 2/7 Bn, diary 23 May 1941, PR02043, AWM.
22 Quoted in Brown, *Blue*, p. 64.
23 A/WOII S O'Brien, 2/7 Fd Amb, letter Jul 1941.
24 Long, *Greece, Crete, and Syria*, p. 307.
25 Lt KR Walker, 2/7 Bn. letter c. Jun 1941.
26 Cpl RC Gordon, 2/7 Bn, 'Report of his escape from Crete by Cpl R.C. Gordon', p. 94, MS 9553, SLV. Walker's conversation is quoted slightly differently in Long, *Greece, Crete, and Syria*, p. 307n.
27 Quoted in Brown, *Blue*, p. 67.
28 Lt MB Edwards, 2/2 Fd Regt, diary 1 Jun 1941, PR88/66, AWM.
29 Lt C Chrystal, 2/3 Bn, diary 21 May 1941.
30 Quoted in Unit History Editorial Committee, *White Over Green*, p. 176.
31 Pte MJ Wilson, 2/4 Bn, letter 5 Jun 1941, PR01343, AWM.
32 2/4 Bn War Diary, May-Jun 1941, p. 14, AWM52, 8/3/4, AWM.
33 Long, *Greece, Crete, and Syria*, p. 263.
34 Long, *Greece, Crete, and Syria*, p. 266.
35 Pte LF Williams, 2/11 Bn, letter 3 Nov 1941.
36 Quoted in Bishop, *The Thunder of the Guns!*, pp. 341–2.
37 Quoted in Long, *Greece, Crete, and Syria*, p. 265.
38 Quoted in Chapman, *Iven G Mackay*, p. 239.

Chapter 6 Syria
1   Gullet, *Not as a Duty Only*, p. 66.
2   Long, *Greece, Crete, and Syria*, p. 424n.
3   Sig TR Neeman, 6 Div Signals, letter Jul 1941, PR01034, AWM.
4   Sig TR Neeman, 6 Div Signals, letter Jul 1941.
5   Long, *Greece, Crete and Syria*, p. 493.
6   17 Inf Bde War Diary, Jul 1941, 'Report on Operations in Syria', p. 12, AWM52, 8/2/17, AWM.
7   Sig TR Neeman, 6 Div Signals, letter Jul 1941.
8   Ivor White, 'Whiteye's Army Memoirs', p. 13.

9 Sig TR Neeman, 6 Div Signals, letter Jul 1941.
10 17 Inf Bde War Diary, Jul 1941, 'Report on Operations in Syria', p. 23.

Chapter 7 Return to Australia
1 6 Australian Division General Staff Branch, War Diary Jul-Aug 1941, AWM52, 1/5/12, AWM.
2 Quoted in Chapman, *Iven G Mackay*, p. 240.
3 Sgt RH Bourke, 2/1 Bn, letter Jan 1942, AWM PR88/125.
4 Gullett, *Not as a Duty Only*, p. 67.
5 6 Australian Division General Staff Branch War Diary, 3/9 Mar 1942. The text of the speech is on pp. 79–80.
6 16 Bde War Diary, 26 Mar 1942, AWM52, 8/2/16, AWM.
7 Lt AH Robertson, 2/7 Bn, letters 10 May, 31 May 1942, MJC.
8 L/Cpl FJ Quinn, 2/6 Bn, collection of wartime poems, PR85/209, AWM.
9 The Divisional Headquarters apparently had no war diary between April and July 1942, and the Northern Territory Force War Diary shows that 6th Division Headquarters personnel arriving in Darwin became part of that Force's Headquarters. AWM52, 1/5/27, Apr 1942. Major-General Boase claimed later that he had been confirmed in command of 6th Division on returning to Australia from Ceylon. In August, the 6th Division HQ was located at Seymour, Victoria. The official history says it was only reconstituted on 21 September, and that the division had never existed 'as such' since leaving the Middle East. McCarthy, *South-West Pacific Area*, p. 244.
10 Sandover, 'Home', quoted in Johnson *The History of the 2/11th (City of Perth) Australian Infantry Battalion*, p. 123.
11 2/2nd Battalion War Diary, 5 Sep 1942, AWM52, 8/3/2, AWM.

Chapter 8 Kokoda to the Sea
1 Clift, *The Saga of a Sig*, p. 141.
2 McCarthy, *South-West Pacific Area*, p. 280.
3 Clift, *The Saga of a Sig*, p. 144.
4 Spragg, *When Good Men Do Nothing*, pp. 132–3.
5 16 Inf Bde War Diary, 6 Oct 1942, AWM52, 8/2/16, AWM.
6 Tarlington, *Shifting Sands and Savage Jungle*, pp. 72–3
7 2/1st Battalion War Diary, Oct 1942, AWM52, 8/3/1, AWM.
8 Pte RG Robertson, 2/2 Bn, letter 15 Dec 1942, 2DRL 1304, AWM.
9 16 Inf Bde War Diary, 3 Oct 1942, AWM52, 8/2/16, AWM.
10 Pte RG Robertson, 2/2 Bn, letter 15 Dec 1942.
11 Australian War Memorial, *Japanese Army Operations in the South Pacific Area*, p. 194.
12 Pratten, 'The "Old Man"', p. 255. Cullen's criticism is in: James, *Field Guide to the Kokoda Track*, p. 302; the claim that some men adored him is in: Clift, *The Saga of a Sig*, p. 153.
13 Parbery, *Alf's War*, 26 Oct, p. 101.
14 McCarthy, *South-West Pacific Area*, p. 302.
15 McCarthy, *South-West Pacific Area*, p. 302.
16 Quoted in McCarthy, *South-West Pacific Area*, p. 303.
17 16 Inf Bde War Diary, 29 Oct 1942.
18 Clift, *The Saga of a Sig*, p. 154.
19 Quoted in Tarlington, *Shifting Sands and Savage Jungle*, p. 82.
20 McGammon & Hodge, 'The Kokoda Trail', quoted in Marshall (ed.) *Nulli Secundus Log*, p. 90.

21 Cpl NL Shoemark, 'War Dog', quoted in Marshall (ed.) *Nulli Secundus Log*, p. 99.
22 Quoted in Givney, *The First at War*, p. 308.
23 McCarthy, *South-West Pacific Area*, p. 321.
24 Baker, *Paul Cullen*, p. 146.
25 16 Bde War Diary, 13 Nov 1942.
26 McCarthy, *South-West Pacific Area*, p. 386.
27 Hard-fighting: McCarthy, *South-West Pacific Area*, p. 394.
28 2/2 Bn War Diary, 21 Nov 1942, AWM52, 8/3/2, AWM.
29 16 Inf Bde War Diary, 10 Dec 1942.
30 2/3 Bn War Diary, 24 Dec 1942, AWM52, 8/3/3, AWM.
31 Horner, *The Gunners*, p. 346.
32 Bolger & Littlewood, *The Fiery Phoenix*, p. 209.
33 Bolger & Littlewood, *The Fiery Phoenix*, p. 209.
34 John Hynes, letter to the author, 7 Mar 2007.

Chapter 9 Wau-Salamaua
1 Quoted in Hay, *Nothing Over Us*, p. 266.
2 Ross (ed.), *The Seventeenth Australian Infantry Brigade*, p. 31.
3 Capt JJ May, 2/7 Dental Unit, diary 29 Jan 1943, PR87/135, AWM.
4 Capt JJ May, 2/7 Dental Unit, diary 4 Feb 1943. See also Hay, *Nothing Over Us*, p. 273.
5 Maj HLE Dunkley, 17 Bde, letter 23 Mar 1943, PR84/35, AWM.
6 Lt AH Robertson, 2/7 Bn, letter 8 Feb 1943, MJC.
7 Quoted in Department of Information, *Jungle Trail*, pp. 42 & 46, where the implication is that this was Savige's term.
8 McNicoll, *The Royal Australian Engineers*, vol. 3, p. 174.
9 Dexter, *The New Guinea Offensives*, p. 39.
10 Department of Information, *Jungle Trail*, p. 6.
11 Pearson, *Brothers, Battlers and Bastards*, p. 110.
12 Ross (ed.), *The Seventeenth Australian Infantry Brigade*, p. 35.
13 Hay, *Nothing Over Us*, p. 320.
14 Cpl R Jones, 2/5 Bn, letter 1943, PR01329, AWM.
15 Bennett, *Rough Infantry*, pp. 161–2.
16 Walker, *The Island Campaigns*, p. 363.
17 Maj HLE Dunkley, 17 Bde, letter 23 Apr 1943.
18 Maj HLE Dunkley, 2/7 Bn, letter 29 Jun 1943.
19 Bennett, *Rough Infantry*, p. 173.
20 2/7th Battalion War Diary Jul 1943, A Company report week ending 9 Jul 43, AWM52, 8/3/7, AWM.
21 2/7 Bn War Diary, 20 Aug 1943.
22 Department of Information, *Jungle Trail*, p. 61.
23 Reproduced in Ross (ed.), *The Seventeenth Australian Infantry Brigade*, p. 121.
24 Department of Information, *Jungle Trail*, p. 54.
25 Gullett, *Not as a Duty Only*, p. 112.

Chapter 10 The Longest Wait: Australia 1943–4
1 Wounded members did the same from the balcony of the Sydney Town Hall at a 16th Brigade march in Jan 1944.
2 Quoted in Unit History Editorial Committee, *White Over Green*, p. 344.
3 Hay, *Nothing Over Us*, p. 410.
4 Bolger & Littlewood, *The Fiery Phoenix*, p. 209, p. 300.

5 Lt BH MacDougal, 2/3 Bn, letter 20 Mar 1945, 3DRL 457, AWM.
6 Bishop, *The Thunder of the Guns!*, p. 545.
7 Des Wyles, quoted in Bishop, *The Thunder of the Guns!* p. 553. As mentioned in Chapter 7, there had been a smaller 'divisional parade' at Julis in August 1941.
8 From 1943 the anti-tank regiments were officially called 'Tank Attack Regiments'. This clumsy designation was not used by the official historian or the units' postwar associations.
9 Unit History Editorial Committe, *White Over Green*, p. 222.

Chapter 11 Aitape–Wewak
1 Quoted in Bolger & Littlewood, *The Fiery Phoenix*, p. 310.
2 Gnr R Flew, 2/2 Fd Regt, diary 22 Dec 1944, PR00526, AWM.
3 Capt OU Williams, 2/4 Bn, letter 19 May 1944, PR00057, AWM.
4 Lt MJ Wilson, 2/4 Bn, letter 26 Dec 1944, PR01343, AWM.
5 Pte RR Dove, 2/4 Bn, diary Dec 1944, MJC.
6 Trigellis-Smith, *All the King's Enemies* pp. 270–1.
7 Lt GH Fearnside, 2/3 Bn, letter 1 Feb 1945, PR85/071, AWM.
8 Fearnside, *Half to Remember*, pp. 184–5.
9 Walker, *The Island Campaigns*, p. 353.
10 O'Leary, *To the Green Fields Beyond*, p. 296.
11 Lt BH MacDougal, 2/3 Bn, letter 20 Mar 1945, 3DRL 457, AWM.
12 Cpl FJ Quinn, 2/6 Bn, diary 16 Mar 1945, PR85/209, AWM.
13 Long, *Final Campaigns*, p. 327.
14 Long, *Final Campaigns*, p. 342.
15 Hay, *Nothing Over Us*, p. 439.
16 Ken Kell, 'The Early Years', p. 63.
17 Bishop, *The Thunder of the Guns!*, p. 623.
18 Long, *The Final Campaigns*, p. 347.
19 Capt OU Williams, 2/4 Bn, letter 19 May 1945.
20 O'Leary, *To the Green Fields Beyond*, p. 314.
21 Lt MJ Wilson, 2/4 Bn, letter 14 Jun 1945, AWM PR01343.
22 Pte AE Wallin, 2/5 Bn, diary 21 Jun 1945, MS10172, SLV.
23 Pte AE Wallin, 2/5 Bn, diary 4 Jun 1945.
24 Pte AE Wallin, 2/5 Bn, diary 9 Jul 1945.
25 Pte AE Wallin, 2/5 Bn, diary 20 Jul 1945.
26 6 Australian Division General Staff Branch War Diary, 15 Aug 1945, AWM52, 1/5/12, AWM.
27 Quoted in Clift, *War Dance*, p. 410.

Chapter 12 Conclusion
1 Hay, *Nothing Over Us*, p. 470.
2 Sgt KCT, 2/6 Bn, 'Reflection on Armistice', 16–17 Aug 1945, in MS10346, SLV.
3 Sgt KCT, 2/6 Bn, 'Reflection on Armistice', 16–17 Aug 1945.
4 Lt MJ Wilson, 2/4 Bn, Letter 12 Aug 1945, AWM PR01343.
5 Lt MJ Wilson, 2/4 Bn, Letter 12 Aug 1945. See also Trigellis-Smith, *All the King's Enemies*, p. 307.
6 Quoted in Grey, *Australian Brass*, p. 119.
7 McNicoll, *The Royal Australian Engineers*, vol. 3, p. 251.
8 Maj B French, 2/6 Bn, diary 1 Oct 1945, PR85/219, AWM.
9 Grey, *Australian Brass*, p. 119.
10 Quoted in Long, *The Final Campaigns*, p. 340.

11 Text in AWM Photograph 101095.
12 6 Australian Division General Staff Branch War Diary, 6 Jan 1946, AWM52, 1/5/12, AWM.
13 William Dexter, 'The Battalion – My Home', p. 152.
14 Maj B French, 2/6 Bn, diary 13 Dec 1945.
15 Quoted in Pratten, 'The "Old Man"', p. 314.

Appendix 1: 6th Division Casualties
1 Sources for these figures include: unit histories; official history volumes; the AWM Roll of Honour <www.awm.gov.au>; Reid, *A Great Risk in a Good Cause: Australians in Greece and Crete April–May 1941*.

Appendix 2: 6th Division Honours and Awards
1 Marshall (ed.), *Nulli Secundus Log*, p. 101.
2 Lenore Vincent, letter to the author, Mar 2007.

Bibliography

Bibliographical note: a guide to further reading on the 6th Division

The Australian War Memorial's superb website allows readers to read the official diary entries for the divisional, brigade and battalion headquarters, though unfortunately not for artillery and other branches. Those available are often dauntingly big documents, but fascinating. The website also contains brief histories of each of the battalions.

Those seeking publications on the division have some excellent choices, though there should be more. Every infantry battalion and field regiment has a published history. Each is of value, but the quality varies greatly. Of the 16th Brigade histories, the 2/2nd is probably the best, and that battalion also has a worthwhile wartime history (*Nulli Secundus Log*) and Barter's more academic treatment (*Far Above Battle*). All three of the 17th Brigade histories are good, as is the wartime publication about the brigade, *17th Infantry Brigade*. Of the 19th Brigade histories, the 2/4th's *White Over Green* is beautifully produced and well written. The 2/3rd Field Regiment's history, *Thunder of the Guns!*, is also outstanding. The fine writing, excellent illustrations and unusually reflective quality of the Cavalry (Commando) Regiment's history, *To the Green Fields Beyond*, make it one of the best Australian unit histories.

Those keen to understand the division's many fine leaders could start with Chapman's enjoyable biography of Mackay. Horner's biography of Blamey, Grey's of Robertson and Keating's of Savige are important too. Kevin Baker's biography of Paul Cullen gives insights into this complex, brave and outspoken 'Thirty-Niner' and the men he led so well. John Mole's biography of his cavalryman father is a beautifully produced tribute.

There are a few illuminating personal memoirs by some men who were at the sharp end. 'Jo' Gullett's *Not as a Duty Only* is arguably the best Australian memoir of the war. Ken Clift's *Saga of a Sig* and Bob 'Hooker' Holt's *From Ingleburn to Aitape* are much earthier than blue-blood Gullett's, but give considerable insight into the thinking of many 6th Division originals. By contrast, Clift considered his fellow signaller Alf Parbery the 'cleanest' man, morally and physically, he'd ever known, and Parbery's wartime diaries are collected in the moving *Alf's War*. Griffith Spragg, a 2/3rd Battalion soldier who became a psychiatrist, wrote a powerful memoir entitled *When Good Men Do Nothing*. Norman Johnstone's *'Dearest Geraldine'* includes revealing letters from a 2/4th Battalion veteran of Libya, Greece and Crete. Peter Charlton's depiction of the *Thirty-Niners* contains some valuable reminiscences of their war, especially in the Middle East.

The 6th Division's individual campaigns have received desultory coverage, but the official histories are the eternal standby. The more I research, the more I'm left in awe of these works. Gavin Long wrote three volumes that cover most of the division's campaigns. The first volume, *To Benghazi*, provides masterly coverage of the raising of the 6th Division and its first campaign. I wonder whether anyone could persevere through every word of the volume on Greece, Crete and Syria, but many of its accounts of 6th Division battles are excellent. The last volume,

The Final Campaigns, covers an exceptionally complex range of political and military matters, and for Aitape–Wewak provides impressively detailed accounts of operations.

Peter Ewer's *Forgotten Anzacs*, published just before this book went into production, is a very readable account of operations in Greece and Crete, based largely on interviews with veterans. Among the many books about Papua in 1942, few offer detailed coverage of the 16th Brigade's substantial contribution. Though it is not perfect, McCarthy's *South-West Pacific Area: First Year* is my favourite official history volume. It is still easily the best account of the 16th Brigade battles. Paul Ham's *Kokoda* adds some interesting material.

Phil Bradley's book on Wau is required and fascinating reading on that topic. His forthcoming work on Salamaua will also be invaluable. Moremon's DVA booklet is a good introduction. Dexter's official history volume threatens to overwhelm readers with the details of the numerous actions in this area, but gives a strong impression of the heights, figurative and literal, reached by the redoubtable 17th Brigade. The Aitape–Wewak campaign is well covered by Long, though it deserves a new study. On this campaign, as all others, the unit histories are a good source of anecdote and atmosphere.

PERSONAL WARTIME TESTIMONIES
HW Adeney, Bdr to Sgt, 2/2 Fd Regt, letters 1939–42. SLV MS10868.
JK Atock, Pte, 2/7 Bn, letters 1940–1. AWM 3DRL 6372.
PM Barrett, Spr, 2/8 Fd Coy, letter 1941. MJC, donor: W Barrett.
RC Beilby, Spr, 2/1 Fd Coy, diary 1940–1. SLV MS10019.
RH Bourke, Sgt, 2/1 Bn, letter 1942. AWM PR 88/125.
J Browning, Pte, 2/4 Bn, letter 1941. AWM PR03192.
J Butler, Pte, 2/23 Bn, diary 1941. AWM 3DRL 3825.
RF Cameron, Pte, 2/1 Bn, letter 1941. AWM 3DRL 506.
KA Carroll, Lt, 2/6 Bn, diary 1939–40. AWM 3DRL 1003.
SL Carroll, MM, Pte, 2/11 Bn. Wartime report on his experience on Crete. AWM 3DRL 6045.
C Chrystal, Lt to Capt, 2/4 Bn, diaries 1940–2, letter 1941. MJC, donor: P Chrystal.
G Clark, Gnr, 2/1 Fd Regt, diary 1941. AWM PR01035.
AS Cobb, Gnr, 2/1 AT Regt, diary 1941. SLV MS10131.
RJW da Fonte, Sgt, 2/8 Bn, diary 1941. MJC, donor: 2/8 Bn Association.
RR Dove, Pte, 2/4 Bn, diary 1944–5. MJC, donor: RR Dove.
HLE Dunkley, DSO, MC, Maj, 2/7 Bn and 17 Bde, letters 1941–43. AWM PR84/35 and MJC, donor: L Jones.
MB Edwards, Lt, 2/2 Fd Regt, diary 1941. AWM PR88/66.
GH Fearnside, Lt, 2/3 Bn, letters 1944–5. AWM PR85/71.
TH Fellows, Lt, 2/8 Bn, letter 1941, AWM PR00411.
R Flew, Gnr, 2/2 Fd Regt, diary 1944–5, AWM PR00526.
B French, Maj, 2/6 Bn, diary 1945. AWM PR85/219.
CW Golding, Capt, 2/1 Bn, letter 1941. MJC, donor: G Griffiths.
RC Gordon, Cpl, 2/7 Bn. 'Report on his escape from Crete by Cpl R.C. Gordon', 1941. SLV MS9553.
A Hackshaw, Pte, 2/11 Bn, diaries 1940–1. AWM 3DRL 6398.
J Harkness, Lt, 2/2 Bn, letter 1941. AWM PR88/89.
L Howard, Gnr, 2/2 Fd Regt, letter 1941. AWM PR00428.
F James, Gnr, 2/2 Fd Regt, diary 1941. AWM PR00607.
R Jones, Cpl, 2/5 Bn, letter 1943. AWM PR01329.
C Kelly, Pte, 2/7 Bn, diary 1941. AWM PR02043.
G (Bill) Laybourne Smith, Capt, 2/3 Fd Regt, letters 1939–41. MJC, donor: H Laybourne Smith.

E Loubet, Spr, 2/1 Fd Coy, diary 1940–1, letter 1941. AWM PR01676 and MJC, donor: P Connor.
BH MacDougal, Lt, 2/3 Bn, letter 1945. AWM 3DRL 457.
E MacLeod, Pte, 2/11 Bn, letter 1941. MJC, donor: E MacLeod.
JJ May, Capt, 2/7 Dental Unit, diary 1943. AWM PR87/135.
TR Neeman, Sig, 17 Bde Sigs and 6 Div Sigs, letters 1940–3. AWM PR01034 and MJC, donor: TR Neeman.
S O'Brien, A/WOII, 2/7 Fd Amb, letter 1941. SLV MS10616.
A Parsons, Cpl, 2/3 Fd Coy and 2/5 Bn. Wartime memoir of travels 1940–2. AWM 3DRL 3908.
SHWC Porter, Maj, 2/5 Bn, letters 1939–40. SLV MS11477.
FJ Quinn, L/Cpl to Cpl, 2/6 Bn, diaries 1941, 1943, 1945. Also a collection of wartime poems. AWM PR85/209.
AH Robertson, Lt, 2/7 Bn, letters 1942–3. MJC, donor: H Lind.
RG Robertson, Pte, 2/2 Bn, letter 1942. AWM 2DRL 1304.
HW Thomas, Sgt, 2/7 Bn, diary 1941. AWM 54, Item No. 253/1/10.
KCT, Sgt, 2/6 Bn. Reflection on armistice August 1945. SLV MS10346.
RK Turner, L/Cpl, 2/11 Bn, letter 1941. AWM PR83/42.
AJ Ulrick, Pte, 2/2 Bn, letters 1939–41. AWM PR82/177.
IW Walker, Cpl, 2/7 Bn, letter 1941, AWM PR00178.
KR Walker, Lt, 2/7 Bn, letter 1941, AWM PR00178.
AE Wallin, Pte, 2/2 AGH and 2/5 Bn, diaries 1941–45. SLV MS10172.
LF Williams, Pte, 2/11 Bn, letters 1941. MJC, donor: M Barr.
OU Williams, Capt, 2/4 Bn, letters 1944–5, AWM PR00057.
ER Wilmoth, Lt, 2/8 Bn, letter 1941. AWM PR86/370.
JL Wilson, Spr, 2/2 Fd Coy, diary 1940–1. SLV MS10169.
MJ Wilson, Pte to Lt, 2/4 Bn, letters 1941–5, AWM PR01343.

UNPUBLISHED POSTWAR REMINISCENCES
William Dexter, 'The Battalion – My Home', n.d., AWM PR01182.
Philip Hurst, 'My Army Days', AWM MSS1656.
Ken Kell, 'The Early Years', 1994, AWM PR01312.
R Singleton, 'The Memoirs of a Young Soldier', 1996, AWM PR01917.
Ivor White, 'Whiteye's Army Memoirs', 2005. Donor: Ivor White.

GOVERNMENT AND ARMY DOCUMENTS
Australian War Memorial
AWM Roll of Honour, <www.awm.gov.au>.
AWM52, 1/5/12, 6 Australian Division General Staff Branch War Diary.
AWM52, 1/5/27, 12 Australian Division General Staff Branch Northern Territory Force War Diary
52, 8/2/16, 16 Inf Bde War Diary.
52, 8/2/17, 17 Inf Bde War Diary.
52, 8/3/1, 2/1 Bn War Diary.
52, 8/3/2, 2/2 Bn War Diary.
52, 8/3/3, 2/3 Bn War Diary.
52, 8/3/4, 2/4 Bn War Diary.
52, 8/3/7, 2/7 Bn War Diary.

PUBLISHED WORKS
Unit histories
2/2nd Field Regiment, *Action Front: Official History of the 2/2nd Field Regiment*, Co-Creations Pty Ltd, Melbourne, 2006. Electronic copy.
Bentley, A, *The Second Eighth*, 2/8 Battalion Association, Melbourne, 1984.
Bishop, Les, *The Thunder of the Guns! A History of 2/3 Australian Field Regiment*, 2/3 Australian Field Regiment Association, Sydney, 1998.
Bolger, WP and Littlewood, JG, *The Fiery Phoenix: The Story of the 2/7 Australian Infantry Battalion 1939–46*, 2/7 Battalion Association, Parkdale, 1983.
Clift, Ken, *War Dance: The Story of the 2/3 Aust. Inf. Bn.*, PM Fowler and 2/3rd Battalion Association, Kingsgrove, 1980.
Givney, EC (ed.), *The First at War: The Story of the 2/1st Australian Infantry Battalion 1939–45*, Association of First Infantry Battalions, Earlwood, 1987.
Hay, David, *Nothing Over Us: The Story of the 2/6th Australian Infantry Battalion*, Australian War Memorial, Canberra, 1984.
Haywood, EV, *Six Years in Support: Official History of the 2/1st Australian Field Regiment*, Angus and Robertson, Sydney, 1959.
Johnson, KT, *The History of the 2/11th (City of Perth) Australian Infantry Battalion*, John Burridge Military Antiques, Swanbourne, 2000.
Marshall, Jock (ed.), *Nulli Secundus Log*, 2/2nd Australian Infantry Battalion, Sydney, 1946.
O'Leary, Shawn, *To the Green Fields Beyond: The Story of 6th Division Cavalry Commandos*, Wilke Group, Zillmere, 1975.
Ross, A (ed.), *The Seventeenth Australian Infantry Brigade*, 17th Brigade, 1944.
Trigellis-Smith, S, *All the King's Enemies: A History of the 2/5th Australian Infantry Battalion*, Headquarters Training Command, Georges Heights, 1994.
Unit History Editorial Committee, *White Over Green: The 2/4th Infantry Battalion*, Angus and Robertson, Sydney, 1963.
Wick, S., *Purple Over Green*, The History of the 2/2 Australian Infantry Battalion, 2/2 Aust. Inf. Bn Association, Guildford, 1978.

Official histories
Australian War Memorial, *Japanese Army Operations in the South Pacific Area: New Britain and Papua Campaigns, 1942–43*, translator Steven Bullard, Australian War Memorial, Canberra, 2007.
Dexter, David, *The New Guinea Offensives*, Australian War Memorial, Canberra, 1961.
Long, Gavin, *Greece, Crete and Syria*, Collins/Australian War Memorial, Sydney, 1986.
— *The Final Campaigns*, Australian War Memorial, Canberra, 1963.
— *The Six Years War*, Australian War Memorial, Canberra, 1973.
— *To Benghazi*, Collins/Australian War Memorial, Sydney, 1986.
McCarthy, Dudley, *South-West Pacific Area – First Year: Kokoda to Wau*, Australian War Memorial, Canberra, 1959.
Walker, Allan S, *Middle East and Far East*, Australian War Memorial, Canberra, 1956.
— *The Island Campaigns*, Australian War Memorial, Canberra, 1957.

Other published works
Baker, Kevin, *Paul Cullen: Citizen and Soldier*, Rosenberg, Dural, 2005.
Barker, Theo, *Signals: A history of the Royal Australian Corps of Signals 1788–1947*, Royal Australian Corps of Signals Committee, Canberra, 1987.

Barter, Margaret, *Far Above Battle: The Experience and Memory of Australian Soldiers in War 1939–45*, Allen and Unwin, Sydney, 1994.
Bennett, Cam, *Rough Infantry: Tales of World War II*, Warrnambool Institute Press, Brunswick, 1985.
Brown, Wayne, *Blue: The remarkable exploits of 'Blue' Reiter MC, MM, MID*, Wayne Brown, Warana, 2006.
Chapman, Ivan D, *Iven G Mackay: Citizen and Soldier*, Melway Publishing, Melbourne, 1975.
Charlton, Peter, *The Thirty-Niners*, Macmillan, Melbourne, 1981.
Clift, Ken, *The Saga of a Sig*, KCD Publications, Randwick, 1972.
Dennis, Peter, Jeffrey Grey, Ewan Morris & Robin Prior (eds), *The Oxford Companion to Australian Military History*, Oxford University Press, Oxford, 1995.
Department of Information, *Jungle Trail*, Sydney, 1944.
— *The Battle of Wau*, Brochure No. 1, n.d.
Fearnside, GH, *Half to Remember: The reminiscences of an Australian infantry soldier in World War II*, Haldane Publishing Co, Sydney, 1975.
Forty, George, *The First Victory: O'Connor's Desert Triumph*, Guild Publishing, London, 1990.
Fulton, ETW, *No Turning Back: A Memoir*, Pandanus Books, Canberra, 2005.
Green, Olwyn, *The Name's Still Charlie*, University of Queensland Press, St Lucia, 1993.
Grey, Jeffrey, *Australian Brass: The Career of Lieutenant General Sir Horace Robertson*, Cambridge University Press, Cambridge, 1992.
Griffiths-Marsh, Roland, *The Sixpenny Soldier*, Angus and Robertson, North Ryde, 1990.
Gullett, Henry ('Jo'), *Not as a Duty Only: An infantryman's war*, Melbourne University Press, Carlton, 1984.
Hadjipateras, Costas & Maria S Fafalios (eds), *Crete 1941 Eyewitnessed*, Efstathiadis Group, Attikis, 1993.
Handel, Paul, *The Vital Factor: A History of 2/6th Australian Armoured Regiment 1941–46*, Australian Military History Publications, Loftus, 2004.
Holt, Bob, *From Ingleburn to Aitape*, R Holt, Brookvale, 1981.
Hopley, JB, 'Stevenson, John Rowlstone (1908–1971)', *Australian Dictionary of Biography*, Volume 16, Melbourne University Press, 2002, pp 305–6.
Horner, David, *Blamey: The Commander-in-Chief*, Allen & Unwin, Sydney, 1998.
— *Crisis of Command: Australian Generalship and the Japanese Threat, 1941–43*, Australian National University Press, Canberra, 1978.
— *General Vasey's War*, Melbourne University Press, Carlton, 1992.
— *High Command: Australia's struggle for an independent war strategy, 1939–45*, Allen & Unwin, Sydney, 1992.
— *The Gunners: A History of Australian Artillery*, Allen & Unwin, Sydney, 1995.
James, Bill, *Field Guide to the Kokoda Track*, Kokoda Press, Lane Cove, 2006.
Johnstone, Norman, *'Dearest Geraldine': Letters from a soldier*, Publishing Services, Loftus, 2003.
Keating, Gavin, *The Right Man for the Right Job: Lieutenant General Sir Stanley Savige as a Military Commander*, Oxford University Press, Melbourne, 2005.
Lind, LJ, *Escape from Crete*, Australasian Publishing, Sydney, 1944.
Lindsay, Neville, *Equal to the Task: The Royal Australian Army Service Corps*, Historia Productions, Kenmore, 1991.
McAllester, Jim & Syd Trigellis-Smith, *Largely a Gamble: Australians in Syria June–July 1941*, Headquarters Training Command, Sydney, 1995.
McDonald, Neil, *Damien Parer's War*, Lothian Books, South Melbourne, 2004.

McDonald, Neil & Peter Brune, *200 Shots: Damien Parer, George Silk and the Australians at war in New Guinea*, Allen & Unwin, Sydney, 1998.
McNicoll, Ronald, *The Royal Australian Engineers 1919 to 1945: Teeth and Tail*, Volume 3, Corps Committee of the Royal Australian Engineers, Canberra, 1982.
Mole, John, *Farmer, fighter, forester and father: the diaries of Bryan Mole explored*, John Mole, North Ringwood, 2003.
Moremon, John, *Wau-Salamaua*, Department of Veterans' Affairs, Canberra, 2003.
Parbery, Frances & Stephen Parbery, *Alf's War: With the Sixth Infantry Division*, Loftus, 2005.
Pearson, Arthur, *Brothers, Battlers and Bastards*, Boolarong Press, Maroochydore, 1995.
Reid, Richard, *A Great Risk in a Good Cause: Australians in Greece and Crete April–May 1941*, Department of Veterans' Affairs, Canberra, 2001.
Ritchie, Henry, 'The Yeomen of Old England', in Kenneth Rankin (ed.), *Lest We Forget: Fifty Years On*, Kenneth Rankin, Odiham, 1989.
Silk, George, *War in New Guinea: Official War Photographs of the Battle for Australia*, FH Johnston, Sydney, 1943.
Spragg, Griffith, *When Good Men Do Nothing*, Australian Military History Publications, Loftus, 2003.
Tarlington, George, *Shifting Sands and Savage Jungle*, Australian Military History Publications, Loftus, 1994.
Wavell, Sir Archibald, *Speaking Generally*, Macmillan, London, 1946.
Wigmore, Lionel, *They Dared Mightily*, Australian War Memorial, Canberra, 1963.
Wilmot, Chester, *Tobruk 1941*, Angus and Robertson, Sydney, 1945.

Internet articles
Paul Handel, 'Matilda Tanks at Retimo on the Island of Crete', <www.defence.gov.au/army/ahu/books_articles/Articles/Matilda_Tanks.htm> accessed 26 May 2008.

Theses
Garth Pratten, 'The "Old Man": Australian battalion commanders in the Second World War', PhD Thesis, Deakin University, 2005.

Index

42nd Street, 96, 238

Adachi, Hatazon, 195, 234
Adelaide River, 128
Adeney, Harold (2/2 Fd Regt), 61, 85, 91
aircraft, 27
    Aitape–Wewak, 195, 200, 207, 225, 228
    American, 216
    German, 72, 74, 78, 88–99, 101
    Italian, 22, 27, 28, 31, 65
    transport, 158, 213
    Wau, 160
Aitape, 191, 193, 202, 203, 205, 225
Aitape–Wewak campaign, 192–232, 234, 244
Alexandria, 64, 85
Aliakmon River, 70
Allen, AS 'Tubby' (16 Bde), 7–8, 18, 19, 26, 28–31
Allen, Les 'Bull' (2/5 Bn), 120, 175
American forces, 133, 148, 150, 153, 164, 170, 174, 175, 192, 196
    32nd Division, 150
Amiriya, 25
Andrews, Bill (2/4 Bn), 98
Apex Hill, 98
Armstrong, Clive (2/3 Bn), 81
artillery, 79, 119
    18-pounders, 15
    25-pounders, 15, 23, 30, 65, 73, 74, 149, 189, 198, 200, 216, 223
    Aitape–Wewak, 198, 210, 228, 231
    anti-aircraft guns, 22–3
    anti-tank guns, 37, 53, 69, 101, 109, 118, 151
    Bardia, 30–2
    British, 69
    Crete, 89, 95–7
    Greece, 68, 75–7
    howitzers, 226
    Italian, 39, 49, 52, 54, 62, 63
    Japanese, 207, 210
    'Long Toms', 217
    mountain guns, 142, 146
    Papua, 149–50, 154
    reorganisation in SWPA, 128–9, 190
    Tobruk, 46, 52
    Wau, 159
    Wau-Salamaua, 174
Atebrin, 181, 201
Athens, 65, 74
Atherton Tableland, 181
Atock, James (2/7 Bn), 43
Australian army
    armies, **First**, 203
    corps, **I**, 66, 125
    divisions, 2–3, **3rd**, 165, 173; **7th**, v, 1, 8, 61, 66, 107, 109, 114, 125, 133, 142, 187, 190, 234; **8th**, v, 1; **9th**, v, 1, 187, 190
    forces, **Blackforce**, 149–50, 152–4; **Bullforce**, 150, 154; **Farida**, 220, 222; **Habforce**, 114; **Hayforce**, 205, 207, 212; **Kanga**, 156, 162, 175; **Lustre**, 64, 71, 74, 77; **Mackay**, 67–70; **Savige**, 70–1; **New Guinea**, 156
    headquarters, **3rd Division**, 163, 165, 180; **6th Division**, 4, 31, 121–3, 133, 252n9
    armour and cavalry, **2/4th Armd Regt**, 213–5; **6th Div Cav Regt (also 2/6th Cav (Cdo) Regt)**, 4, 27, 51, 55, 58–9, 61–3, 106–10, 114, 118–20, 127–8, 150, 187, 193–6, 201, 216, 256; **7th Div Cav Regt**, 106
    artillery, **2/1st Anti-Tank Regt**, 4, 23–4, 53, 67, 69, 114, 128, 190, 220, 226; **2/1st Fd Regt**, 4, 22–3, 30–2, 42–3, 55–8, 75–7, 128, 149–50, 152–4, 159–60, 190, 216–7, 228, 230; **2/2nd Fd Regt**, 4, 15, 23, 25, 61, 76, 85, 88–9, 97, 128, 189–90, 200, 210, 222; **2/3rd Fd Regt**, 4, 23–4, 46–7, 65, 67–9, 74, 77–9, 87–9, 95–6, 100–1, 103–4, 128, 189–90, 198, 228, 230, 256

engineers, 24; **2/1st Fd Coy**, 4, 24, 27–8, 32–3, 35, 45, 70, 126, 165–6; **2/2nd Fd Coy**, 4, 24, 39, 217, 222; **2/3rd Fd Coy**, 24–5; **2/8th Fd Coy**, 4, 25, 39, 75, 88, 126, 158, 163, 166; **2/1st Field Park Company**, 25; **2/2nd (later 2/22nd) Fd Pk Coy**, 4, 32, 126, 222

independent companies and commando squadrons, **2/3 Ind Coy**, 164, 166; **2/7th Ind Coy**, 193; **2/7th Cdo Sqn**, 193, 196; **2/9th Cdo Sqn**, 193, 207, 220–1; **2/10th Cdo Sqn**, 193–4, 205, 206–7, 220

infantry brigades, 3; **16th**, 3, 7–8, 10, 11, 13–14, 16–17, 20, 25, 27, 31, 36, 40, 46, 51, 60, 64–5, 67, 75, 77, 105, 114, 126, 130–1, 133–49, 181, 186, 200, 207, 215–6, 220, 231, 256–7; **17th**, 3, 8, 10, 13, 14–15, 17, 27, 37, 40–1, 44, 51, 59, 60, 64–6, 71, 75, 77, 114, 116, 118, 120, 126, 130, 133, 150, 155–80, 181, 186, 213, 223, 225–6, 256–7; **18th**, 9; **19th**, 3, 9, 17, 20, 27, 31, 41, 46, 59, 60, 64–5, 67, 76–7, 89, 125–6, 128–30, 133, 181, 186, 200, 216, 221, 227, 231; **21st**, 107, 114, 116, 146–7, 186; **25th**, 107, 134, 144, 146–7; **29th**, 179; **30th**, 149

infantry battalions, 3–4; **2/1st**, 13, 22, 32, 36, 40, 46–7, 81, 88, 105–6, 111, 124, 137–46, 148–9, 183, 188, 202–4, 215, 237, 240; **2/2nd**, 3, 16, 19, 35–6, 40, 44, 46–7, 70, 71–3, 81, 88–9, 94, 99–101, 103–4, 124, 130–1, 136–8, 140–4, 147–9, 183, 204, 207–10, 215, 239, 246, 256; **2/3rd**, 3, 8, 36–7, 40, 46, 49, 51, 71, 73, 81–3, 88, 107, 111–4, 116–20, 123, 133, 137–40, 143–4, 146–7, 149, 183, 200, 210–3, 231–2, 235, 256; **2/4th**, 3, 9, 19–20, 22–3, 49, 51–2, 56, 60–1, 68–70, 81, 85, 88, 90–3, 98–9, 125, 128, 190–1, 196–7, 200, 217–8, 221–2, 227, 233, 237, 256; **2/5th**, 3, 12, 16–17, 20, 37, 70–1, 78–9, 88, 107, 109–10, 114, 116–20, 150, 156, 158–9, 161, 163–5, 169–76, 200, 205, 223, 225–6, 239, 246; **2/6th**, 3, 10, 38–9, 41–2, 47, 78, 88, 109, 126, 156–8, 160–2, 168–9, 176–7, 179, 182–3, 187, 207, 213, 215–6, 233, 235; **2/7th**, 3, 20, 21, 37–8, 47–8, 88–9, 95–7, 104, 124, 150–2, 158–60, 162, 164–8, 176–9, 186–7, 193, 205–7, 212, 226–7; **2/8th**, 3, 9, 49, 53, 68–70, 88–9, 95–7, 128, 200, 218, 222, 227–30, 235; **2/11th**, 3, 9, 41, 50, 53, 55–6, 59, 60, 67, 70–1, 85, 88–9, 93–4, 99–104, 128–30,

183, 197–200, 218–22, 241; **2/12th**, 9; **2/17th**, 52; **16th Bde Composite**, 88, 89, 95; **17th Bde Composite**, 88, 89, 95; **23rd/21st**, 128; **3rd**, 137; **49th**, 149; **2nd New Guinea Bn**, 223; **3 RAR**, 82

machine gun battalions, **2/3rd**, 220–1
pioneer battalions, **2/1st**, 83; **2/2nd**, 114, 118

Australian New Guinea Administrative Unit, 193

medical units, **2/1st Fd Amb**, 4, 65; **2/2nd Fd Amb**, 4, 162, 175–6; **2/7th Fd Amb**, 4, 87, 97, 207, 235; **2/2 AGH**, 45; **2/5 AGH**, 176

ordnance, **2/1st Army Fd Workshop**, 4; **2/41st LAD**, 189; **2/46th LAD**, 162

Provost Companies, **6th Div Prov Coy**, 29–30

Service Corps, **6th Div**, 4, 60, 65, 74; **6th Div Supply Column**, 53–4

Signals, **6 Div Sigs**, 4, 25, 31, 55, 88, 172–3, 187; **'J' Sec**, 140; **'K' Sec**, 54–5, 114

Australian government, 7–8, 126, 233
Australian Imperial Force
  First, 1, 7–8, 18, 29, 42, 65
  Second, 1, 3, 7, 10, 19, 62, 63, 110, 126, 127, 133, 146, 182, 191, 226, 238, 239
Aytoun, William (2/1 Fd Coy), 167

Bader, Ron (2/7 Fd Amb), 235
Bardia, 1, 10, 12, 15, 48, 53, 54, 62, 63, 133, 137, 142, 239–59
  Post 11, 39, 40, 42, 238
  Post 47, 35
Bassula, William (2/8 Bn), 227
'Battle of the Ridges', 169
Bauer, George (2/1 Fd Amb), 65
Bawden, Dick (2/4 Bn), 197
bayonets, 20, 35, 37, 41, 47, 87, 93, 96–8, 144, 157, 190
Beddome, Bob (2/5 Bn), 239
Bedells, JG (2/11 Bn), 102
Beilby, Richard (2/1 Fd Coy), 27–8, 35, 37
Beirut, 107, 112, 114
Bena Bena, 180
Bennett, Cam (2/5 Bn), 178
Berryman, Mick (17 Bde Sigs), 54
Berryman, Sir Frank (6 Div), 10, 110, 121, 178, 191
Bessell-Browne, Ian (2/3 Fd Regt), 87, 95
Black Cat Track, 156, 162
Blain, Reg (2/2 Bn), 124, 137
Blamey, JM (2/2 Bn), 148

Blamey, Sir Thomas, 1, 2, 8, 9, 25, 62, 67, 70, 71, 121, 133, 139, 149, 155, 156, 163, 167, 183, 190–2, 196, 203, 209, 256
Blot, The, 228
Boase, Allan (16 Bde), 121, 123, 126, 133, 252
Bobdubi Ridge, 164, 170, 179
Boiken, 213, 232
Bosgard, AK (2/2 Bn), 83
Bowden, Jim (2/7 Bn), 212
Bower, Albert (2/1 Fd Coy), 45
Brallos Pass, 71, 76, 238
Brand, David (2/11 Bn), 50
Bren carriers, 20, 35, 40, 46, 50, 60, 65, 71, 73, 107–9, 113, 121, 128, 133, 150–2, 183
British forces, 31, 52, 66, 69, 70, 87, 89, 113, 114
    7 RTR, 31–5, 37
    7th Armoured Division, 26, 31, 46, 55
    Habforce, 114
    Royal Navy, 81
Brooker, John (2/5 Bn), 18
Brooks, William (6 Div Prov Coy), 29
Brown, Jim (2/4 Bn), 197
Brown, Stanley (2/4 Bn), 191
Buckley, AA (2/2 Bn), 83
Buisaval Track, 156, 158
Bulldog Track, 166
Bulolo, 163
Buna, 20, 150–3
Burgess, Jim (2/8 Bn), 49
Burma, 125–6
Burrell, John (2/1 Bn), 22
But, 204, 207, 209, 210, 215

Cade, Peter (2/4 Bn), 68
Cairns, 188
Cameron, Lin (2/5 Bn), 174
Campbell, Ian (2/1 Bn), 89, 99–100, 103–4
camps and barracks, 7–8, 15, 65, 182, 185, 237
Canea, 85, 96
cannibalism
    see Japanese forces
Cape Wom, 234, 238
    accidental air attack on, 216
Capuzzo, Fort, 28–30, 106
carriers, 'native', 143, 162, 173, 212
    'native sentries', 213
Carroll, Keith (2/6 Bn), 10
Carson, Arthur (2/3 Bn), 138
casualties, 105, 183, 231, 241–5
    Bardia, 44–5
    Crete, 103

    Greece, 82
    Kokoda campaign, 147
    Papua, 149
    Tobruk, 52
Catterns, Basil (2/1 Bn), 139, 140, 148
Ceylon, 125–7, 130
Channell, DR, (2/1 Bn), 99
Chappel, BH, 89, 99
Chilton, Fred (2/2 Bn), 36, 82, 239
Chowne, Bert (2/2 Bn), 209
Chrystal, Cecil (2/4 Bn), 22, 69, 91, 98
Churchill, Sir Winston, 61, 126
Clift, Ken (16 Bde Sigs), 29, 55, 133, 141, 256
Coconuts, The, 179
Colbert, Ken (2/3 Bn), 232
Colman, Alwyn (2/3 Fd Regt), 79
Colombo, 125, 127
Connor, Gerry (2/2 Bn), 16
Cooper, William (2/1 Bn), 21
Copeman, Jim (2/3 Bn), 112, 232
Corinth Canal, 78
Craig, Felix (6 Div AASC), 74
Crawford, Alec (2/2 Fd Coy & 2/8 Fd Coy), 39
Cremor, WE (2/2 Fd Regt), 88
Crete, 1, 19, 21, 38, 48, 50, 52, 54, 59, 81–106, 111, 185, 197, 198, 223, 234, 237, 243, 251, 256, 257, 260
Crystal Creek, 158, 161, 163, 174
Cullen, Paul (2/2 Bn & 2/1 Bn), 95, 138–40, 148, 203, 240, 256
Curtin, John, 125
Cyrenaica, 26, 61, 62, 109

da Fonte, Ron (2/8 Bn), 49
Dagua, 204, 209
Damascus, 107, 111–14, 185
Damour, 114–18
Dandriwad River, 194
Daniel, Jack (2/6 Bn), 213
Danmap River, 106, 194, 196–7, 203, 232
    flooding of, 200
Daqoun, Wadi, 116
Davie, John (2/6 Bn), 188
Dawson, Brian (2/1 Fd Coy), 32
'deep thinkers', 145
Deir Mar Jorjos, 116–17
Derna, 31, 50, 55–60, 238
Dexter, Bill (2/6 Bn), 239
disease, 185, 231
    see also malaria
Dogreto Bay, 202
Donoghue, Timothy (2/3 Bn & 2/2 Bn), 185
Doran, Roy (2/7 Bn), 179, 180

Dougherty, Sir Ivan (2/4 Bn), 68, 98–9, 239
Dove Bay, 219
Dove, Reg (2/4 Bn), 197
Dunkley, Harry (2/7 Bn & 17 Bde), 164, 177, 178
Dyce, John (2/3 Bn), 235

Eather, Ken (2/1 Bn), 13, 32, 144
'economic conscripts', 11–12, 14
Edwards, Marcus (2/2 Fd Regt), 97
Egypt, 16, 22–4, 43, 45, 53, 61, 64, 66, 81, 87, 103, 106
Eichelberger, Robert, 150
Elasson, 74
enlistment, motives for, 11
Eora Creek, 138–41, 149, 238
Erithrai, 75, 77
Escreet, Herbert (2/5 Bn), 169
Ewing, Ian (2/10 Cdo Sqn), 194

Farrell, Nevis (2/4 Bn), 197
Fergusson, MA (6 Div Cav), 62
Fergusson, Terence (6 Div Cav & 2/7 Bn), 150, 151
Ferris, MJ (6 Div Cav), 118
Finlay, 'Jock' (2/1 Fd Regt), 152
flame-throwers, 219
Florina Valley, 67–8
Flude, Bruce (2/8 Bn), 235
Fort Weygand, 111, 112
Francisco River, 167, 181
Free French forces, 107, 112
French, Bevan (2/6 Bn), 235, 239
Frew, John (2/1 Bn), 139
Freyberg, Sir Bernard, 85, 87–9, 95–7, 104
Friend, John (2/5 Bn), 166
Fuller, JSC (6 Div Cav), 63
Fulton, Ted (2/1 Fd Regt), 23, 43

Gannan, Tony (2/7 Bn), 206
Garn el Grein, 27
Gaza, 19
George VI, King, 23
Georgioupolis, 89, 95, 96
German forces, 67
    SS, 69
Giarabub Oasis, 62–3
Gidley-King, George (2/3 Bn), 137
Gill, M (2/7 Bn), 193
Glasgow, Derek (6 Div Cav), 118
Glasgow, Duncan (6 Div Cav), 118
Glasgow, Gordon (6 Div Cav), 118
Goble, Eric (2/6 Bn), 63

Godby, Norman (2/7 Bn), 48
Godfrey, Arthur (2/6 Bn), 42
Goodview Junction, 179, 180
Gorari
    see Oivi-Gorari
Gower, John (2/5 Bn), 117
Grant, Eldrick (2/4 Bn), 52
Great Britain, 7, 18, 22, 24
Greece, 1, 30, 31, 50, 52, 61, 64–85, 89, 96, 103, 105, 106, 111, 124, 142, 191, 221, 223, 232, 234, 243, 245, 250, 251, 256, 257
    Olympus–Aliakmon Line, 67, 70
    Thermopylae Line, 76, 77
    Vermion–Olympus Line, 67
Greek forces, 66–9, 87, 88, 100
Green, Arthur (2/1 AT Regt), 226
Green, Charles (2/2 Bn & 2/11 Bn), 82
Griffiths, Sydney (2/1 Bn), 145
Guadagasal, 163
Gullett, Henry 'Jo' (2/6 Bn), 12, 109, 124, 181, 256
Gurr, John (2/2 Bn), 207

Haifa, 22
Hamilton, Matt (17 Bde Sigs), 54
Hanson, Arthur 'Black Tom' (2/1 Fd Regt), 149
Harvey, Tom (2/2 Bn), 44
Hay, Sir David (2/6 Bn), 205
Haydon, JB (2/1 Bn), 202
Haydon Knoll, 202
Hayfield, 213, 225, 226
Hedderman, 'Smoky' (2/6 Bn), 177
Hennessy, EC (6 Div Cav), 50
Heraklion, 85, 87, 89, 91–2, 98–9, 238
Herring, Sir Edmund (6 Div), 69, 121–3, 125–7, 156, 174, 181
Hewett, Francis (2/8 Bn), 228
Hill 569, 119
Hillcoat, Eric (2/1 Fd Regt), 31
Hocking, Douglas (2/6 Bn), 188
Hoddinott, Frank (2/3 Bn), 133
Hoffmann, Roland (16 Bde), 11
Honeywell, Harry (2/2 Bn), 82, 142
Honner, Ralph (2/11 Bn), 56, 59, 102
honours and awards, 209, 246–7
Horner, David, 83, 256
House Copper, 157
House Tamboran, 212
Hurst, Philip (2/7 Bn), 37–8
Hutchison, Ian (2/3 Bn), 112, 133, 140
Hynes, John (2/1 Fd Regt), 152

Ilimo, 144
Indian forces, 26, 107, 111, 112, 235–6
indiscipline, 43
   see larrikins
Ireland, Robert (6 Div Cav), 106
Isedale, James (2/2 Bn), 207
Isurava, 142

Jackson, James (2/5 Bn), 171
'Jap Track', 157
Japanese forces, 134, 195, 212
   attitudes to, 173
   cannibalism, 16, 138, 197, 198, 228
   night raiders, 227
   night raids, 231
Jerram, RM, 37
Johnson, Ken 'Katie' (2/11 Bn), 50
Jones, Bob (2/5 Bn), 173

'Kangaroo Club', v, 182
kangaroo symbol, v, 60
Kell, Kenneth (2/1 Fd Regt), 216
Kemsley, William (2/1 Bn), 137
Kenna, Ted (2/4 Bn), 221
Kerslake, Norman (2/7 Bn), 38
Khalde, 119
Kiarivu, 226, 227
Killey, George (2/3 Fd Regt), 87, 93, 95
King, Roy (2/5 Bn & 16 Bde), 116–19, 187, 207, 209
Kokoda campaign, 132–46, 194, 234
Kokoda Track, 19, 120, 123
Komiatum, 156, 167, 169, 177, 181
Komiatum Ridge, 180
Kumusi River, 146

Lababia Ridge, 167, 169, 178
Lae, 155, 156, 167
Lamb, DJ (2/3 Bn), 73, 111
Lamont, George (2/6 Bn), 169
Larissa, 65, 71–4, 223
larrikins, 2, 12, 18
Lavarack, Sir John, 107, 114, 125
Laver, Harold (2/6 Bn), 177
Laver's Knoll, 177, 180
Lawry, PC (2/1 Bn), 102
Laybourne Smith, Bill (2/3 Fd Regt), 47, 48, 68, 70, 71, 74, 79, 96, 97
Le Souef, Leslie (2/7 Fd Amb), 87
Lea, Francis (6 Div Cav), 195
Leahy's Farm, 160
Leask, JC (2/5 Bn), 117
leave, 127, 131
Lebanon
   see Syria

Leonard, George (2/1 Bn), 124
Lewitz, John (2/1 Fd Regt), 153
Libya, 1, 15, 22, 26, 27, 52, 61, 63, 66, 83, 185, 197, 223, 239, 242, 245, 256
Litani River, 109
Lloyd, John (16 Bde), 133, 137, 139, 142, 144, 148, 149
Lloyd, WL, 111
Lomax, CEN, 113
Long, Gavin, 215, 217, 256, 257
Long Ridge, 204
Loubet, Eric (2/1 Fd Coy), 32, 46, 49, 52
Louch, TS (2/11 Bn), 55–60

MacArthur, Douglas, 133, 139, 167, 191, 196
Macarthur-Onslow, D (6 Div Cav), 55, 57
MacDougall, Ian (2/7 Bn), 38
machine guns, 15, 20, 64, 65, 89, 102, 136, 139, 146
Mackay, Sir Iven (6 Div), 8–10, 27, 30–2, 37, 41, 44, 52, 55, 67, 69, 70, 82, 85, 104, 121–3, 162, 256
mail, 31
malaria, 201, 215, 216
Maleme, 87, 88, 95, 96
Manning, Herbert 'Bull' (2/1 Fd Regt), 150
Manns, Thomas (2/1 Bn), 237
Maprik, 201, 204, 206, 207, 212–13, 223, 225
marches through cities, 13–15, 129–31, 182
Margetts, Douglas (6 Div Sigs), 114
Martin, Harold (2/2 Bn), 207
Masterson, Andrew (2/5 Bn), 226
Matapau, 198
Matthews, Fred (2/2 Bn), 143
McAuley, Dick (2/5 Bn), 239
McCabe, Jack (attached 16 Bde), 141
McCormack, Fred (2/5 Bn), 239
McDonald, 'Meggsie' (2/7 Bn), 48
McDonald, Stan (2/9 Cdo Sqn), 219
McFeeters, Charles (2/10 Cdo Sqn), 194
McGoldrick, Alfred (2/1 Bn), 144
McGovern, Gordon (2/1 AT Regt), 226
McGrath, Leonard (2/6 Bn), 177
McGuiness, 'Mac' (2/2 Bn), 149
McKeague, RD (6 Div Sigs), 55
McLennan, HH (2/2 Bn), 209
McNally, Frank (2/5 Bn), 161
McVicar, Fred (2/5 Bn), 173
Menzies, Sir Robert, 7, 121
Merdjayoun, 109, 114

Milak, 206–7
Miles, Cyril (2/5 Bn), 223
military police, 29
militia, 7–8, 10
Mills, Tom (6 Div Cav), 109
Milne Bay, 133, 150, 156
Minga Creek, 217
Monastir Gap, 67
Moriarty, Boyd (2/1 Bn), 99, 100
Morse, Bill (2/5 Bn), 12
Morshead, Sir Leslie, 50
mortars, 206
Moten, Murray (17 Bde), 156–9, 163–4, 177–9, 181, 187, 205, 212
Mott, Cliff (2/3 Fd Regt), 103
Mubo, 156, 163, 167–70, 181
Muir, RAC (17 Bde), 158
Murdoch, MH (2/3 Bn), 112
Murphy, Henry (2/1 Bn), 203

Nambut Hill, 202, 203
Nassau Bay, 167, 169–70, 213
Nauro, 135
Neeman, Tom (17 Bde Sigs & 6 Div Sigs), 34, 74, 114–17, 120
Nelson, St ED (2/7 Bn), 96
Netherlands East Indies, 125
New Guinea, fighting in, 134
New Zealand forces, 53, 66–7, 72–4, 77, 87, 95–6
Nicholas, Ted (2/2 Bn), 149
Nicholson, Jack (2/2 Fd Coy), 39
Ninahau River, 207
Northern Territory, 127–8, 133

O'Brien, Stan (2/7 Fd Amb), 97
O'Connell, KE (2/1 Fd Regt), 153
O'Connor, Sir Richard, 26–7, 31, 42, 52, 61
O'Sullivan, John (2/1 Fd Regt), 31
Observation Hill, 170
officers, 2, 185, 239
    future AIF leaders, 2, 130, 187
    transferred to militia, 128
Oivi-Gorari, 142–6
Old Vickers, 179
Olive Oil factory, 100
Operation Brevity, 106–7
organisation of 6th Division, 3–4
'originals', 185, 215
Oro Bay, 153
Orodubi, 180
Owen guns, 179, 188, 193
Owers' Corner, 133, 136

Palestine, 1, 9, 18–24, 45, 82, 105, 107, 109–11, 121, 125
Palmyra, 114
parades, divisional, 190
Parbery, Alf (16 Bde Sigs), 140, 256
Parbury, Philip (2/3 Bn & 2/7 Bn), 111–13
Parer, Damien, 21, 56
Parkes, John (2/2 Bn), 207
Parkin, Douglas, 219
Parkin, Roy (2/11 Bn), 221
Parsons, Alf (2/3 Fd Coy & 2/5 Bn), 44
Pauley, 'Blue' (2/11 Bn), 50
Peppercorn, Jack (2/3 Bn), 133
Perivolia, 95, 100–3
Perkins, Ken (2/10 Cdo Sqn), 207
Pett, LG (2/3 Bn), 140
Philippine Islands, 191, 231
Pickett, Arthur (16 AT Coy), 37
Pinios Gorge, 71–4, 82
Pirois, Frank (2/5 Bn), 239
Popondetta, 147, 149
Port Moresby, 133, 137, 149, 156, 162
Porto Rafti, 79
prisoners of war, 236
Pritchard, Aubrey (2/2 Bn), 210
Pritchard, Keith (2/7 Bn), 179, 180
Pye, 'Corny' (2/5 Bn), 197, 225

Queensland, 129–30, 206
Quinn, Fred (2/6 Bn), 213

rations, 147
    Kokoda, 136
    Tobruk, 46
Razor Spur, 200
Reddish, John (6 Div RAA), 187
Redmond, Neil (2/10 Cdo Sqn), 207
Refshauge, WD (2/2 Fd Amb), 177
Reid, John (2/1 Bn), 22
reinforcements, 1, 124, 185, 188, 225, 239
Reiter, 'Blue' (2/7 Bn), 97
Rethymnon
    see Retimo
Retimo, 87, 89, 92–5, 99–104, 238
Reynolds, Ernest (2/7 Bn), 20
Reynolds, Jack 'Trout' (2/5 Bn), 226
Roberts, David (2/3 Bn), 37
Robertson, Alexander (2/7 Bn), 164
Robertson, Sir Horace (19 Bde & 6 Div), 9–10, 50, 55–6, 60, 231, 234–5, 238, 256
Rogers, Bernie (2/11 Bn), 50
Rogers, Dave (2/11 Bn), 50
Russell, Bill (2/7 Bn), 162
Russell, Douglas (2/3 Fd Regt), 79

Russell, Vincent (2/1 Bn), 144
Ryan, Bill (2/2 Bn), 18
Ryan, WP (2/2 Bn), 137

Salamaua, 155, 156, 164, 167–70, 179–81
Sanananda, 44, 147, 149, 154, 155
Sanderson, AG (2/1 Bn), 139
Sandover, Ray (2/11 Bn), 100, 103, 130
Sargent, Abraham (2/4 Bn), 219
Saunders, Reg (2/7 Bn), 124, 185, 212
Savige, Sir Stanley (17 Bde), 10, 41, 71, 114–17, 119, 120, 163–7, 174, 178–9, 253, 256
Searle, Lloyd (2/2 Fd Regt), 15
Sepik River, 196
Servia Pass, 71
Sfakia, 97
Shanahan, James (2/2 Bn), 83
Sherlock, Bill (2/6 Bn), 157–61, 239
Shibarangu, Mount, 228
Shilton, Alwyn 'Blue' (2/5 Bn), 116
ships and convoys, 16–18, 84, 191, 219
    evacuating Crete, 98–99
    evacuating Greece, 79–81
    return from Middle East, 125–6
    return from the Middle East, 127
Sidon, 109, 111
signalling equipment, 74, 88, 116
Sims, Ewart (6 Div Cav), 106
Skindewai, 163
Smibert, RS (2/2 Fd Amb), 177
Smith, Carlyle (2/3 Bn), 112
Smith, John (2/5 Bn), 174
Smith, Radford (2/1 Bn), 144
Smith, Robert (2/2 Bn), 207
Smith, William (2/1 Fd Regt), 31
Sollum, 27, 28, 223
Soputa, 149, 150
St John, Francis (1 A-Tk Regt), 24
Starr, PDS (2/5 Bn), 163
Stavramenos, 93
Stening, William, 177
Stevens, 'Jackie' (6 Div), 187, 196, 197, 201, 204, 209, 219, 222, 227, 231
Stevenson, John (2/3 Bn), 113, 123, 139, 140
stretcher bearers, 209, 228
Strutt, Horace (2/3 Fd Regt & 6 Div RAA), 23, 96
Sturdee, Sir Vernon, 125, 193, 201, 204, 235
Suda Bay, 84, 85, 88, 95, 96
Sullivan, WAJ (2/1 Fd Regt), 216
Sutherland, Roy (16 Bde), 123
Swinton, NC (2/2 Bn), 142
Syria, 22, 105–21, 124, 133, 232, 234, 243

Tambu, Mount, 166, 167, 170, 174, 177, 180, 181, 238, 239
Tambu Bay, 174
tanks, 101, 118, 221
    Australian, 106, 213
    British, 31–7, 46
    German, 69, 70, 72–3
    Italian, 37, 49
    Matilda, 213
    Vichy French, 109, 113, 118
    Vickers, 107, 108
Tarlington, George (2/2 Bn), 136, 142–3
Taylor, Douglas 'Jock' (2/7 Bn), 20, 151
Tazaki, Mount, 227, 237
Tempe, 72, 238
Templeton's Crossing, 124, 137–8
Thermopylae 71
    see also Greece
'Thirty-Niners', 1, 12, 164, 239, 256
Thomas, HW (2/7 Bn), 96
Thompson, Edward (2/5 Bn), 173
Tiller, Bill (2/5 Bn), 171
Tobruk, 31, 45, 46–60, 64, 133
Tokuku Pass, 209, 210
Tong, 196, 197, 225
Torricelli Mountains, 194, 196, 197, 200, 205
traditions, 44
training, 10–16, 18, 20, 25, 127, 128, 187
transport, 53, 54, 73, 74, 79, 82, 93
Trethowan, Jim (2/8 Bn), 228
Trounce, Eric (6 Div Cav), 63
Twomey, Vic (2/1 Bn), 144, 148

Ulupu, 226
uniforms, 12, 27, 33, 41, 70, 108, 133, 135, 146, 193
    leather jerkins, 33, 35, 38

Vasey, George (6 Div & 19 Bde), 10, 18, 70, 76, 82, 85, 89, 96, 99, 121, 133, 142–4, 148, 231
Veria Pass, 67, 70
Vevi, 68–9, 79
Vichy French forces, 107
    Foreign Legion, 109
Victoria Cross, 74, 161, 209, 222
Vincent, John (2/5 Bn), 164, 246

Wakip River, 198
Walker, IW (2/7 Bn), 151
Walker, KR (2/7 Bn), 159
Walker, Theo (2/7 Bn), 96–7
Wallin, Arthur (2/5 Bn), 225, 227

Wandumi, 157–61, 238
War Crimes Commission, 235
Ward, Hon EJ, 11
Warmington, Ken (2/3 Bn), 212
Watson, Tom (2/4 Bn), 191
Wau, 155-80, 257
Wau-Salamaua, 120, 194, 244
Wavell, Field Marshal Rt Hon Earl, 18, 22, 25, 26, 61, 62, 66, 89, 106, 125
Wells, John 'Willie' (6 Div Cav), 107–8
West, Harold (2/1 Bn), 124
Western Australia, 129–30
Wewak, 195, 196, 201, 203, 204, 209, 216–22, 226, 227, 232, 238
White, Ivor (2/5 Bn), 225, 226
Whittle, Jack (2/1 Bn), 21
Willett, Arthur (2/8 Bn), 219
Williams, Owen (2/2 Fd Amb & 2/4 Bn), 177, 197, 217

Wilmot, Chester, 52
Wilson, Bill (2/5 Bn), 161
Wilson, Field Marshal Lord, 67, 69–71
Wilson, 'Mac' (2/4 Bn), 197, 223
Wilton, Cec (2/7 Bn), 150–1
Wiltshire, Bob (2/8 Bn), 128
Wirui Mission, 221–2
Wise, RJ (2/1 Fd Regt), 160
'Wizard of Oz', 36
Wondecla, v, 182–7
Wood, FG (2/6 Bn), 162, 178
Wood, Frank (2/1 Bn), 21
Wood, Stanley (2/11 Bn), 103
Wray, CHW (6 Div Cav), 109

'X' numbers, 3, 79

Yamil No. v, 226
Yeo, Fred (2/11 Bn), 185

Lightning Source UK Ltd.
Milton Keynes UK
UKOW06n2319040914

238106UK00003B/44/P